Leadership 2050

Critical Challenges, Key Contexts, and Emerging Trends

The authors of this edited volume go where others fear to tread. They are to be commended first for recognizing that leadership and followership change over time – and second for using their expertise to project what leadership and followership might look like decades from now. Though as the editor himself admits, "prediction is very difficult, especially about the future," this book is a worthy look into an admittedly cloudy crystal ball.

– Barbara Kellerman, James MacGregor
Burns Lecturer in Leadership, Harvard Kennedy School

Leadership 2050 exemplifies effective collaboration between scholars and practitioners in two distinct fields – Strategic Foresight and Leadership. Together, the contributors to this volume illuminate the challenges leaders will face over the next 35 years. Much like the World Future Society, *Leadership 2050* promotes awareness of the changing context for leadership and encourages creative solutions. It is a wonderful resource for leaders in all contexts looking to respond effectively to a complex and still emergent conditions. I heartily endorse!

– Amy Zalman, Ph.D., CEO & President, World Future Society

In 1970, futurists Alvin and Heidi Toffler observed, "Change is the way the future invades our lives." This book affirms that leadership is the way we invade the future. The foresight needed to engage in the complexity and demand of "wicked" global problems that become adaptive challenges, the transcendent perspective of being people flourishing in socially just relationships built on trust, and envisioning the expanding digital age, all coalesce in this book. This book is a must read for leaders in all sectors and leadership scholars and educators in all disciplines as a framework to think critically together about these global challenges.

– Susan R. Komives, Professor Emerita, University of Maryland

From global crises to corporate and community concerns, the effective use of personal influence and sanctioned authority today are being challenged and reshaped by new technologies and major shifts in attitudes and expectations. *Leadership 2050* offers a broad yet solidly researched overview of key issues and influences most likely to dominate the global social, political and economic landscape in the decades ahead. This is a book to guide and inspire anyone, from CEO to private citizen, who faces the important task of shaping sound long-range plans, while earning and preserving the trust of co-workers and the public. Any leader who deserves the title can profit from the insights and ideas found in *Leadership 2050*.

– Lane Jennings, Managing Editor, World Future Review

The past 35 years of leadership studies are strewn with achievements. This book is one of them and suggests the best may be yet to come. It is interdisciplinary work at its finest and brings future studies into the mix of its myriad sources. It culls vision and value from the current state of leadership scholarship to emphasize a leadership premised on interconnectedness, peace, sustainability, justice, and social organizations as living dynamic systems. It combined accessibility and solid research makes it ideal for classroom and discussion groups. It faces "wicked problems" that lie ahead of us and suggests the leadership styles and models needed to address them. It is simply wonderful to see a collection that celebrates where the field has been and shapes a direction for its increased relevance in the future. Highly recommended for anyone concerned with the future of the planet and its people.

– Richard A. Couto, Distinguished Senior Scholar, Union Institute

Leadership 2050

Critical Challenges, Key Contexts, and Emerging Trends

Edited by

Matthew Sowcik
Wilkes University, Wilkes-Barre, PA, USA

Anthony C. Andenoro
University of Florida, Gainesville, FL, USA

Mindy McNutt
Wright State University, Dayton, OH, USA

Susan Elaine Murphy
The University of Edinburgh, Edinburgh, UK

International Leadership Association

Emerald

United Kingdom – North America – Japan
India – Malaysia – China

Emerald Group Publishing Limited
Howard House, Wagon Lane, Bingley BD16 1WA, UK

First edition 2015

British Library Cataloguing in Publication Data
A catalogue record for this book is available from the British Library

ISBN: 978-1-78560-349-5
ISSN: 2058-8801 (Series)

ISOQAR certified
Management System,
awarded to Emerald
for adherence to
Environmental
standard
ISO 14001:2004.

ISOQAR
REGISTERED
Certificate Number 1985
ISO 14001

INVESTOR IN PEOPLE

Contents

List of Contributors

Stan Amaladas	University of Manitoba, Winnipeg, Canada
Anthony C. Andenoro	University of Florida, Gainesville, FL, USA
Skye Burn	Social Artist, Researcher, Writer, Bellingham, WA, USA
Susan Cannon	Evolucent Consulting, Seattle, WA, USA; Fielding Graduate University, Santa Barbara, CA
Cathleen Clerkin	Center for Creative Leadership, Greensboro, NC, USA
Barry A. Doublestein	Leadership Solutions, Loganville, GA, USA
Lisa Endersby	National Association of Student Personnel Administrators (NASPA), Toronto, Canada
Philip A. Foster	Maximum Change, Inc., Bell Buckle, TN, USA
Kathy L. Guthrie	Florida State University, Tampa, FL, USA
Jean Houston	Scholar, Philosopher and Researcher, Ashland, OR, USA
Bruce H. Jackson	The Institute of Applied Human Excellence, Highland, UT, USA
Daniel M. Jenkins	University of Southern Maine, Lewiston, ME, USA
Karen K. Johnson	University of Phoenix, Tempe, AZ, USA

Walter T. Lee	Duke University Medical Center, Durham, NC, USA
Timothy C. Mack	AAI Foresight, Freeland, WA, USA
Whitney McIntyre Miller	Chapman University, Orange, CA, USA
Mindy McNutt	Wright State University, Dayton, OH, USA
Maureen Metcalf	Metcalf & Associates, Inc., Huntersville, NC, USA; Capital University, Columbus, Ohio, USA
Michael Morrow-Fox	Metcalf & Associates, Inc., Huntersville, NC, USA
Susan Elaine Murphy	The University of Edinburgh, Edinburgh, UK
Donnette J. Noble	Roosevelt University, Chicago, IL, USA
Richard M. Pfohl	Navigos, Tolland, CT, USA
Michael A. Piel	IceBridge Research Institute, Manizales, Colombia
Sebastian Salicru	PTS Consultants Pty Ltd, Sydney, Australia
Rian Satterwhite	University of Oregon, Eugene, OR, USA
Kate Sheridan	Christopher Newport University, Newport News, VA, USA
Matthew Sowcik	Wilkes University, Wilkes-Barre, PA, USA
Nicole L. P. Stedman	University of Florida, Gainesville, FL, USA
Jeffrey L. Suderman	Suderman Solutions, Palm Desert, CA, USA
Icarbord Tshabangu	Leeds Trinity University, Leeds, UK

Foreword

This book helps us think at once about the demands our world is likely to face in the next 35 years and the leadership our communities will need to both survive those challenges and thrive. How will we grow the future out of the present? How will we prepare people for the practices of leadership our children and grandchildren will need? What is our work, in our lifetimes, to build a scaffold for the next generations?

The authors in this volume have worked these questions with courageous imagination and insight. As they suggest, we live at an opportune moment. Human beings can discover as never before our interdependence and commonality to bridge across national, religious, economic, and ethnic identities. We can pool our talents, resources, and spirit, locally and broadly, to create the synergies and capitalize on our differences to evolve toward a sustainable, peaceful, and just world.

The adaptive pressures challenge us: severe inequity; disrespect and violence toward women and disenfranchised peoples; rapid climate change and devastation of the natural environment; our industrial and numbing brutality toward animal life; population growth that exceeds the economic and political capacities of our cities, countries, and international relationships; and the wars, chaos, and terroristic violence that follow when, as Yeats wrote after World War I, "the center cannot hold."

Leadership is likely to matter.

To introduce this volume, I suggest two key areas for our thinking and research as we look to the future: the dynamics of adaptive change, and the practices of authority and leadership.

Adaptive Change

I believe we need to comprehend much more fully than we currently do the dynamics of adaptive problem-solving, not only generically, but also across the diverse contexts that require informed and skilled differences in leadership practice. To draw on the metaphor of evolutionary biology, adaptive processes involve three tasks: identifying the cultural DNA that should be conserved, identifying the cultural DNA that should be lost, and innovating new capacity so that people can bring the best of their culture's history into the future. In countless local and global ways, we will need to learn how to sift through what to conserve from the riches of our heritage, what to discard, and what innovations will enable us to move forward.

Knowing how to move between local and global adaptive work will be crucial because different contexts require different local adaptations. As Tim Mack describes here, the practice of leadership in mobilizing adaptive change requires being able to listen carefully and adjust accordingly to the subtle cues any particular environment provides.

We need a great deal of research to capture lessons from past adaptive successes and failures, micro and macro, to identify the generic and contextual variables, and to suggest guidelines for leadership that can engage people in adaptive work across the great spectrum of families, organizations, and communities to evolve successful solutions.

One such frontier is the need to understand how the practice of leadership can help people renegotiate and refashion historical loyalties and narratives to build on the essential wisdom of a familial or cultural narrative, but depart to create sustainable modifications and innovations for the adaptive contexts in which we find ourselves. How can we refashion narratives both to give people the freedom to change and to provide anchoring orientation and guidance for the change process itself?

For example, we see both historically and in our time that, in response to the disorienting local and global challenges we face, too often we react by retreating to primary loyalties and narratives for the security of identity and absolute thinking, but lose then the ability to engage in the complex task of sifting through our heritage to discern what to hold onto and what to change. We see this among some progressives and conservatives alike. The leadership of people, organizations, and institutions that will mobilize adaptive work within and across the boundaries of our local frames of reference, and draw upon our extraordinary human capacity, will require, I believe, a deep understanding of the practices of adaptive change within and across contexts.

Authority and Leadership

"The center cannot hold." The essays in this book suggest a second major opportunity and frontier for practitioners, scholars, and teachers of leadership: to more fully and clearly distinguish leadership from both formal authority and informal authority (e.g., moral and charismatic authority). I see three key sources of practical leverage derived from clarifying the conceptual relationship among leadership, formal authority, and informal authority.

First, we need to deepen our understanding of the ways that authority relationships and authority structures can productively and trustworthily provide holding environments for families and communities that are stressed now and will be in the future so that they can engage in civilized forms of collective problem-solving. Holding environments are constructed, not only of the horizontal bonds described as social capital, but also of the vertical bonds of authority relationships. Indeed, we might do well to expand our understanding of social capital to include both the horizontal and vertical bonds that hold a community together and create the matrix for collective problem-defining and problem-solving.

As I've written elsewhere, authority can usefully be defined as a relationship in which one party entrusts power to another party in exchange for services. Power entrusted for service. Often these are formalized roles, for example, in job descriptions or legal authorizations, and sometimes these roles are left informal (e.g., in a "go to person" to whom people look to champion their perspective or inspire hope but who may not hold a high, or even any, position). Both formal and informal roles of authority are made up of authorizations, and both are crucial to the daily operation of families, organizations, and societies. Neither, however, constitutes leadership in and of itself. One may lead from a formal authority position, but many do not. One may lead with abundant informal authority (trust, credibility, admiration, respect), but many do not. Many squander both of these sources of relational power and fail to lead.

The first key reason to distinguish leadership from both formal and informal authority is to focus our attention on authority itself, and the practices of renewing our human capacity to engage in healthy and respectful authority relationships – to renew our ability to trust – to strengthen the vertical bonds that hold us together. Distinguishing leadership from authority pushes us to investigate the virtues and value of authority structures in our lives, and at the same time the ways authorities become untrustworthy.

My argument here is that trust is the basis of all authorizing relationships, and therefore, to raise the quotient of trust in our societies we need to train people who gain authority positions to be trustworthy. At the very same time, we also need to renew the ability of people who have been scarred by violations of trust, either in their own lifetime or in the past generations they carry, to discern trustworthy behavior and risk trusting again. In a world in which authorities have too often violated trust, for example, through colonial oppression, sexual abuse, or police brutality toward minority citizens, distrust is often enculturated, preventing good citizenship, governance, and healthy communal life. Renewing the trust of citizens toward authorities, requires, I believe, that we both prepare and train authorities to be trustworthy, and at the same time address the fact that many of us have become distrusting toward authority in ways that are counterproductive.

I believe we can do this. I've seen it happen in my 32 years of leadership education in classrooms of 112 people mostly at midcareer from 40 countries many of whom represent traumatized histories and cultures of endemic distrust. People can be trained to notice from their past practice and to anticipate in the future for themselves the corrupting temptations of authority they will likely experience, create anchors to maintain their own trustworthiness, and develop the skill to repair the historic distrust of their people by learning, for example, how to acknowledge historic injustice and trauma, and how to be on the receiving end of historic anger with grace.

The second key source of leverage that comes from distinguishing leadership from authority is that it helps us build practical theory to guide the practice of leadership from authority positions. We need case work for teaching and research that explains the frequent failure of people in high positions of authority to exercise leadership. How is authority a constraint, and not only a set of resources, for the practice of leadership? We need research and theory that informs people in roles of authority about the constraints of authority for leadership, and that provides practical theory to manage and transcend these constraints. For example, in my work advising George Papandreou, the Prime Minister of Greece from 2009 to 2011, we faced the generic dilemma: how in a democracy do you disappoint the expectations of your own party's constituents and dispense widespread economic pain that may take years to resolve? In my current work with the Colombian President, Juan Manuel Santos, on the current peace negotiations with the FARC, we are analyzing the challenge: how do you prepare a traumatized people for peace when peace requires accepting significant psychological, economic, and political costs? The leadership of adaptive change from authority positions is something we need to understand much better than we currently do.

The third key source of leverage that comes from distinguishing leadership from authority is the way it helps us to prepare future generations for the practice of leadership from all walks of life, with and without authority, from wherever one sits. To fully democratize the availability of leadership as a practice that nearly anyone might do, we need to decouple it from positions of authority. Indeed, many of the authors in this volume provide illustrations of people who exercise leadership without office, simply because they see a collective problem and then mobilize whoever is within reach to address it. They do not wait. They care and they act.

Looking toward the future, our world will need more than ever leadership that comes simultaneously from many places to distribute the work of change to the local level. For many of our future challenges, our problems will lie within the hearts, minds, and behavior of people, and so the solutions will lie there as well. When the people are the problem, the people are the solution. Therefore, we need a theory and practice of leadership available to citizens from all walks of life. We need to educate children and adults to see that leadership as a practice is available to them simply because they care and engage, regardless of their social dominance or authority.

This book points ahead to the work to be done in every realm of our lives throughout the globalizing world: families working to survive and thrive in challenging conditions; businesses in complex environments tackling tough trade-offs squaring values of profitability, long-term sustainability and social justice; and public organizations, nonprofits, and social entrepreneurs working to build collaborative capacity across boundaries to transform cultures of dependency into communities of engaged citizenship and distributed leadership.

Ron Heifetz

Section I
Envisioning Leadership in 2050

" **P**rediction is very difficult, especially about the future." These humorous words, attributed to Niels Bohr, help to frame both Section I and *Leadership 2050* (Whitehead, 2012). There are very few certainties about the future — one of those is that 35 years from now, in 2050, the world will be very different than it is right now. Change is inevitable. The second certainty is that any prognostication today, particularly about leadership in 2050, is going to be inaccurate and incomplete. However, this book is not about predicting leadership in 2050. This book is about exploring, based on current knowledge and understanding, the issues, drivers, and contexts that may influence leaders and followers over the next 35 years. In addition to the aforementioned certainties are a number of themes which you will see emerge from each of the articles in this book. These themes help to establish boundaries and provide an avenue to discuss integrated solutions to address the complex, adaptive challenges we will face as a global population.

1980—2050

From the perspective of time, we are closer to the year 2050 than we are to 1980. Think about some of the changes that have occurred in the ways we have studied and practiced leadership over the past 35 years. In 1980, we had not yet begun to focus on systems thinking and complexity theory. Moreover, the importance of studying and appreciating followership had not entered into the leadership studies discourse. In 1980, it would still be another decade before Salovey and Mayer (1990) coined the term *emotional intelligence* and Daniel Goleman (1996) made it a "must have" in leadership development programs. From the standpoint of leadership education, it was also in the early 1990s that the first degree-granting school of Leadership Studies at the University of Richmond, started offering classes (Riggio, Ciulla, & Sorenson, 2003). Finally, it wasn't until 1999, two decades later, that the International Leadership

Association was formed (A Brief History of the International Leadership Association, 2012).

However, even with all the changes that have happened in the study and practice of leadership over the past 35 years, it would be shortsighted not to acknowledge the tremendous impact a number of leadership scholars and events had leading up to the progress made over the last 35 years. It was over 80 years ago that Mary Parker Follett (1933) wrote about the importance of followership (Kellerman, 2014). Concepts like social and multiple intelligence, discussed by scholars like Thorndike (1920) and Gardner (1975), were both precursors to emotional intelligence. Thirty six years ago, in 1979, the University of San Diego launched the first Ph.D. program in Leadership Studies, which was one of the forerunners to the leadership education movement (University of San Diego, n.d.).

Finally, 37 years ago, Burns published *Leadership* (1978), which "is still considered the seminal work in the field of leadership studies (Leadership Legacy Program, 2014)." Not only did Burns' book impact the way we study and practice leadership, it can be argued that due to his success, it lead him down the path to help launch the International Leadership Association. There was no way, in 1980, to predict with certainty the state of leadership in 2015. However, what is clear is the possibility did exist to look out across the landscape of leadership and identify different drivers, issues, and context that might shape the study and practice of leadership.

The same is true now and is the basis for this book. We have the opportunity in 2015, to look toward the future of leadership and identify those drivers, issues, and contexts that might shape the study and practice of leadership. When talking about Mary Parker Follett in her book *Hard Times: Leadership in America*, Kellerman (2014) pointed out, "ultimately, she wrote, leaders should see 'all the future trends and unite them' − decisions made today must anticipate tomorrow." One theme that surfaced throughout this book is that the past and the present can guide us toward the future. Today offers those clues to better understand the theories, models, and competencies, which will become increasingly important over the next three and a half decades.

The Future Is a Context with Issues

"Leadership is the process by which leaders and followers develop a relationship and work together toward a goal (or goals) within an environmental context shaped by cultural values and norms" (Perruci, 2011, p. 84). Perruci's definition highlights the important role environmental context plays in leadership. Currently, our response to natural disasters, the emergence of leadership in joint public/private ventures, integrity at all levels of government, the technology revolution, an aging global population, the rise of new economic powers, youth culture, and the impact of rapid globalization, are just a few examples of contexts impacting the leadership process and the fluid interaction between leaders and followers.

In her book *Hard Times: Leadership in America* (2014), Kellerman, highlights the importance of "contextual expertise" within the leadership system. "Contextual expertise" consists of the knowledge a leader should take into account, prior to engaging in the leadership process. One theme that emerged throughout Leadership 2050 is the importance the authors place on understanding the past, present and future context in order to lead.

Another theme that can be seen in *Leadership 2050* is a focus on the issues associated with overcoming the "contextual odds" (Kellerman, 2014, p. 306). However, as the authors define and outline possible futures to help provide "contextual expertise" it is important to remember that complex systems are not easily simplified. For example, imagine if this book was published on September 10, 2001. The events that played out the next day, on September 11, 2001, reshaped the landscape and the "contextual expertise" we have to explore the future. However, the problem that arises when utilizing context and issues to explore the future, is that the events, which will have a significant impact on the future, have not yet happened.

People Make Up the Future

Whether it is the rise of machines or a zombie epidemic, Hollywood has enjoyed playing to our fears and we have responded in box office sales. When computers became a reality so did our fear of technology. As we have increasingly seen epidemics like human immunodeficiency virus (HIV), swine flu, and Ebola, we have translated those fears into a zombie apocalypse. Although this has made for great entertainment, like the Terminator and The Walking Dead, one theme that is consistent throughout this book – and as close to a certainty as we can get – is the future consists of people. As Baker (2014) stated in her article, The Future is about People,

> We must remember that the future is not only a time, but it is a place. In fact, these places of the future will be inhabited by people with innate characteristics that mirror who they were yesterday, who they are today, and who they will be tomorrow.

Additionally, she noted that since people will make up the future, we can assume that certain human characteristics, like the need to explore, the need for interpersonal relationships, and the need to find answers to our questions, will very likely be present in 2050 as they are in 2015.

The many authors of this book have also embraced the notion that people make up the future. In *Leadership 2050*, you will not be reading any new leadership theories resembling Leader-Zombie Exchange Theory. Instead, the authors focus on many of the elements that are likely to remain constant regardless of change. Elements like the importance of emotions, creativity, communication, social justice, adapting, context, and time, all of which impact leaders and followers today, and are likely to have an impact into the distant future.

People Make Up the Present

As important as it is to point out that the future is made up of people, it is equally important to remind ourselves that people make up the present. This is the basis for the third theme that can be found throughout the book. As humans, it is our nature to want to predict the future. For centuries, whether reading tea leaves, palms, or stars, humans have tried to predict future outcomes. Today, even though we understand that the future is unknowable and cannot be predicted, we still have an unwavering desire to prognosticate. An outcome of this need to define the future has promoted predictions in all fields of study, for example:

- The electric energy need of Turkey in the year 2050 will be approximately 1173 billion kilowatt-hours (Yumurtaci & Asmaz, 2004).
- It is predicted that personal travel in North America will increase from the 1990 value of about 23,000 passenger-km per capita to 58,000 passenger-km per capita by the year 2050 (Moriarty & Honnery, 2004).
- The overall consumption of metals in 2050 will be five times greater than the current levels. Demand for metals such as Gold, Silver, Copper, Nickel, Tin, Zinc, Lead, and Magnesium is expected to be several times greater than the amount of their respective reserves (Halada, Shimada, & Ijima, 2008).
- The population of the labor force that will be 55 years and older will grow from 13% in 2000 to 24% in 2050 (Toossi, 2012).
- It is estimated that in 2050 the planet will have about 9.4 billion people, which is in excess of 30% more than today (World Bank, 2014).

One element of forecasting is attributing statistics to the prediction. As shown above, statistics can be used to help frame the prediction, while additionally helping to make the authors point. Throughout the book you will find that different authors use different statistics to make a point. For example, the human population statistic for 2050 noted above appears in Chapter 6. However, in Chapter 9, Nicole L. P. Stedman and Anthony C. Andenoro point out that the total population by the year 2050 will be 9.6 billion. Finally, in Chapter 2, Jeffrey L. Suderman and Philip A. Foster suggest that number could be nearing 10 billion people.

The use of different statistics is not an oversight or a mistake by the authors. There is a basic tension that exists when utilizing statistics to predict the future. The statistics often depend upon the outcome of a number of different current and future variables, which often times are not known until closer to the year that is being predicted. For example, when looking at population growth, variables like fertility, mortality, and immigration all play a role in the growth or decline of the population in different countries. A change in any one of these variables can shift the projected numbers. For example, in 2013, the UN updated previously low population predictions due to the increase in fertility rates in some developing nations (UN Press Release, 2013).

Additionally, when utilizing statistics to describe the future, it is common practice to provide a few possible scenarios. Once again, looking at population growth, the UN produced three main scenarios looking at variables like fertility rate in both industrialized and developing countries (Haub, 2013). Specifically in population growth, the UN has provided statistics on Low, Middle and High variants. The Low variant is calculated at one-half child less than the Medium variant, while the High variant is one-half child more than the Medium variant. Taking these variables into account it is estimated that the world population in 2050 is project at 8.3 billion at the low end, 10.9 billion at the high end, and 9.6 billion at the medium variant (Haub, 2013).

Scholars, Practitioners, and Students

In addition to taking on the rather ambitious task of exploring those issues, drivers, and contexts that will likely impact the future of leadership, the authors of this book also took on the challenge of making this book accessible to a broad audience. Foresight and our ability to forecast what contexts and issues will define leadership in the future can provide a valuable roadmap to those currently studying and practicing leadership. Very intentionally a diverse set of authors were selected to contribute to *Leadership 2050*. Whether it was a purposeful split between practitioners and academics or providing various viewpoints from authors from the United States,

Canada, the United Kingdom, Australia, and Colombia, this book looks to draw on multiple expertise to explore the future.

As much as we hope this book has a positive impact on current scholars and practitioners of leadership, the book was also written to be accessible by those individuals who will make up the future. Our intention was to provide students with a valuable roadmap to address the complex adaptive challenges of the future. If we can provide different avenues for students to answer questions like "leadership for what?" and identify the major challenges shaping leadership theory, thought, and application in the future, students will better understand the critical role leadership will play now and into the future.

Leadership 2050: Section I

In the introductory section of *Leadership 2050*, the authors provide a primer for those interested in studying leadership and the future. Timothy C. Mack, drawing on his years of experience as former President of the World Future Society and Executive Editor of *World Future Review*, uses foresight analysis to raise a number of questions about the possible challenges facing leaders over the next 35 years. In Chapter 2, Suderman and Foster, provide an in depth overview of strategic foresight and scenario planning, in order to offer plausible changes to the field of leadership. In both cases, the authors, who have a background in futurist studies, set the stage for the issues, contexts, and integrated solutions that follow throughout the book.

Matthew Sowcik

References

A Brief History of the International Leadership Association. (2012, December). *International leadership association*. Retrieved from http://www.ila-net.org/about/history.htm

Baker, N. (2014). The future is about people. *The Futurist*, 2014 Issues of The Futurist, *48*(4), July−August. Retrieved from http://www.wfs.org/futurist/2014-issues-futurist/july-august-2014-vol-48-no-4/future-about-people.

Burns, J. M. (1978). *Leadership*. New York, NY: Harper & Row Publishers.

Gardner, H. (1975). *The shattered mind: The person after brain damage*. New York, NY: Alfred A. Knopf.

Goleman, D. (1996). Emotional intelligence. Why it can matter more than IQ. *Learning*, *24*(6), 49−50.

Halada, K., Shimada, M., & Ijima, K. (2008). Forecasting of the consumption of metals up to 2050. *Materials transactions*, *49*(3), 402−410.

Haub, C. (June, 2013). United nations raises projected world population. Population Reference Bureau. Retrieved from http://www.prb.org/Publications/Articles/2013/un-world-projections.aspx

History and Facts. (n.d.). University of San Diego. Retrieved from http://www.sandiego.edu/soles/about-soles/history-and-facts.php

Kellerman, B. (2014). *Hard times: Leadership in America.* Redwood City, CA: Stanford University Press.

Moriarty, P., & Honnery, D. (2004). Forecasting world transport in the year 2050. *International journal of vehicle design, 35*(1), 151–165.

Perruci, G. (2011). Millennials and globalization: The cross-cultural challenge of intragenerational leadership. *Journal of Leadership Studies, 5*(3), 82–87.

Riggio, R. E., Ciulla, J., & Sorenson, G. (2003). Leadership education at the under-graduate level: A liberal arts approach to leadership development. In S. E. Murphy & R. E. Riggio (Eds.). *The future of leadership development.* (pp. 223–236). Mahwah, NJ: Lawrence Erlbaum Associates.

Salovey, P., & Mayer, J. D. (1990). Emotional intelligence. *Imagination, Cognition, and Personality, 9,* 185–211.

Thorndike, E. L. (1920). Intelligence and its uses. *Harper's Magazine, 140,* pp. 227–235.

Toossi, M. (2012). Projections of the labor force to 2050: a visual essay. *Monthly Labor Review, 3,* 135.

UN Press Release. (June, 2013). *World population projected to reach 9.6 billion by 2050 with most growth in developing regions, especially Africa – says UN.* Retrieved from http://esa.un.org/unpd/wpp/Documentation/pdf/WPP2012_Press_Release.pdf

Whitehead, J. (2012). *What you need to know about strategy.* Hoboken, NJ: Wiley.

World Bank. (2014). *Population estimates and projections.* Retrieved from http://datatopics.worldbank.org/hnp/popestimates

Yumurtaci, Z., & Asmaz, E. (2004). Electric energy demand of Turkey for the year 2050. *Energy Sources, 26*(12), 1157–1164.

1

Leadership in the Future

Timothy C. Mack

Introduction

After consulting, writing, and speaking in the foresight and strategic leadership arena for the past several decades, it has become clear to me that the challenges of leadership are growing and not shrinking. The range of tools and information sources continues to expand, so does the complexity of the global environment. As the CEO of the World Future Society, the largest foresight-focused association, I traveled to every continent but Antarctica, and had the chance to dialog with leaders in the private sector, academia, and government. My previous professional opportunities within the industry (WPP Ltd, the largest strategic communications conglomerate), government (the US Congress), and academia (Harvard's Kennedy School and the National Academy of Sciences) provided access to on-the-ground details of the threats and opportunities facing leaders globally.

It is my conviction that the study of the future and the study of leadership are quite similar in a number of ways. Both are very broadly relevant concepts, with interactive impacts across a range of sectors. When thinking about what is relevant to either, it is difficult not to respond, "What is not?" Accordingly, I will propose at the outset that the future of leadership is the future of humanity, and effective leadership guides us all as we steer our course between opportunities and threats. As such, any discussion on the future of leadership will necessitate a greater understanding of the many challenges facing the future of all of us.

I confess that at times I wonder whether the upcoming challenges facing humanity might not prove overwhelming. This sort of pessimism is not new. In the 21st century, although expanded technological capabilities have certainly led to higher volumes of digital connectivity, this often results in lower relevant interactivity and message sharing, especially when developing strategic policy, business intelligence, and environmental analysis. I am not using the term "environmental" here in the context of global warming or pollution but instead in a foresight context, which involves identification of all those factors that might influence the direction of trends affecting leadership in the future.

Although it is a common distinction, I have not made a hard and fast distinction between leadership and management. Leadership does have an almost spiritual ring to it when couched in terms of vision, unique personal dynamics, and rising above the dross of management detail, but I see the management/leadership separation as a liability rather than strength, as it leaves leadership without the assistance of experienced implementation of skills.

Challenges Facing the Leaders of the Future

WALL OF WHITE NOISE

Twenty-first century technology has been transforming business and organizational communications in ways that are not always for the better. Contrary to Thomas Friedman's optimism in *The World Is Flat* (Friedman, 2005), too much information can become a problematic wall of white noise. In such an environment, all voices can have equal authority and authenticity, which can cause cultural dysfunction. One symptom of this dysfunction is the rise of buzzwords and secret professional languages. Another is the tendency to tune out important content as a result of constant communication overload.

While there are many consequences of this communications overloading, one worth noting is the growing loss of dialog in many leadership settings. For example, team building is now often seen as just "too much hard work," which can be accompanied by an illusion of total self-reliance. A common expression of this is the phrase, "Not always right but never, ever in doubt." If validation is perceived as unnecessary, then weak assumptions are seldom critically assessed or challenged. How this will play out as generations age and evolve is not likely to follow straight-line projections but instead follow the more complex path woven by the interaction of the range of shifting values that we have been observing.

At a cultural level, this loss of dialog is likely to lead to an increasing loss of mutual trust across society. Where the Internet was once a vast experiment (much as open-source programming and cultural and technology laboratories such as BarCamps continue to be today), it now contains swirling currents of hidden intent, social subjugation, and outright fraud. In an organizational context, this is a systemic problem that may affect the underlying channels of communication critical to organization health and growth. The challenge in this troubling trend is, "How can a leader be heard against this din of white noise?" One strategy is to work to enhance the dialogic nature of leadership communications by enhancing the value, relevance, and uniqueness of the information being offered, thereby increasing the likelihood of it being noticed, considered, and acted upon.

RESPONSE TO COMPLEX, MULTI-SECTOR CHANGES

Another trend involves the continuing inability (or lack of inclination) of many governments, organizations, corporations, and NGOs to understand and address potential negative change. To put it in a more specific context, many organizations and companies adapt to change, not when they should but only when they must adapt, but their adaptations are often too late. One result is that there are many looming resource shortfalls now facing humanity. These shortfalls will continue to grow, driven in part by the expanding consumption patterns of global prosperity. Ignoring these shortfalls can only increase their prevalence. Accordingly, systemic solutions and public education strategies concerning diminishing resources should be developed and implemented.

One looming resource shortfall concerns future sources of sufficient fresh water. By 2025, 1.8 billion people will be living in countries or regions with fresh water scarcity (Gleick, 2008). In addition to this, two-thirds of the population might be living under water-stressed conditions. According to the UN water initiative by the Department of Economic and Social Affairs (UNDESA), by 2025 at least 36 countries will have major fresh water and agricultural resource deficiencies, compared to only 20 countries facing that problem today. This represents over 1.8 billion people in physical water scarcity and over two-thirds of the world in water stress conditions (United Nations, 2014a). Essentially, water is distributed unevenly across the globe, both from geological dynamics and from the human-driven impact of waste, pollution, and unsustainable management. Pressure from growing populations, concerns about discarded pharmaceuticals and personal care products interfering with wastewater treatment processes, and high costs of desalination technologies are endangering essential urban water resources worldwide. New technologies, such as greenways and other vegetation filtration systems for recycling gray water outputs, may help, but are being developed too slowly.

UNPLANNED URBANIZATION

The future of urban areas is increasingly becoming the future of the globe, and the need for imaginative innovation is dire. The world urban population will double by 2030, and there will be at least nine cities with populations over 20 million. By 2050 more than 70% of the world's population will live in urban areas with a total global population of nine billion plus (Goldstone, 2010).

Today, 54% of the world's population lives in urban areas, a proportion that is expected to increase to 66% by 2050 (United Nations, 2014b). Projections show that urbanization combined with the overall growth of the world's population could add another 2.5 billion people to urban populations by 2050, with close to 90% of the increase concentrated in Asia and Africa. Largest cities will include Tokyo, Shanghai, Mexico City, Mumbai, San Paolo, Osaka, and largest areas of growth will be in Africa and Asia (United Nations, 2014b).

The critical issue here is Unplanned Urbanization – development without consideration of economic, political, health, and/or environmental consequences. One of the many issues arising from unplanned urbanization is local food sourcing. One urban food solution that holds possibility is self-sustainable, vertical, downtown farms. Proposals such as Dubai's Food City offers a similar solution, with solar energy to power lights, pumps, and conveyer belts, plus chicken and fish fed on plant byproducts. As many of the world's cities are located within 60 miles of an ocean, increased urbanization means increased impact from 1 to 14 meter rise in sea level expected by 2100 – a very sobering prospect.

After agonizing over the impact of the global urban population crunch, it should be noted that many "Smart Cities" are already managing city systems for city needs and keeping the stakeholder connections open. For example, the LIVE Singapore! program provides citizens with real-time fully open data streams concerning public works systems. These sort of examples are multiplying logarithmically and include such thing as health monitoring using mobile tracking and reporting via smartphones, geo-tagged media, and continuous counting, which includes enhanced detail on global migration. All of these data streams are combining into "big data" mega banks that will feed leadership decision-making processes like never before.

DIFFICULTIES OF AN UNPREDICTABLE FUTURE

It may be that humans will not be the only decision-makers involved in meeting the challenges of the future, a possibility that may further complicate finding viable solutions. This assertion should not be read as a validation of the Technological Singularity concept, rather just a recognition that novel factors are increasingly in play. The concept of Technological Singularity, which emerged in the 1950s and was popularized by Vernor Vinge in the 1990s, proposes that by 2030 technological acceleration will create − through computer AI, human biological enhancement, and/or machine-human interface − superintelligence levels exceeding those of any human alive today (Vinge, 1993). The consequences of this extraordinary level of change will be unique in human history and completely unpredictable.

The Digital Universe in 2020, predicts that over 40% of all communications will be entirely machine-generated or M2 − machine to machine − by 2020 (Gantz & Reinsel, 2013). Of course, M2M interpretation and response will be much faster than the typical human conversation, but hopefully less problematic than machine-driven stock and financial instrument trading *circa* 2007, which, if readers remember, did not go so well.

Regardless of whether Metcalf's law, which states that the value of a communication network increases quadratically in relation to user growth, is strictly accurate, any value increases, especially where the capabilities of the whole are far beyond that of individual units, can include unpredicted emergent properties. One example is computer networks that exhibit abilities for which they are not originally designed. As a general rule then, when system complexity increases, predictability decreases.

Essentially, as much as leaders might attempt to predict and peer into the future, novel factors, including, but not limited the possibility of a Technological Singularity, may render a significant portion of any forecast off-target.

DIMINISHING RESOURCES

While there are some counter-forces that can be tactically utilized to offset challenges, including a range of new technologies, public education on consumption practices, and commitments to mutual cooperation, the overarching issue of diminishing resources will continue to hinder progress. Leaders of the future must embrace imagination and innovation as essential to both identification of emerging problems and crafting of workable solutions. Workable means that resources, including political will, are available for solution design and successful implementation in a global context. These problems will not yield a patchwork quilt of varied solutions, as evidenced from the ongoing hodgepodge of climate change solutions.

Many proposed solutions will appear viable in theory, but the challenge is how to build sufficient ongoing support and resources into the implementation stage to yield a successful result.

Accordingly, identification of resources and expertise continue to be challenges to be faced and overcome, even after problem identification and solution suggestions have been developed. This is not to say that reaching beyond one's grasp or "dreaming big" should not be encouraged, but only that a thorough understanding of whether resources needed for a viable solution and the resources actually available match up. In addition to the question of political will, viability will also depend upon sufficiently broad stakeholder buy in and the essential community education needed to forestall the all-too-common knee-jerk change phobia.

There are a plenty of ideas and not a few dynamic strategies already in play. In 2013, the McKinsey Global Institute in Africa report on Internet/e-commerce suggested that there are tipping points coming soon in Africa (Manyika et al., 2013). Financial systems, education, health systems, retail infrastructure, agriculture, and government, to name a few, are all on the verge of exponential growth and change. The interesting thing about tipping points is their slow, then fast pattern. Consider the possibility that Lagos, Nigeria might one day be more economically powerful worldwide than New York City or Beijing. The potential of urban centers in emerging markets is enormous. But, leaders need to anticipate how these dramatic global shifts will affect political, economic, and cultural patterns that have been in place for decades. No one ever said leadership is easy.

DATA COLLECTION: USE AND ABUSE

Leadership information services are getting better just as fast as they are getting worse. What is really happening in these profound transformations of new values, new connections, and new tools is that many old approaches and resources are losing viability or just are vanishing.

Transparency has been a strong meme in government and private sector transactions for some time. This has been driven by NGOs like Transparency International (www.transparency.org) and by the WTO recruitment and implementation process. Furthermore, when every citizen walks around with a camera ready to record misdoings and post them online, when facial recognition software can analyze potential threats from multiple camera feeds placed around our cities, and when digital records are easily penetrated and shared with the world, individual, corporate, and government wrongdoing becomes much more difficult to hide and much more discoverable. Big Brother may be here, as we now watch one another quite closely on social media.

But what, in fact, are the consequences of living in a transparent world? Is leadership effectiveness enhanced by in-depth data on each and every citizen or does big data damage the existing constructive and viable relationships, which currently provide the enabling "grease" that keeps organizations moving effectively?

In his 2013 book, *Who Owns the Future*, Jaron Lanier argued that any collected aggregate data should be considered the property of those from whom or about whom it was collected, that is, seeing it as a personal property of the primary source and therefore necessitating a payment for its use (Lanier, 2013). That could be interesting during the price setting process, but it gets more complicated when the public use of such data for the common good comes into play. For example, epidemiological behavior such as influenza outbreaks could be tracked and managed based on group movement and communication patterns using Smart Phone info, such as has been done with Google Flu Trends (Google, 2015).

But, when does this cross from the public good into questionable national security territory? The ability of any government to identify "influencers" in any public or private network, track behavioral indicators of growing mental illness, and follow the travel of memes, especially political ones — seen by some governments as a social contagion — further complicates this question. Of course, much of this observation could be self-initiated, such as "selfie" sonograms and blood work phone apps, but again the question is who gets what information first and what do they do with it? When we are fully aware of where everyone on the planet is and what they are doing, will this reshape the definitions of public safety and national security? For example, will some soon-to-be-fully-observed individual behaviors such as rock-free climbing or body surfing during storms be seen by governments or machine analysis as too dangerous to be allowed? China's Golden Shield Program, for example, aims to use facial recognition to track everyone of the PRC's 1.3 billion people throughout their day. And while some people oppose the business practices of data giants like Google though conventional public policy initiatives like the European Right to be Forgotten, it is possible that in the future, privacy may become an issue generating political conflict and even terrorism.

Leadership, Management, and Change

The world around us is continuing to change dramatically, as does the world of leadership and management, driven by new technological capabilities and cultural shifts. Accordingly, we all need to better understand how the skills needed for effective 21st Century leadership, that is, communication (language, verbal/writing, thinking/emotion, listening); science (curiosity and ability to judge validity); thinking and reasoning (mindfulness, macro-level thinking, complexity, context, questioning assumptions); problem solving; and self discipline must all be rethought and rebuilt upon for the 21st century. For one, the basic cognitive skills that formed the foundation of education in the last century are becoming the very first candidates for expert software systems. What are not likely to be duplicated by an AI are the creative and collaborative problems skills; new technology assessment; change adaption and management; and cross disciplinary analysis. In other words, the ability to identify, understand, interpret, and communicate relevant new knowledge, as it constantly adapts to environments in constant transformation (Schleicher, 2010).

One major leadership ideal over the next 35 years should be that message "send and receive" dynamics are in balance. In other words leadership requires a balanced dialog. Meeting that ideal is challenging, however, as even such touted connectivity approaches as viable "word of mouth" marketing are very often unilateral in practice. Learning to listen from both sides of a connection is not a small accomplishment. It involves realizing that there are multiple paths to desired conclusions and that offering choices is critical, especially in light of growing research on the diversity of human learning styles.

Dialog between leaders and followers is now technologically possible almost everywhere around the world, thereby performing a number of useful tasks, including the following:

- Building potential channels of connectivity;
- Building new attitudes (ideally positive);
- Providing feedback, both positive and negative (mistakes happen and it's better to hear about them early, before they are unfixable); and
- Creating special interest groups focusing on personal interests.

But some potential changes in leadership structure and practice are moving much more slowly. It continues to be a cliché that while women are considered better at dialog than men, they hold fewer leadership positions globally, although this is improving (Pew Research Center, 2014). In the United States, while more than 50% of college graduates and 30% of business managers are now women, only 5% or 1 out of every 20 senior management positions in high-profile Fortune 500 corporations are filled by a female (Grant Thornton, 2014; McMillian, 2012).

In an arena that sometimes seems to change at glacial speeds, it is not yet clear what sorts of shocks will bring about significant shifts or what the cascading results will then be. Perhaps, the revolution in social media (already a part of education, business communications, and organizational decision-making) will bring critical and difficult issues (such as glass ceilings) to the fore, stimulating more committed policy change than previously. Similarly, the growing flow of information along horizontal and non-hierarchical pathways will certainly alter organizational structures as well.

INFORMATION RELEVANCE AND NEW TOOLS

One of the most pervasive analytical leadership tools arising in the still relatively new 21st century is "Big Data," or the computer-driven ability to collect and analyze information at levels not previously possible. Leaders will increasingly use Big Data to drive policy changes, which as a new tool still under development, is likely to suffer a few missteps over the next few years. As the almost supernatural aura of Big Data's early promise fades away, it still marks a "sea change" in the level and quality of information available to leaders in the future. Explanations such as, "I didn't see it coming," or "We don't work down at that level in the C Suite," will be swept aside, leaving leaving top leaders with few viable excuses for their failure to foresee the problem in question.

I believe that one significant advantage Big Data will provide tomorrow's leadership/management arena is the ability to obtain unique and valuable content "ahead of the crowd," so to speak. This is likely to involve the use of relevant foresight tools, some of which I discuss below.

During the last century, communications technology designers saw their primary challenge as overcoming information scarcity, thus leading to the "fire hose" approach and resulting in maximum data throughput. Without relevant measures that work for everyone, this information deluge is likely to continue. One arena where message and dialogic relevance is being addressed is in work surrounding the "attention economy." In general, the research underway is a mash-up of psychology, epistemology, and system dynamics, overlain upon a communications dynamics platform. When tied to leadership, those mechanics usually go forward in three basic steps: a leadership communiqué enters the "field of attention" of an individual or a community; then, ideally, the attention of that target audience is grabbed; and finally, an action of some sort is taken (or not taken). These concepts have come out of the marketing world, where the action taken or not taken is often a purchase. However, the potential desired action could also encompass a wide range of political, behavioral, or professional choices tied in with patterns of citizen or organizational actions.

This research on the dynamics of attention has generated interest in new decision-making tools that may be able to weave useful fabrics of thought and action. While there is a temptation to flirt with the pejorative term "mind control," these approaches can also be viewed as simply more effective communications. These attention-relevant tools include elements that improve messages, such as visualization (often through interactive graphics and even animation) or translation (defined here as a successful restatement of message concepts in terms relevant to the listener).

Another rapidly developing area of social analytics is "rapid experimentation" or applied predictive technologies (APT), which aim to map cause-effect relationships between tactical change and any resulting benefits for the change initiator. This often involves sorting out the change drivers and weighing their impact value. These sort of tools are largely software-driven and are becoming favorites among innovative big data analysts.

USING FORESIGHT TOOLS IN LEADERSHIP

In the final pages of this chapter, I would like to mention some tactics and tools that may prove useful to leadership teams. Much has been written by others over the years on the use of such classic foresight tools as scenarios, backcasting, and Delphi studies, and I recommend the reader to that voluminous literature. However, I will take a few moments to discuss a developing technique known as the search for "weak signals."

The promise of being able to create one's own in-house foresight research center is an enticing but not a necessary one. Weak signal approaches can be built around external and often virtual foresight research groups. As one example, social media entrepreneurs such as LinkedIn have long supported self-organizing special interest groups as relatively independent sub-groups within the larger LinkedIn structure (such as those dedicated to the practice of foresight). Regardless of how such communal teams are built and managed, the goal is to broaden stakeholder networks through distributed intelligence approaches. This "distributed intelligence" process involves looking for robust outcomes (defined as offering the most utility in the broadest number of settings). Accordingly, it is important to cross-analyze measures of meaning such as social values, market dynamics, and attitude shifts, and triangulate the analytical outcomes.

This avoids the common 'zone out' that results from to see everything at once and the related failure to properly prioritize issues. Interweaving different skill sets and mindsets often requires both collaboration and teamwork, which may in fact consist of consistently exhibiting good manners. For example, listening is usually a passive activity, but it takes some serious digging to find out what a critical naysayer in a foresight team really means and how that affects one's own position. Finally, if the research and analysis process isn't very messy, you are probably not accomplishing much or even doing it right.

The search for weak signals, properly done, can enhance one's ability to spot problems early, share them with allies, and extend the senses of the organization beyond organizational boundaries. Locating leading edges of developments or warnings early enough is critical. That means calling attention to developing trends neither too late or too soon, as too late does no one much good (like yesterday's news) and comes close to embracing "conventional wisdom," while too soon can also be problematic, with an overly visionary leadership team ending up too far ahead of other stakeholders and accordingly and out of connection with "real world" dynamics.

Thus, building a functional mythology of pre-emptive and proprietary visioning on behalf of a leadership team involves a never-ending balancing act. For example, weak signals issues may be threats or opportunities and the real challenge is to know which is which relatively early on in the process. Weak signals are actually "suggestive" trends. Interpreting them takes significant time, focus, and experience. Not all leadership teams enjoy such luxuries and those that do must use them wisely.

The reader might notice the use of the phrase "leadership team," because I want to strongly reinforce that the search for weak signals simply cannot yield useful results as the exercise of a single visionary leader or analyst. It must be a team effort and ideally a community effort, involving coordinated work among concerned and relevant stakeholders to yield viable results over the longer term. As such, the broader the search process and the greater the number of scanning participants, the higher the chances of yielding relevant and useful data.

One highly successful example of distributed intelligence is Intellipedia, which arose in the US Intelligence Community after the shock of being blindsided on September 11, 2001. As of January 2014, Intellipedia had 1113 content pages used by 255,000 analysts at the top secret level (Mathers, 2014). Intellipedia also offers a window on one of the most common responses to sharing sensitive data, which is resistance in cultures where limitations on distribution are common. But it was noted at the time of its founding by Michael Wertheimer, Asst. Deputy Director for Analysis at the Office of the Director of National Intelligence, that the key is risk management, and not risk avoidance, which requires good information throughout that process (Shrader, 2006).

However, no matter how exemplary participants feel their horizon scanning systems are, it is essential to avoid over confidence. The literature is full of what are called "black swans" or "wild cards." These consist of events of very low likelihood but very high systemic impact that seem to "come out of nowhere" and catch senior management entirely by surprise. In 2009, MIT's *Sloan Management Review* asserted that less than 20% of global companies have an ability to spot, interpret, and act on weak signals, implying that management promises of *fully manageable risk* to stakeholders or stockholders is a significant mistake (Schoemaker & Day, 2009).

As well, new solutions to global challenges can also generate what are termed "unexpected consequences" or new and sometimes worse disorders arising from a problem fix. The ideal is to begin to identify threats and opportunities early enough to conceptualize, develop, and integrate well-thought-out responses. Tomorrow's leaders will need to understand change and how change occurs within systems. They will need to prioritize the most probable changes to pay attention to and prepare for the possible, the probable, and the preferable – the last one being the most complex, as it requires achieving working consensus, which becomes more challenging each day we proceed into the increasingly contentious 21st century.

CONCLUSION

In this article, I have endeavored to outline some of the major challenges facing leaders over the next few decades. And naturally, one of the most likely suspects is the disruptive force of new technologies. However, because the forces shaping change outcomes are more often dialectic, I believe that a description of force and counterforce is more accurate. Accordingly, those technologies will likely be constructive as well as disruptive.

Ideally, leaders will map the resulting range of dynamic trends, with their relative weights, hoping for a set of options that can guide the weighing of choices concerning potential threats and opportunities. Not a clear and simple roadmap, surely, but a catalyst for robust change response strategies (again, those strategies that may achieve the best responses across the maximum number of potential situations) for coping with continually accelerating change amid diminishing resources. Finally, while some feel that functional change management is a 'will o' the wisp,' but if it is successful, it is clearly worth pursuing.

In summary, to be valuable to leadership, foresight work should:

- Be focused and targeted,
- Be original and imaginative,
- Provide economic, personal, and cultural payoffs,
- Offer enrichment and learning, and
- Include localization detail, to account for unique cultural and logistic contexts.

Foresight teams and trend analysis tools can enhance leadership strategies and help prepare for sea changes. But with time and staff resources increasingly dear, the following guidelines should be taken seriously. As a rule, good leaders should:

- Look for futures that can be influenced (should be malleable),
- Look for futures that are relevant to the situation in question (should be appropriate),
- Look for futures that include a sufficiently broad range of trends (should be robust),
- Look for futures that are flexible and responsive to continuing change (should be relevant),
- And don't take just one look — keep looking! nothing stands still!!

References

Friedman, T. (2005). *The world is flat: A brief history of the twenty-first century*. New York, NY: Farrar, Straus & Giroux.

Gantz, J., & Reinsel, D. (2013). The digital universe in 2020: Big data, bigger digital shadows, and biggest growth in the far east. *IDC iView: IDC Analyze the Future*. Retrieved from http://www.emc.com/collateral/analyst-reports/idc-digital-universe-western-europe.pdf. Accessed on December 9, 2014.

Gleick, P. H. (2008). *The world's water 2008–2009: The biennial report on fresh-water resources*. Washington, DC: Island Press.

Goldstone, J. (2010). The new population bomb: Four megatrends that will change the world. *Foreign Affairs*, January-February.

Google, Flu Trends. (2015). Retrieved from https://www.google.org/flutrends/us/#US. Accessed on February 12, 2015.

Grant Thornton. (2014). Women in Business: From Classroom to Boardroom.

Lanier, J. (2013). *Who owns the future*, New York, NY: Simon & Schuster.

Manyika, J., Cabral, A., Moodley, L., Moraje, S., Yeboah-Amankwah, S., Chui, M., & Anthonyrajah, J. (2013). *Lions go digital: The Internet's transformative potential in Africa*. Seattle, WA: McKinsey & Company. Retrieved from http://www.mckinsey.com/insights/high_tech_telecoms_internet/lions_go_digital_the_internets_transformative_potential_in_africa. Accessed on November 28, 2014.

Mathers, J. (2014). *FOIA request of Intellipedia usage statistics*. Retrieved from www.muchrock.com. Accessed on January 14, 2015.

McMillian, L. (2012). Gender, organizational behavior &, organizational culture: What studies tell us about how women lead in business. *International Review*, 1(1–2) 33–45.

Pew Research Center. (2014). Women and Leadership.

Schleicher, A. (2010). The case for 21st century learning. OECD education directorate.

Schoemaker, P. l., & Day, G. (2009). *How to make sense of weak signals*. Cambridge, MA: MIT Sloan Management Review. Spring.

Shrader, K. (2006, November 2). *Over 3,600 intelligence professionals tapping into Intellipedia*. Washington, DC: Associated Press. Retrieved from www.usatoday.com http://usatoday30.usatoday.com/tech/news/techinnovations/2006-11-02-intellipedia_x.htm. Accessed on January 18, 2014.

United Nations. (2014a, November 24). *Water for life program "Water Scarcity."* Retrieved from www.un.org/waterforlifedecade/scarcity.shtml. Accessed on January 21, 2015.

United Nations. (2014b). Economic and social affairs. World Urbanization Projections.

Vinge, V. (1993). The coming technological singularity. *Whole Earth Review, 81,* 88–95.

Envisioning Leadership in 2050: Four Future Scenarios

A Case for Relevant 2050 Leadership — Preparing for Change

Jeffrey L. Suderman and Philip A. Foster

> Since the future lacks facts and empirical data, it is less comfortable to work in than the present.
>
> Bishop and Hines (2012, p. 148)

A review of leadership, past, and present, reveals continued evolution and development in our understanding of leadership theories and practices. From Machiavelli to Robert Greenleaf or from Fredrik Taylor to Peter Drucker, leadership has changed over time. One cannot help but wonder how it will continue to evolve in the future.

While we cannot know the future, we can be certain that leadership in 2050 will be different from what it is today. There is immense strategic value in anticipating change and, specifically, anticipating change which will help us understand the future of leadership. The purpose of this chapter is to help readers imagine the future of leadership in two ways. First, it will introduce readers to the academic discipline of strategic foresight and explain how it helps organizations prepare for the future. Second, it will apply the tools of foresight to the topic at hand — what will leadership look like in 2050? This will provide an introductory theoretical understanding of foresight as well as a practical application of how it can be used to anticipate change and develop future agility.

What Is Strategic Foresight?

> Foresight helps organizations build a set of internally consistent and imagined futures in which decisions about the future can be played out, for the purpose of changing thinking, improving decision making, fostering human and organizational learning and improving performance.
>
> Chermack (2011, p. 16)

Successful leaders and organizations are learning to adapt amidst an era which is defined by complexity and constant change (Ashley & Morrison, 1995, p. 5; Nanus, 1992, p. xvii). Adaptation requires leaders to make sense of a world filled with "bewildering complexity and uncertainty" Hammond (1998, p. 13). Herein lays our challenge: consideration of the future requires us to grapple with uncertainty. Two ways leaders can proactively respond to future uncertainty are through either a control model or an agility model. The **future control model** seeks to use processes that predict the future. Concepts such as risk management or Taylorian mechanistic methodologies adhere to tenets of control management. Alternately, the **future agility model** encourages leaders to embrace uncertainty and respond by equipping themselves with knowledge which helps them understand plausible futures.

The disciplines of strategic foresight or future studies adhere to the latter ideology. Foresight does not seek to predict the future. Rather, it seeks to foster future agility by breaking mental models that hinder our ability to identify emerging change (Ashley & Morrison, 1995, pp. 36–37). This agility provides leaders with the ability to respond quickly when changes occur. A pioneer in the field of foresight, Pierre Wack (1984), aptly summarized this when he wrote, "In our times of rapid change and discontinuity, crisis of perception – the inability to see a novel reality emerging by being locked in obsolete assumptions – has become the main cause of strategic failure." Foresight seeks to create an organization that understands its current environment, has thoughtfully considered their future and then applies this knowledge in order to create a preferred future.

Foresight is based on the premise that the future is inherently unknowable, and efforts to get it exactly right are futile (Hines & Bishop, 2006, p. 85). Foresight exercises are used to expand the depth and range of possibilities for organizations to consider, thereby reducing the likelihood and magnitude of surprise. Forecasting alternative futures does not mean developing detailed plans for every contingency. Rather, it equips organizations to monitor the external environment for leading indicators, signs, or guideposts that suggest events are heading toward one or more of the alternatives (Hines & Bishop, 2006, p. 85). The outcomes of these processes enhance individual and corporate nimbleness – the ability to respond quickly – in an environment where no one knows what will happen next (Strategy Foresight Partners, 2011).

The discipline of strategic foresight has been a growing component of strategic planning processes. A study by The Economist Intelligence Unit (2008) revealed that two-thirds of companies have used foresight in some capacity and another 30 percent plan to do so in the future. The Royal Dutch Shell Company popularized scenario planning as a result of their anticipation of Mideast oil embargoes of the 1970s, the collapse of the Soviet Union in the 1980s, and the emergence of the environmental movement in the 1990s (Shell Global, 2013). Similarly, AutoNation, a US car retailer, increased their profitability during the US financial crisis through the use of foresight. They pondered wild possibilities like, "what if consumers were to replace cars every five years instead of every three?" as well as, "what would occur if consumer financing became more difficult to achieve?" (Niles, 2009). Thinking through these future scenarios enabled them to prepare for and prosper in a future affected by economic recession, one that left many auto retailers bankrupt (Niles, 2009). Foresight helps organizations intelligently plan for today through thoughtful consideration of the future.

Chermack (2011) suggests that effective foresight makes uncertainty a part of the plan (p. xv). Foresight does not provide a future blueprint. Rather, it is a process that provides insights, which allow us to respond in the present in an informed and strategic way.

How Do You Utilize Strategic Foresight?

> Scenarios are not about the future, but always about the present. Knowledge of the future must be used to influence the decisions that we make today.
>
> Wilkinson and Kupers (2014)

A cake is a common object. However, the ingredients we use to make a cake differ widely in their form, usage, and outcome. The same principle holds true for the ingredients of strategic foresight. There are dozens of theories, tools, and methodologies that can be used to conduct foresight. Each of these tools may be used to achieve different goals and outcomes. Therefore, the material that follows provides a glimpse of a few foresight tools. It is neither exhaustive nor should our process be viewed as a preferred methodology. For the purposes of this chapter, we have utilized an approach called scenario planning. The following section provides a high-level summary of the scenario planning steps we utilized as we examined the future of leadership. This section will be followed by application of these principles to the subject at hand, the future of leadership.

DEFINE THE ISSUE

The first step in scenario planning is clearly defining the specific future you want to explore and then develop a taxonomy or domain of knowledge about this subject. In this case, the International Leadership Association asked, "What will leadership be like in the year 2050?" While this question evokes a great deal of subjective imagery about leadership, the process of scenario planning involves more than simply imagining a plausible future. Instead, we must compile taxonomies of knowledge from diverse sources. The domain we utilized for this chapter was qualitative expert-generated data derived from a review of current literature. We studied over 100 expert-written articles on varying subjects related to the future context of leadership and business. The research from this step provides the essential knowledge base required for step 2.

SCANNING AND IDENTIFYING KEY THEMES

In step 2, the goal is to identify and summarize emergent research themes in a spreadsheet. This "scanning" process allows key issues to organically emerge from the data. To do this, we reviewed our data from step 1 and asked the following:

1. What phenomena have we identified that could affect the future of leadership?
2. Are there meaningful differences in these phenomena – measured over time?
3. How/where might these phenomena fit in Social, Technological, Economical, Environmental, Political framework (STEEP)? and
4. What are the plausible implications of these phenomena?

These questions were derived from our work in step 1 as we began to define the issues or questions we sought to answer.

From these extrapolated trends, we began to identify the frequency with which a particular theme or concept presented itself. In addition, we assessed the potential level of impact (high or low) and the probability (high or low) of these themes. This resulted in the identification of issues that had both high impact and high probability when applied to our core issue about the Future of Leadership in 2050. These themes form the basis for the next step of identifying driving forces.

IDENTIFYING DRIVING FORCES

Once enough relevant data has been collected and summarized, we turn our attention to identifying driving forces. This involves assessing the issues identified in step 2 and determining how they could impact your organization (significant revision – it previously included content related to trend ID from step 2). These issues are contextualized to your organization by determining which independent external forces will accelerate or restrain the pace of change (Accel-Team, 2012). This step in the process requires us to review our summary of trends and themes and ask, "What will the impact of this be on our organization?" For example, in the previous step we identified the impact of technology as a key theme in leadership literature. Further discussion about this led to the development of a driving force about the impact of technology on leadership – will it have a humanizing or a dehumanizing affect?

This step in the process helps identify areas of future uncertainty and also helps us develop alternatives. These help break our mental models or assumptions about what the future will look like. Driving forces identify emerging patterns that enable us to respond to threats or seize opportunities presented by change (Hickman, 2010, p. 2). The identification of key drivers provides us with information which is foundational to the development of plausible futures as described in step 4.

DEVELOP SCENARIOS

Our list of key drivers and their potential implications are used to develop future scenarios. A simple way to do this is to utilize a Johari window. By crossing two key drivers and their driving forces we create a Johari window with four future scenarios.

These scenarios are a means to *stress test* an organization's current strategy or to develop a new strategy based on the insights it provides. In our example below, the two primary driving and restraining forces were used to create a Johari window, which provided four different scenarios about what leadership could look like in 2050.

In order to make each scenario understandable, a story is written for each of the four quadrants. These vignettes help us understand what these futures would look like and to create mental models about how this future may affect us. The purpose of scenarios is to help us formulate new ideas and analyze alternative futures. Scenarios are not designed to predict the future. Rather, they should help us consider "*what if*" in relation to our current strategy.

APPLY LESSONS LEARNED

Finally, we must act on what we have learned. Our insights from step 4 are then assessed in light of an organization's current strategy and used to develop new strategies. Applying the lessons learned includes communicating the results, developing action agendas, and institutionalizing strategic thinking. This step also includes the development of leading indicators, which are markers that help us identify whether a scenario is growing or decreasing over time. This step begins to activate our response to the "*what if*" question mentioned above.

Thus far we have outlined what strategic foresight is as well as provided a high-level summary of a scenario development process. Next, we will utilize this process to examine what leadership could look like in 2050.

Applying Strategic Foresight: The Future of Leadership

Leadership is inherently shaped by the environment in which it is practiced. What will this environment look like in 2050?

The **first stage** of our process (Define the Issue) was very clear — what will leadership look like in 2050? This question was the foundation for our work in **stage 2**, Scanning and Identifying Key Themes, and required considerable research. Over 100 articles, most less than 12 months old, were assessed for early signs or leading indicators of what that future may look like. The results of these were compiled into a summary list as follows:

SOCIAL
The graying of the workforce
Generation Y/Z
Empowered workforce, self-
    led, leaderless

The psychology of work
The rise of soft-skilled
    workers
Skill specialization
Rise of social networking

Need for strong
   organizational culture

TECHNOLOGICAL
The maker movement –
   distributed
   manufacturing
Bio-machinery
Smarter robots
Internet of things
Information overload –
   big data
Disruptive technology

ENVIRONMENTAL
Environmental movement
Reclaiming the environment
Environmental crisis

ECONOMIC
Intrepreneurs and
   entrepreneurs
VUCA
Changing business lifecycle
Increasing need for
   anticipation
Social impact of business
Rise of collaboration
Prosumers
Changes in reward
   structures

POLITICAL
Corporate social
   responsibility
Post-capitalist society
Value pluralism

Even though the scenario development process is not complete, these results alone demonstrate the value of monitoring changes in our emerging environment.

In **step 3,** identifying driving forces, we assessed how the themes derived from phase 2 have the potential to significantly affect organizations. A typical scanning and driver identification process brings together several experts from numerous fields of study to ensure that diverse ideas are considered (Chermack, 2011; Hines & Bishop, 2006; Ralston & Wilson, 2006). Since the goal of foresight is to break mental models, it is critical that different opinions and perspectives are present. However, for the purpose of this article, we used a vicarious group of experts in the form of a literature review of articles, which assess emerging organizational and leadership trends. The results were qualitatively assessed and then summarized in a list of drivers of change. These issues met the criteria of having high importance and high impact in relation to our question about the future of leadership. The summary of the top external drivers is as follows:

1. Will the practice of leadership place more emphasis on the role of a singular leader or embrace shared leadership teams?
2. Will a workforce with increasing flexibility in workplace/workspace congregate at headquarters (mother-ship) or decentralize and work anywhere (cloud)?
3. Will shifts in social and technological norms require leaders to become specialists or generalists in their skills?

4. Will the increasingly diverse nature of workplace norms (generational and cultural) divide our workforce or draw them together? Will it create strength or weakness?
5. Will the effects of globalization catalyze or fragment our workplaces and organizations?
6. Will our environment cause us to focus on control or flexibility as the success ingredient for leadership and our organizations (Cameron & Quinn, 1999, p. 34)?
7. Will our environments cause our organizations to become more inward facing or outward facing (Cameron & Quinn, 1999, p. 34)?
8. Will ongoing technological advances result in dehumanization or humanization of the workplace and organizations?
9. Will ongoing technological advances cause our leadership and workplaces to integrate and draw closer together or fragment and pull apart?

It is important to note that this is not an exhaustive list of drivers. Thoughtful readers will add their own insights and ideas. Our hope is that these concepts will stimulate further conversations and work related to key leadership drivers and the future of leadership. To borrow a wonderful quote, "This framework is designed to give the user a domain in which to exercise judgment" (Chermack, 2011, p. 29).

Once a broad list of drivers or signals has been identified, we moved on to **step 4**, scenario development. This stage evaluates the list of drivers and narrows them to two key signals (Chermack, 2011, p. xv; Hines & Bishop, 2006). These drivers should encompass the ethos of as many driving forces as possible, have high levels of uncertainty as well as be logical and plausible (Ralston & Wilson, 2006, pp. 112–114). Any of the drivers noted above (as well as ones you will add) could be used to create many different scenarios. In fact, our hope is that others will use and adapt these ideas to develop other future leadership scenarios. However, for the purpose of this exercise, the two core drivers that we chose focused on the form of leadership and the impact of technology on the leadership process. Specifically, they were:

How will changes in the context in which we practice leadership change the form of leadership?

Focus on the role of "me" as the leader (individual)	← →	Focus on the importance of "we" as a leader (group/team)

How will ongoing changes in technology and culture affect the heart of leadership – people?

Dehumanize the ⟵⟶ Humanize the
workplace   workplace

These drivers were then crossed to form a Johari window, also referred as an Axis of Uncertainty. This creates four future leadership scenarios. In order to help others understand the meaning of these scenarios, titles and stories are created for each quadrant (Chermack, 2011, pp. 147–149; Ralston & Wilson, 2006, p. 125). These stories allow us to communicate the implications of these plausible futures to others who may or may not have been involved in the scenario development process and further extrapolate the context of these futures. The following section will provide you with a visual overview of the four scenarios, their story titles, and a brief summary of what each leadership story could look like in the year 2050. The figure below outlines the four future leadership scenarios, and pages 12–17 provide a story which paints a picture of leadership in the year 2050 for each scenario.

THE FUTURE OF LEADERSHIP

Scenario 1: Bio-Circuitry Leadership

The Metaphor: In the movie *Edge of Tomorrow*, soldiers are partnered with a personal armored body suit with which to wage war. Similarly, in this scenario, there is minimal separation between humankind and machinery/technology and very often, humans must adapt to the needs of technology instead of technology being adapted to meet our needs.

Credo: Knowledge is Power

Leader Type: Coordinator, Controller, Organizer, Synthesizer, Monitor

Team Orientation: Performance, Teaming with Technology, Efficiency, Individualistic, Specialists

Story: As the world's population nears 10 billion, organizations are pressed on all sides by demographic, geographic, and technological shifts. These pressures along with the pace of change and growth of technology cause leaders to spend most of their time managing processes and not people. In fact, people are secondary when compared to the importance of technology in solving the challenges of our world. Technology itself has forced workers toward an ever increasing amount of specialized knowledge. Leadership has also become more specialized and singular. Thirty years ago, the term "silo" was considered a negative concept of non-integration. Today, the silo strategy is an intentional means to ensure that we have specialized leaders who can oversee and control complexity. These specializations have resulted in a re-definition of the classical great-man leadership theory but now, the core of this definition focuses on the acquisition of specialized competencies and technological enhancements instead of an inherent leadership ability. As a result of the heavy emphasis on knowledge, the workplace focuses on process, systemization, and efficiency. People fit into these processes and are parts within a dynamic and complex techno-system – an upgrade of Taylorian theory. The organization and the leaders within them are a complex blend of the best of both worlds: machines and humanity. The era of bio-circuitry leadership means that organizations have leveraged people and technology into a seamless system. It is difficult to distinguish between who people are and what they do because of how effectively human capacity is enhanced and blended with technology.

Scenario 2: High-Pod Leadership

The Metaphor: The pea pod is a single unit in which several sub-units exist. Although each individual pea is unique and distinctive, it is only by combining them into one pod whereby we achieve results better than a single part can achieve. Each pod is connected to a larger network, the vine, in which many peas and pods operate together to achieve results which bend technology to serve the needs of the society.

Credo: Power to the People

Leader Type: Innovator, Entrepreneur, Synthesizer, Specialist

Team Orientation: Coupling Innovators with Altruistic Goals, Human Development, Transformation, and Multidisciplinary Collaboration

Story: Although the pace of change and the role of technology continue to increase, the goal has shifted from "more" to "better." We are discovering new ways to utilize technology which are increasing our quality of life and re-humanizing our world. Leadership has responded to the growth in knowledge by creating pods of specialization. When linked together, these mini-idea factories create a network which embody the adage, "the whole is greater than the sum of its parts." These partnerships and networks, once focused on systems and processes, have shifted to a focus on people and re-humanization. Although the knowledge specialization of leaders is increasing, they also realize their limitations of a singular leadership. As a result, specialists have become adept at linking various pods of specialty together. People embrace the paradox of specialization and generalization by becoming subject-matter experts and by building teams or using partners to provide overarching competencies. Leaders build teams both within and outside their organizations. They are driven by goals of transformation, agility, and innovation. Humanity and quality of life are important goals in the lives of leaders and their supporting pods.

Scenario 3: Murmeration Leadership

The Metaphor: Murmeration is the phenomenon we observe when a flock of thousands of starlings fly together as one. As they weave and dance through the air, their form changes and evolves but they remain visible as one entity. This leadership scenario mimics murmeration by blending many unique and complex parts into an overarching whole.

Credo: People-Powered Projects

Leader Type: Innovation, Entrepreneurship, Visionary, Mentor, Team-Builder

Team Orientation: Empowering, Self-Leadership, Transparency

Story: The form of organizations has evolved and we no longer rely on one ideal structure to accomplish our mission. The complexity of our world has been matched by evolving organizational norms which shift as needed to perform complex and multidisciplinary tasks. Organizations are considered temporary in nature and as a result are best described as cloud based – existing and operating as needed. Human capital, now referred to as cloud workers, is composed of many individuals who contract with an organization to complete tasks on a shared organizational platform. Cloud workers are considered as fractional employees, are organizationally transient, and they often work with several firms at a given time. Employees may be distributed anywhere on earth or galactically, and some employees are robotic artificial intelligence workers. The lines are blurred between human capital and robotic capital in this new era of cloud organizations as both work together to complete objectives. Organizations are driven by networked human structures rather than by hierarchical systems. Organizations are self-led and individuals are empowered to get the work done. Hierarchies have collapsed into a network of connected workers. The internet of everything has given way to the humanity of everything. A people-centric approach has overtaken task as king. Macgregor's theory Y is embraced as the driving force behind productivity and competitive advantage. The company structure is defined by those who work there and evolves as projects come and go.

Scenario 4: Automaton Leadership

The Metaphor: By definition, an automaton is a moving mechanical device made in imitation of a human being. This leadership scenario flips this model. As a result of the relentless progression of technology, human capital will be shaped into a group of robot-like devices to accomplish the betterment of our world.

Credo: Processing People

Leader Type: Driver, Competitor, Producer, Micromanagement

Team Orientation: Competing, High-Structure, Top-Down, Groupthink

Story: The economic collapses of the early twenty-first century coupled with a decreasing fulltime workforce led to a wide acceptance of technologies in everyday life. Because of the pace of technological growth and a dire need for individuals to find work, employment laws protecting human capital could no longer be sustained. Individuals of working age now apply for and are fitted with docking harnesses which permit them to connect directly into the work grid. The Internet of everything now includes humans themselves. Individuals strap themselves into a work pod, and the docking hardness connects their entire body into the Internet. These tech pods read and sense thoughts and movements as all individuals are now integrated directly into technology. Leaders now have a direct control over the individual workers. While each worker maintains a certain level of free will, leaders are able to maintain a closer control over their every thought and action. Working pods are the twenty-first century equivalent of the cubical office space where work activities are monotonous, routine, and where every action is tracked. Employees no longer have a say in many of their work conditions and as a result of control-based leadership, act and think in a collective manner. Opportunities for advancement are few and are based on strict analytics. Organizations are no longer defined by human capital and geographic space but by the size of their human network, operational efficiencies, and terabytes of data. Organizations have since abandoned expensive buildings in favor of the cloud and engage the world within a virtual holographic context. The lines between reality and virtual are merged as individuals spend most of their waking time connecting to the network. Leadership uses detailed analytics to track productivity and efficiencies and control individuals through data. The leadership function has evolved into hyper-micromanagement as organizational traffic control – monitoring and micro-managing every detail.

SIGNPOSTS

While each of these scenarios is plausible, only time will tell which elements will become most dominant. As a result, it is useful to establish leading indicators — also called signposts — of each scenario as a means to track their progress or lack of progress (Ralston & Wilson, 2006, pp. 167–68). Here are some of the indicators we developed for each of the scenarios listed above:

1. **Bio-Circuitry Leadership**
   (a) Emphasis on technology over people
   (b) Merging of biology and technology
   (c) Emphasis on the management of processes and systemization
   (d) Rise of specialized knowledge
   (e) Increased emphasis on silo strategy

2. **High-Pod Leadership**
   (a) The mindset that more is better
   (b) Emphasis on technology to re-humanize the world
   (c) The paradoxical blending of specialists and generalists
   (d) Networking of people and systems for greater efficiencies
   (e) Emphasis on transformation, agility and innovation

3. **Murmeration Leadership**
   (a) Flattening of organizational hierarchies
   (b) Emergence of temporary organizations
   (c) Cloud based workers
   (d) Blending of human capital and robotics
   (e) People-centric approach to human capital

4. **Automaton Leadership**
   (a) A new emphasis on the great man theory
   (b) Integration of technology into humanity
   (c) Internet of everything and everyone
   (d) Organizations reside in a virtual holographic context
   (e) Emphasis on results and efficiencies

Conclusion

The physicist, Niels Bohr once stated, "Prediction is very difficult, especially about the future." His humorous sound-bite contains a lot of truth! This chapter presents an outline of what leadership could look like in 2050. We are confident that aspects of these scenarios will become reality while others will fade into oblivion.

As we circle back to where we began, we are reminded that, "the future is inherently unknowable and efforts to get it exactly right are futile" (Hines & Bishop, 2006, p. 85). While elements of these stories may seem far-fetched, their usefulness will not be measured by their accuracy. Instead, we have used the discipline of foresight to present a range of possibilities to help us consider leadership in the year 2050. This helps us achieve several important outcomes: making sense of an issue, helping determine an optimal strategy, anticipating what could occur, and facilitating adaptive learning (Chermack, 2011, p. 83).

Therefore, the success of this foresight process will be measured by how effectively we process these insights. These images should begin to evoke changes in how we view and engage with our eventual future. As you assess these leading indicators you will be able to ascertain which leadership future we are heading toward (Hines & Bishop, 2006, p. 85). In addition, thoughtful consideration of scenarios causes us to ask critical questions such as, what is our preferred future and how can we foster it? This knowledge, whether gleaned here or elsewhere, becomes a means by which you can proactively prepare for the future. This is leadership agility.

References

Accel-Team. (2012). *Force field analysis*. Retrieved from http://www.accel-team.com/techniques/force_field_analysis.html. Accessed on July 25, 2012.

Ashley, W. C., & Morrison, J. L. (1995). *Anticipatory management: 10 power tools for achieving excellence into the 21st century*. Leesburg, VA: Issue Action Publications.

Bishop, P. C., & Hines, A. (2012). *Teaching about the future*. New York, NY: Palgrave MacMillan.

Cameron, K., & Quinn, R. (1999). *Diagnosing and changing organizational culture: Based on the competing values framework*. Reading, MA: Addison-Wesley.

Chermack, T. J. (2011). *Scenario planning in organizations: How to create, use and assess scenarios*. San Francisco, CA: Berrett-Koehler.

Hammond, A. (1998). *Which world? Scenarios for the 21st century*. Washington, DC: Island Press.

Hickman, G. R. (2010). *Leading organizations. Perspectives for a new era* (2nd ed.). Thousand Oaks, CA: Sage.

Hines, A., & Bishop, P. (2006). *Thinking about the future: Guidelines for strategic foresight*. Washington, DC: Social Technologies.

Nanus, B. (1992). *Visionary leadership*. San Francisco, CA: Jossey-Bass.

Niles, D. (2009). The secret of successful scenario planning. *Forbes*, August 3. Retrieved from http://www.forbes.com/2009/08/03/scenario-planning-advice-leadership-managing-planning.html

Ralston, B., & Wilson, I. (2006). *The scenario planning handbook: Developing strategies in uncertain times*. Mason, OH: Thomson South-Western.

Shell Global. (2013). Sowing the seeds of strategic success. *Impact Magazine*, Issue 1. Retrieved from http://www.shell.com/global/products-services/solutions-for-businesses/globalsolutions/impact-online/read-full-issues/2013/issue-1/sowing-the-seeds-of-strategic-success.html. Accessed on August 25, 2014.

Strategy Foresight Partners. (2011). *The strategy foresight partnership*. Retrieved from http://www.strategyforesight.org/index.php?option=com_content&view=article&id=48&Itemid=53. Accessed on September 6, 2014.

The Economist Intelligence Unit. (2008). Risk 2018: Planning for an unpredictable decade. *The Economist Group.* New York, NY. Retrieved from http://www.slideshare.net/Management-Thinking/risk-2018-planning-for-an-unpredictable-decade. Accessed on September 11, 2014.

Wack, P. (1984). *Scenarios: The gentle art of re-perceiving.* Unpublished manuscript, Harvard Business School.

Wilkinson, A., & Kupers, R. (2014). *The essence of scenarios: Learning from the Shell experience.* Amsterdam: Amsterdam University Press.

Section II
Future Leadership Drivers,
Issues, and Contexts

epending on which side of the aisle one sits, predictions regarding the global future in 2050 can be filled with optimism or fraught with pessimism. Gorbachev, former leader of the Soviet Union, quoted in the New York Times Opinion Page described it in this way, "The future is not predetermined. It depends on what we do today" (Gorbachev, 2012). Thus, we can either react to or take control of what lies ahead. Unlike the past 35 years, we know that from now till 2050 and beyond, the world will become far more globalized facing challenging issues such as population growth and ageing; the expansion of urban centers; global warming and climate change; the depletion of natural and other resources, including potential food shortages; rapid technological advances; changing economic dominance; and far more interdependence among nations than currently exists. Therefore, it is incumbent upon leaders today to take charge and be proactive to ensure that the leaders of tomorrow are equipped with the resources, skills, and tools needed to adapt to these ever evolving challenges.

The chapters in this section of *Leadership 2050* purposefully take us from broad issues to specific contexts impacting the future of leadership. In Chapter 3, Donnette J. Noble begins by examining broad drivers and issues related to social justice that will be exacerbated in the future without intervention or attention today. Noble then outlines a variety of critical social issues of the future, and suggests that socially responsible and socially just leadership ensure equitable treatment for all. Her piece provides us a glimpse of disparities that will only be intensified without intervention and suggests that we incorporate social justice into our leadership education and scholarship.

Next we move into specific issues and drivers, when Rian Satterwhite, Whitney McIntyre Miller, and Kate Sheridan leads us directly from Nobel's social justice point of view into an understanding of the complexities and "wicked problems" associated with sustainability and peace. He frames the challenges of social, environmental, and ecological justice in the future and what must be done to address these issues from a leadership perspective. In Chapter 4, they posit that social and environmental justice are intricately linked to peace and that leaders in the future must address these challenges from a systems perspective with an eye toward meaning making and distributed leadership. Moreover, leadership educators must be adaptive, understand current leadership challenges, and evolve to fit the leadership needs of the day.

The next two chapters utilize our knowledge of the past to inform our understanding of the future. If the past is prologue, then Stan Amaladas broadens our perspective by examining the issues and drivers of the past, to suggest positive change for the future. In Chapter 5, Stan takes us on a journey through the last three centuries, examining society's self-focused behavior through the lenses of three writers, Rousseau, Marx, and Weber. This notion that self-serving behavior, or private reason, has existed at least for the last 300 years reminds us that leaders must be vigilant in broadening their perspective to incorporate social reason, and address the concerns of private reason in order to mobilize communities for the betterment of the future.

Like the preceding chapter, Icarbord Tshabangu challenges us not only to reflect on the political contexts of past, but also the contemporary contexts of today. He suggests we seek to understand the world's political systems, economics, and education as they inform future leadership development and democratic education necessary to address democracy and meet future challenges of the citizenry. In Chapter 6, Tshabangu examines the variety of historical perspectives of political systems and concludes that democracy has and will continue to rise significantly by 2050. This distributed leadership, in large part, is a result of the advances of technology, which resulted from access to vast quantities of information. Regarding the future of distributed leadership, he sees a move that allows the exercise of power and influence by followers and a valuing of many involved in decision-making.

Finally, the last two chapters focus on specific contemporary contexts, which will have huge implications for the future. Barry A. Doublestein, Walter T. Lee, and Richard M. Pfohl, implore the healthcare profession to be proactive, rather than reactive, lest the profession become irrelevant and lack the strategies to be innovative. They suggest that the issues and challenges of healthcare will be more critical in 2050 if we don't act decisively today to address the complexities and shortfalls of a burdened system. In Healthcare 2050: Anticipatory Leadership to Address the Challenges of the Future, the authors offer "anticipatory leadership" as a strategic response to future challenges including the shortages of physicians and the quality of patient-centered care.

In Chapter 8, Daniel M. Jenkins, Lisa Endersby, and Kathy L. Guthrie, discuss the changing digital landscape and how these changes will inform leadership education into the future. The authors examine how technological advances that are boundless will fuel leadership development and education. They postulate that higher education will be available in far more venues and platforms, competency based, and often utilizing virtual worlds. This chapter takes an in-depth look into the shifting landscape of leadership education and provides guidance as we move toward 2050.

Mindy McNutt

Reference

Gorbachev, M. (2012). The earth in 2050. *The New York Times*, June 21. Retrieved from http://www.nytimes.com/interactive/2012/06/22/opinion/global-agenda-magazine-the-earth-in-2050-interactive.html

Leading for Tomorrow in a World Yearning for Social Justice

Donnette J. Noble

Introduction

The global citizens of 2015 are living in contested spaces and precarious places; there is a growing frustration with the *status quo* and we hear increasing demands for fairness. People of privilege, whether or not they believe they are privileged, are finding less and less comfort in the way we were, or the way we are, because those who are not of privilege are increasingly demanding a share of the pie, whatever that pie might be, and they will likely remain undeterred in their quest to gain their fair share, a perceived true equality.

Borders are being violated, cultures called into question, traditional values renounced, beliefs challenged, resources diminished, opportunities squandered, and yes, even our collective humanity is being slowly stripped of its virtue. Yet, amidst the clashing of self-serving ideologies, time-honored practices, and simple survival, there is within many people a desire to right wrongs and achieve true equality as they promote harmony and balance among people in their natural and constructed environments. Achieving equality, harmony, and balance, let alone sustaining it, over the next 35 years will be exceedingly difficult given the projected addition of more than two billion people to the global population (Kochhar, 2014) and the added strain their number will place on the limited resources, services, and opportunities already being sought by the seven billion people currently inhabiting the planet.

The world's social and environmental trajectory, replete with increasing disparities of wealth, resources, and opportunity, is unsustainable (Ehrlich & Tobias, 2014). Therefore, it is critical that leaders expand their focus to encompass a broader accountability and embrace leadership that is centered on social justice — the fair and impartial distribution of resources, opportunities, and benefits of society to all of its members regardless of position, place, or other exclusionary criteria (Johnson, 2008). There is an unequal distribution of power impacting most social collectives, and it is the most powerful in society who can impose interpreted knowledge that marginalizes and de-legitimizes the competing knowledge claims of the less powerful (Johnson, 2008).

Amid the goals of socially just leadership are equity (the fair and just treatment of people), awareness (a realization), and agency (Gale, 2014). Agency, according to Emirbayer and Mische (1998, p. 963), is a:

> temporally embedded process of social engagement, informed by the past (in its habitual aspect), but also oriented toward the future (as a capacity to imagine alternative possibilities) and toward the present (as a capacity to contextualize past habits and future projects within the contingencies of the moment).

It is a critical component in terms of the activism that is necessary to promote a more balanced and equitable order, to combat silence, to defeat erasure and invisibility, to resist harm, and to redress grievances (Gale, 2014; Shields, 2004).

CONDITIONS AND PROJECTIONS

Current Trends

Among the most significant factors contributing to social injustice is economic inequality, a worsening condition evidenced by gaps of income and asset distribution; disparities that have been widening dramatically since the 1980s (United Nations, 2006). In 1987, when *Forbes* began tracking the world's billionaires, there were only 140 of them and they had a combined net worth of some $295 billion. By 2014, there were 1,645 billionaires controlling the world's economy with an aggregate net worth of $6.4 trillion — a nearly 22-fold increase in fewer than three decades. Despots, dictators, and royal families, however, whose wealth is the result of positions of power are not included on the list of the world's wealthiest people (Donlan & Kroll, 2014). Of the 1,645 billionaires who make up the current list, four percent, approximately 66 of them, own assets equal to the total combined assets of the three and a half billion people who currently occupy the lower economic half of the world's population (Moreno, 2014).

There is a significant correlation between economics and social and human development (Marmot & Bell, 2012; Rabiei, 2014; Stavrakantonaki, 2014) and the inequalities that result. Discrepancies occur in the distribution of work and remunerated employment; access to knowledge, education, and healthcare; provisions for a safe environment; and opportunities for civic and political representation and participation (United Nations, 2006) which all contribute to the trend away from social justice. Even in the most developed nations, equality has not yet been fully achieved (Kerbo, 2012).

Population

The global population is expected to exceed nine billion by 2050 with nearly nine out of every ten people living in developing nations and six out of every ten living in India, replacing China as the world's most populous nation (Hagmann, 2001; Kochhar, 2014). Even with the staggering death tolls from AIDS and epidemic disease in Africa and Asia, most of the projected global population growth will be in these areas while the growth in developed nations will remain stable or decline (Hagmann, 2001; Kochhar, 2014). Additionally, by 2050 the number of people worldwide age 65 or older is expected to triple (Kochhar, 2014; WHO, 2012) and 70 percent of the population will live in urban areas (WHO, 2010).

Labor Market

Trends over the last two decades indicate that the economic growth generated by financial globalization has not favored most participants in the labor market, as low employment elasticities, growing inequality, and persistent informalization of labor continue to demonstrate. While a small minority has profited from this growth, such favorable consequences are highly asymmetric. It is the same workers, who did not fully benefit from the economic growth, who are now suffering disproportionately following the recent economic crisis resulting in a substantial increase in the number of households living in poverty (van der Hoeven, 2010).

More than 61 million jobs have been lost since the start of the global financial crisis in 2008 and there are currently 201 million people without jobs; that number is expected to grow by another three million in 2015. The International Labour Organization (ILO) predicts that unemployment will continue to worsen in the coming years resulting in increases in inequality and civil unrest (Hurtado, 2015). Additionally, the ILO (2014) predicted that by 2050 for every four people of working age, six people will be depending on that income and that the "effects of climate change, disasters, pollution, environmental degradation and resource depletion [will] have serious negative implications for economic growth, employment and social development" (p. 39).

Education

The high levels of educational inequality throughout the world consistently result in lower levels of innovation, lower levels of production efficiency, and the continued transmission of poverty across generations. Currently there is a concentration of economic benefits to elite groups of educated people but, as the global population continues to increase substantially, not only does equitable access to education make good economic sense it is becoming a moral imperative. That is, increased access to education will help people realize their full potential and enhance their value to society (Porta, Arcia, Macdonald, Radyakin, & Lokshin, 2011).

There are approximately 69 million adolescents in low-income countries who are receiving no post-primary education; four million new classrooms are urgently needed to accommodate those who are not in school. More than 40 percent of out-of-school children are living in conflict-ridden poor countries and millions of children are forced out of school every year due to natural disasters. Additionally, while the gender gap in education has decreased, women still account for two-thirds (500 million) of the world's illiterate adults (UN Global Education Initiative, n.d.). By 2050, educational attainment, while challenging for developing nations, will be critical in terms of developing the human capital necessary to spur economic growth and mitigate the confluence of negative impacts resulting from the burgeoning population (Lloyd, 2001).

Healthcare

In a single year, 2012, more than six million of the world's children ages five or younger died from preventable causes and more than a billion people every year do not receive the healthcare they need (Forsyth, 2013); the common denominators are a lack of access to care and a lack of money to pay for it. Economic stability is inarguably linked with health and longevity. The overall life expectancy at birth between 1960 and 2007, for example, rose by ten years (from 69 to 79 years of age) in high-income nations while the average life expectancy in sub-Saharan Africa rose by only six years from age 40 to age 46 (Walraven, 2011). A child born in Afghanistan in 2010 was faced with a 20 percent chance of dying before the age of five as compared to a less than one percent chance for a child born in North America or Western Europe during the same time (Walraven, 2011). Even in relatively rich nations (Finland, the Netherlands, the United Kingdom, and the United States), poor people die, on average, five to 15 years younger than people with financial means (Walraven, 2011).

As life expectancies increase, the World Health Organization (2012) predicted that the number of older adults who will no longer be able to look after themselves will quadruple in developing nations by 2050 and the number of cases of dementia and Alzheimer's as the population ages will more than triple. Aside from the significant continuation of communicable diseases, most notably HIV/AIDS, the magnitude of non-communicable diseases (NCDs) (cardiovascular disease, cancer, chronic respiratory diseases, and diabetes) will evolve into a staggering economic burden with a negative impact on the global gross domestic product (GDP) as the number of cases rise substantially by 2050 (Bloom et al., 2011).

Safety Net

According to Lekovic (2012), the natural imperative of the economy is to serve humankind. Therefore, it is necessary to create efficient systems of welfare and social support in order to empower individuals. In transition countries [those moving from centrally planned government or state run economies to free market economies (Che & Shen, 2013)] in particular, the prevailing neo-liberal concepts of deregulation, liberalization, and privatization have almost completely marginalized the social development component. The consequences of these policies have been devastating and have perpetuated high unemployment, increased poverty, the concentration of wealth, and wide-spread social insecurity (Lekovic, 2012; Theoharis, 2007).

Civic and Political Engagement

While one cannot claim that inequality and poverty alone create civil unrest and political violence, the argument has been made that such conditions spark political violence and provide a prime breeding ground for ongoing conflict (Kerbo, 2012). Domhoff (1990, 2006) concluded that, indeed, it is the people from the so-called upper class who populate the positions of most significance within the major economic and political institutions and influence their related policy-forming processes. As we look toward 2050, tensions between political and cultural goals will likely continue (Bernstein, 2010) if not increase.

Environmental Concerns

Food insecurity today results in one out of every five people in the developing world being chronically undernourished. The United Nations Food and Agricultural Organization (FAO) estimated that food production worldwide must increase 70 percent by 2050 in order to accommodate projected population increases and production must double in developing nations during the same period (Powledge, 2010).

And then there is the matter of climate change. Educated predictions about which crops in what regions will suffer most from temperature rises, erratic precipitation patterns, and the other anticipated effects of climate change have been made. The consensus is that Africa will lose a significant portion of its maize crop and the rice-growing regions of Southeast Asia will be similarly affected (Powledge, 2010) thus straining food production even further.

Nearly one-quarter of the world's population faces an economic water shortage as a result of the lack of infrastructure to take water from streams or aquifers. Water use has been growing at more than twice the rate of population and in slightly more than a decade, nearly two billion people will be living in countries with absolute water scarcity and nearly two-thirds of the world's population may find themselves under conditions of water stress (UNDESA, 2014).

MARGINALIZATION AND IMPENDING PREDICAMENTS

Due to time and circumstance, millions of people around the world, despite their contributions or despite their desire to be recognized as valuable members of a community, remain largely invisible to policy and decision-makers in governments and industries and are therefore, socially vulnerable (Hurst, Termine, & Karl, 2007). Social vulnerability can, in turn, lead to human rights violations, racism, discrimination, ethics violations, corporate greed, political corruption, and human atrocities (Abouzeid, 2011; Barr & Drury, 2009; Bernstein, 2010; Braungart, 1984; Bynoe, 2004; Fayong, 2008; Gautney, 2011; Hamayotsu, 2011; Harris, 2006; Langdon, 2011; Meek, 2011; NPR, 2011; Polese, 2011; Thorn, 2009; Valocchi, 2005).

The world is in a state of flux and what it will look like in 2050 is not an absolute but we do know at this moment that, while there are billions of people sharing the planet, they are living in parallel universes as they walk the tightrope of the human continuum from its past to its future (Ehrlich & Ornstein, 2010). There are enormous chasms between the haves and have nots, and such situations create stunning opportunities for leaders to emerge as positive forces for good. The leaders of tomorrow could reshape life to create a more harmonious, just, sustainable, peaceful, and prosperous world (Parks, 2005). Perhaps the greatest challenge for leaders over the next 35 years will be how to shift their mindsets to ensure they are leading in socially *just* ways inasmuch as "the ways in which people understand their own relationship to the past, future, and present, make a difference [in] their actions" (Emirbayer & Mische, 1998, p. 973).

Leadership

Multiple interpretations of the term *leadership* exist yet there is no unequivocally uniform definition (Chemers, 2000; Jago, 1982; Kellerman & Webster, 2001; Lord, Brown, Harvey, & Hall, 2001; Pfeffer, 1977; Rockman & Waterman, 2008; Sashkin, 2004); regardless, it is an instrument of social influence (Fritz, Lunde, Brown, & Banset, 2004; Yukl, 2013). The study of leadership is frequently parsed along lines of specialization such as agricultural (Kelsey & Wall, 2003), environmental (Egri & Herman, 2000), spiritual (Fry, 2005), supervisory (Greer & Plunkett, 2007), or sustainable (Hargreaves & Fink, 2006); however, injustice transcends nearly every socially constructed boundary, and can be found in virtually any society or arena. When it comes to the array of competing forces and current disparities of the human condition, it is critical that scholars, practitioners, and others contribute to the leadership discourse and process by making clear distinctions among attitudes and approaches that are socially *responsible* and those that are socially *just*.

SOCIALLY RESPONSIBLE LEADERSHIP

Socially responsible leadership, which includes an element of self-judgment, encompasses moral and/or legal standards of conduct, internal obligations, concern for others, and concern for consequences (DeHoogh & Den Hartog, 2008; Pless & Maak, 2011; Waldman & Galvin, 2008). It is a relational and ethical phenomenon and occurs in conjunction with social processes among "those who affect or are affected by leadership and have a stake in the purpose and vision" of the relationship (Maak & Pless, 2006, p. 103); and therein lies the crux of the issue. "To not be responsible is to not be an effective leader" (Waldman & Galvin, 2008, p. 327) but to whom the responsibility is owed is problematic inasmuch as "responsible leadership is not the same concept in the minds of all" (Waldman & Galvin, 2008, p. 328).

Socially responsible leadership, a multilevel theory that connects a variety of factors (Pless & Maak, 2011), involves accountability, dependability, authority, and in some cases, empowerment and eudaemonism, as well as producing advantages for certain constituencies (Cameron, 2011). Following the rules and protecting the interests and assets of stakeholders while operating within legal parameters equates to being responsible, but is that enough? Logic overlaid with compassion for humanity would indicate otherwise; it is not enough to be simply responsible. It is quite possible for an individual or an organization to extoll their commitment to be socially responsible while at the same time failing to adhere to the most basic tenets of social justice. According to Augustinian theory, "it's not what you do that matters but rather the state of mind with which you do it" (Moore & Bruder, 2008, p. 291). In other words, a sense of duty may compel a leader to act responsibly but it is the presence of empathy within a leader that will more likely bring social justice to fruition.

SOCIALLY JUST LEADERSHIP

Socially just leadership is both a process and a goal to ensure that all individuals and groups within a society enjoy equal access to participation within that society and that the distribution of resources is equitable in an environment of psychological and physical safety (Bell, 2010). Conceptually, justice seeks the fair distribution of resources and pursues the correction of failed social structures and models that perpetuate stratification and produce injustice and inequality (Kerbo, 2012). Functionally, justice relies on a set of principles that help to guide people in determining what is right or wrong, regardless of culture, and it is one of the four virtues of classical moral philosophy, including courage, temperance, and prudence (CESJ, 2014). Justice also reflects the human striving for universal values and "compels people to look beyond what *is*, to what *ought to be*" (CESJ, 2014, para. 11) in an effort to improve current systems for the good of every person

"Hopes [for] creating a just society have captured the human imagination for years" (Johnson, 2008, p. 301). However, the notion of fusing leadership and social justice is a comparatively recent phenomenon and it is as though we are standing at an intersection of subjective reality and "historically marginalizing factors" (Poutiatine & Conners, 2011, p. 142). The future of socially just leadership hinges on the recognition and respect of a common humanity, an acknowledgment of the existence of unfair and unjust social systems, and a keen observation of disruptions to various social structures.

Social justice demands unwavering attention and must be addressed broadly at every level and within every aspect of society, not just within the framework of socially responsible leadership. Historically, many leadership education and preparation programs have been underprepared to address the elements of social justice and, in practice, were not necessarily focused on understanding the inequities in society or tackling the challenges of equity work (Brown, 2006). However, imbued with a solid understanding of the past, an increased awareness of the nuances of the present, and with a watchful and curious eye on the future, such programs can be transformational as they lead efforts toward social justice and dramatically impact the path of just causes.

Fortunately, there are those who are willing to frame leadership as a quest for equity as well as redress in the transition from one system to another (Jansen, 2006). Logically it becomes incumbent upon leaders to take a principal role in protecting the world's most vulnerable populations and to draw attention to matters of injustice in a legitimate effort to persuade others to forge alliances, strategize, give voice to voiceless, and become vessels of positive and transformative change by embracing the precepts of social justice. This endeavor requires both inductive and deductive reasoning; induction to serve as the starting point to determine what is of greatest concern and to establish certain truths about that concern followed by deduction which moves beyond known or assumed propositions in search of additional truth(s) (Copi, Cohen, & McMahon, 2011).

While Bogotch (2002) contended that there are no absolutes when it comes to models for socially just leadership, there are various themes that highlight the concept and drive the practice. Socially just leaders (Furman, 2012):

1. are proactive change agents who are intimately aware of the issues of oppression, marginalization, and exclusion and they are actively engaged in transformative leadership behaviors;
2. are uncharacteristically courageous, persistent, and wholly committed to a social justice agenda;
3. believe that inclusion and authentic participation is the only way to facilitate opportunities for empowerment and to create mechanisms and spaces for democratic processes;
4. rely on quality communication that supports a relationship-driven, holistic, and morally grounded approach to equity; and
5. engage in regular self-reflection as a means to examine their own previously held assumptions or biases.

The themes that help define socially just leadership, in turn, inform the creation of frameworks for leadership education and development programs that contain actionable steps that can be used toward the resolution of all manner of ills. A basic framework for incorporating social justice into leadership scholarship, programs, and practices includes (Furman, 2012; Parker & Shapiro, 1992): (1) an understanding of social justice and its implications in various arenas; (2) self-reflection to determine one's place within the matrix of being; (3) assessing the specifics of injustice and inequality; (4) identifying, challenging, and countering discrimination and prejudice; (5) analyzing mechanisms that maintain the status quo of social stratification; (6) identifying strategies to challenge power and hierarchical structures; and (7) creating alliances to compel change.

When values that support social justice can be brought into the consciousness of others, they can be validated and taught. Such values include (Hockenos, 2011): (1) solidarity; (2) confidence – trusting in others and their abilities to play an integral role in transformative change; (3) reliability – congruence between one's actions and one's words; (4) commitment to shared effort – a willingness to accept responsibility; and (5) being principled, yet flexible – knowing where one stands without being rigid.

Conclusion

In reach of warranted conclusions, one must evaluate competing claims for truth, critique arguments, recognize inconsistences, detect logical fallacies, and construct formal arguments (Copi et al., 2011) and who better than leaders to do this? Leaders possess a unique ability to inspire others and, perhaps, there is no area more suitable for motivation than the fair and just treatment of all people regardless of who they are or what their circumstance. As Luthans and Slocum (2004) have addressed, humankind is face with "an unprecedented economic, technological, sociopolitical, and [a] moral/ethical tumultuous sea of change" (p. 227). It is time we jettison ineffective leadership theories and practices and think strategically about redesigning leadership approaches to meet the challenges of today's dynamic environments and the emerging demands of tomorrow (Crossan, Vera, & Nanjad, 2008).

An autocratic approach to 2050 is not a viable option, "We live in an era of unprecedented globalization and interdependence, where the impacts of policies, decisions, and initiatives in one place can ripple across the globe" (Clark, 2012, para. 23) and this encapsulates the necessity for repositioning leadership approaches. If "humans make sense of their future by reflecting on the past" (English, Papa, Mullen, & Creighton, 2012, p. 5) it is incumbent upon us to recognize that changes in lifestyles, social indices, communications, production, and consumption patterns have changed dramatically (Johnson, 2008) and it calls into question the legitimacy of current practices. The leaders of today need to support a panoply of tomorrows by creating a culture of innovation and shared values that foster good returns on investments (both economically and in terms of human capital) and will result in the kind of social cohesion that supports sustainable development and success in myriad areas.

To begin meeting the challenges we must recognize collectively that we each have a critical role to play in creating a hopeful and sustainable future to the greatest extent possible. This is best addressed through an adapted multi-perspective view on leadership

(Pappas, 2012) that includes: (1) a *consciousness* that unites individual values, beliefs, and percepts to a respect for nature, hopes for humanity, and connections to spirit; (2) *behavior* that allows for passionate and purposeful action and courage in one's convictions; (3) a *culture* of inclusion and deference for varied worldviews; and, (4) a *multidimensional* approach to problem solving, services, collaboration, and sustainable programs.

It is unrealistic to think that disparities in the human condition will cease to exist by 2050. Inarguably, the notions of *greater than* and *less than* have been present in the minds and creations of humankind for as long as the civilized world has existed. Nevertheless, the evolution of intellect and the growth of compassion can become critical factors in support of the indomitable human spirit leading to equity, balance, and true social justice. Inspiration arises from the depths of worthy purpose and is the energizing force that evokes possibility and fuels the capacity to stay the course; it is the wellspring of courage that resists inadequate solutions (Parks, 2005) and stands firm in the conviction that, when voices and actions are unified, the seed of transformative change will take root and the challenges of 2050 will be met.

References

Abouzeid, R. (2011). Bouazizi: The man who set himself and Tunisia on fire. *Time*. Retrieved from http://www.time.com/time/magazine/article/0,9171,2044723,00.html

Barr, D., & Drury, J. (2009). Activist identity as a motivational resource: Dynamics of (Dis)empowerment at the G8 direct actions, Gleneagles, 2005. *Social Movement Studies, 8*(3), 243–260.

Bell, L. A. (2010). Theoretical foundations: What is social justice? In M. Adams, W. J. Blumenfeld, C. Castaneda, H. W. Hackman, M. L. Peters, & X. Zuniga (Eds.), *Readings for diversity and social justice* (2nd ed., pp. 21–26). New York, NY: Routledge.

Bernstein, M. (2010). Celebration and suppression: The strategic uses of identity by the lesbian and gay movement. In D. McAdam & D. A. Snow (Eds.), *Readings on social movements: Origins, dynamic and outcomes* (pp. 499–518). New York, NY: Oxford.

Bloom, D. E., Cafiero, E. T., Jané-Llopis, E., Abrahams-Gessel, S., Bloom, L. R., Fathima, S., ... Weinstein, C. (2011). *The global economic burden of noncommunicable diseases*. Geneva: World Economic Forum.

Bogotch, I. E. (2002). *Educating for eco-justice and community*. Athens, GA: University of Georgia Press.

Braungart, R. G. (1984). Historical generations and youth movement: A theoretical perspective. In R. E. Ratcliff & L. Kriesberg (Eds.), *Research in social movements, conflicts and change* (pp. 95–142). Greenwich, CT: Jai Press Inc.

Brown, K. M. (2006). Leadership for social justice and equity: Evaluating a transformative framework and andragogy. *Educational Administration Quarterly, 42*(5), 700–745.

Bynoe, Y. (2004). *Stand and deliver: Political activism, leadership, and the hip hop culture.* New York, NY: Soft Skull Press.

Cameron, K. (2011). Responsible leadership as virtuous leadership. *Journal of Business Ethics, 98*, 25–35.

Center for Economic and Social Justice [CESJ]. (2014). Defining economic and social justice. Retrieved from http://www.cesj.org/learn/definitions/defining-economic-justice-and-social-justice/

Che, D., & Shen, L. (2013). The co-development of economies and institutions. *Economics of Transition, 21*(2), 241–268.

Chemers, M. M. (2000). Leadership research and theory: A functional integration. *Group Dynamics Theory, Research, and Practice, 4*(1), 27–43.

Clark, H. (2012, November 7). Lecture: *Our world in 2050: More equitable and sustainable − or less?* Address to the World Affairs Council of Northern California, San Francisco, CA.

Copi, I. M., Cohen, C., & McMahon, K. (2011). *Introduction to logic* (14th ed.). Boston, MA: Prentice Hall.

Crossan, M., Vera, D., & Nanjad, L. (2008). Transcendent leadership: Strategic leadership in dynamic environments. *The Leadership Quarterly, 19*(5), 569–581.

DeHoogh, A. H. B., & Den Hartog, D. N. (2008). Ethical and despotic leadership, relationships with leader's social responsibility, top management team effectiveness and subordinates' optimism: A multi-method study. *The Leadership Quarterly, 19*(3), 297–311.

Domhoff, G. W. (1990). *The power elite and the state.* New York, NY: Aldine.

Domhoff, G. W. (2006). *Who rules America?* (5th ed.). New York, NY: McGraw-Hill.

Donlan, K. A., & Kroll, L. (2014). Inside the 2014 Forbes billionaires list: Facts and figures. *Forbes*, March 3. Retrieved from http://www.forbes.com/sites/luisakroll/2014/03/03/inside-the-2014-forbes-billionaires-list-facts-and-figures/

Egri, C., & Herman, S. (2000). Leadership in the North American environmental sector: Values, leadership styles and context of environmental leaders and their organizations. *Academy of Management Journal, 43*(4), 571–604.

Ehrlich, P. R., & Ornstein, R. E. (2010). *Humanity on a tightrope: Thoughts on empathy, family, and big changes for a viable future.* Lanham, MD: Rowman & Littlefield.

Ehrlich, P. R., & Tobias, M. C. (2014). *Hope on earth: A conversation.* Chicago, IL: University of Chicago Press.

Emirbayer, M., & Mische, A. (1998). What is agency? *American Journal of Sociology, 103*(4), 962–1023.

English, F. W., Papa, R., Mullen, C. A., & Creighton, T. (2012). *Educational leadership at 2050: Conjectures, challenges, and promises.* Lanham, MD: Rowman & Littlefield.

Fayong, S. (2008). Social capital at work: The dynamics and consequences of grassroots movements in urban China. *Critical Asian Studies, 40*(2), 233–262.

Forsyth, J. (2013). Time for universality to reduce inequity. *The Lancet, 382*(9899), 1161–1163.

Fritz, S., Lunde, J., Brown, W., & Banset, E. (2004). *Interpersonal skills for leadership* (2nd ed.). Upper Saddle River, NJ: Prentice Hall.

Fry, L. W. (2005). Toward a paradigm of spiritual leadership. *The Leadership Quarterly, 16*(5), 619–622.

Furman, G. (2012). Social justice leadership as praxis: Developing capacities through preparation programs. *Educational Administration Quarterly, 48*(2), 191–229.

Gale virtual reference library. (2014). *Social Justice, 139*(12), 791–792.

Gautney, H. (2011). What is Occupy Wall Street? The history of leaderless movements. *The Washington Post*, October 10. Retrieved from http://www.washington post.com

Greer, C. R., & Plunkett, W. R. (2007). *Supervisory management* (11th ed.). Upper Saddle River, NJ: Prentice Hall.

Hagmann, M. (2001). The world in 2050: More crowded, urban, and aged. *Bulletin of the World Health Organization, 79*(5), 484–487.

Hamayotsu, K. (2011). Beyond faith and identity: Mobilization Islamic youth in a democratic Indonesia. *Pacific Review, 24*(2), 225–247.

Hargreaves, A., & Fink, D. (2006). *Sustainable leadership*. San Francisco, CA: Jossey-Bass.

Harris, F. C. (2006). It takes a tragedy to arouse them: Collective memory and collective action during the civil rights movement. *Social Movement Studies, 5*(1), 19–43.

Hockenos, P. (Ed.). (2011). *State of the world volunteerism report: Universal values for global well-being*. Denmark: Phoenix Design Aid.

Hurst, P., Termine, P., & Karl, M. (2007). Agricultural workers and their contribution to sustainable agriculture and rural development. Retrieved from http://www. faolio.org/fileadmin/user_upload/fao_ilo/pdf/engl_agricultureC4163.pdf

Hurtado, M. (2015). Global unemployment to increase in next five years, says ILO. *EFE News Service*, January 20. Retrieved from http://ezproxy.roosevelt. edu:2048/login?url=http://search.proquest.com/docview/1646569933?accountid= 28518

International Labour Organization [ILO] (2014). *Report VI: Employment policies for sustainable recovery and development*. Geneva: International Labour Office.

Jago, A. (1982). Leadership: Perspectives in theory and research. *Management Science, 28*(3), 315–336.

Jansen, J. D. (2006). Leading against the grain: The politics and emotions of leading for social justice in South Africa. *Leadership and Policy in Schools, 5*(1), 37–51.

Johnson, B. L., Jr. (2008). Exploring multiple meanings and pursuits of social justice: A reflection on modern, imperative, and postmodern possibilities. *Teacher Development, 12*(4), 301–318.

Kellerman, B., & Webster, S. W. (2001). The recent literature on public leadership reviewed and considered. *The Leadership Quarterly, 12*(4), 485–514.

Kelsey, K. D., & Wall, L. J. (2003). Do agricultural leadership programs produce community leaders? A case study of the impact of an agricultural leadership program on participants' community involvement. *Journal of Agricultural Education, 44*(4), 35–46.

Kerbo, H. R. (2012). *Social stratification and inequality: Class conflict in historical, comparative, and global perspectives*. New York, NY: McGraw-Hill.

Kochhar, R. (2014, March 13). *10 projections for the world population in 2050*. Pew Research Center. Retrieved from http://www.pewresearch.org/fact-tank/2014/02/03/ 10-projections-for-the-global-population-in-2050/

Langdon, J. (2011). Democracy re-examined: Ghanaian social movement learning and the re-articulation of learning in struggle. *Studies in the Education of Adults, 43*(2), 147–163.

Lekovic, V. (2012). Neoliberal marginalization of social component in transition countries. *Montenegrin Journal of Economics*, *8*(3), 55−63.

Lloyd, C. (2001). *World population in 2050: Assessing the projections: Discussion.* Conference Proceedings, Federal Reserve Bank of Boston, 46. Retrieved from http://www.fedinprint.org/items/fedbcp/y2001n46x12.html

Lord, R. G., Brown, D. J., Harvey, J. L., & Hall, R. J. (2001). Contextual constraints on prototype generation and their multilevel consequences for leadership perceptions. *The Leadership Quarterly*, *12*(3), 311−338.

Luthans, F., & Slocum, J. (2004). New leadership for a new time. *Organizational Dynamics*, *33*(3), 227.

Maak, T., & Pless, N. M. (2006). Responsible leadership in a stakeholder society: A relational perspective. *Journal of Business Ethics*, *66*(1), 99−115.

Marmot, M., & Bell, R. (2012). Fair society, healthy lives. *Public Health*, *126*(Suppl. 1), 4−10.

Meek, D. (2011). Propaganda, collective participation and the 'war of position in Brazilian landless workers' movement. *Studies in the Education of Adults*, *43*(2), 164−180.

Moore, B. N., & Bruder, K. (2008). *Philosophy: The power of ideas* (7th ed.). New York, NY: McGraw-Hill.

Moreno, K. (2014). The 67 people as wealthy as the world's poorest 3.5 billion. *Forbes*, March 25. Retrieved from http://www.forbes.com/sites/forbesinsights/2014/03/25/the-67-people-as-wealthy-as-the-worlds-poorest-3-5-billion/

National Public Radio [NPR]. (2011). *The Arab spring: A year of revolution.* Retrieved from http://www.npr.org/2011/12/17/143897126/the-arab-spring-a-year-of-revolution

Pappas, G. (2012). The leadership of Dr. Jane Goodall: A four-quadrant perspective. In J. A. D. Barbour, G. J. Burgess, L. L. Falkman, & R. M. McManus (Eds.), *Leading in complex worlds* (pp. 253−267). San Francisco, CA: Jossey-Bass.

Parker, L., & Shapiro, J. P. (1992). Where is the discussion of diversity in educational administration programs? Graduate students' voices addressing an omission in their preparation. *Journal of School Leadership*, *2*(1), 7−33.

Parks, S. D. (2005). *Leadership can be taught.* Boston, MA: Harvard Business School Press.

Pfeffer, J. (1977). The ambiguity of leadership. *Academy of Management Review*, *2*(1), 104−112.

Pless, N. M., & Maak, T. (2011). Responsible leadership: Pathways to the future. *Journal of Business Ethics*, *98*, 3−13.

Polese, A. D. (2011). Russia, the US, and "the others" and the "101 things to do to win a (colour) revolution": Reflections on Georgia and Ukraine. *Debatte: Review of Contemporary German Affairs*, *19*(1−2), 421−451.

Porta, E., Arcia, G., Macdonald, K., Radyakin, S., & Lokshin, M. (2011). *Assessing sector performance and inequality in education.* Washington, DC: The World Bank.

Poutiatine, M. I., & Conners, D. A. (2011). Teaching leadership for socially just schools: A transformational approach. In J. D. Barbour & G. Robinson Hickman (Eds.), *Leadership for transformation* (pp. 141−158). San Francisco, CA: Jossey-Bass.

Powledge, F. (2010). Food, hunger, and insecurity. *Bioscience*, *60*(4), 260−265.

Rabiei, A. (2014, November). Global approach for comparing the mortality rate from natural disasters and its relationship to the income level and development indices of the countries. In *142nd APHA annual meeting and exposition (November 15–November 19, 2014)*, APHA.

Rockman, B. A., & Waterman, R. W. (2008). *Presidential leadership: The vortex of power*. New York, NY: Oxford University Press.

Sashkin, M. (2004). Transformational leadership approaches: A review and synthesis. In J. Antonakis, A. T. Cianciolo, & R. J. Sternberg (Eds.), *The nature of leadership*. Thousand Oaks, CA: Sage.

Shields, C. M. (2004). Dialogic leadership for social justice: Overcoming pathologies of silence. *Education Administration Quarterly, 40*(1), 279–288.

Stavrakantonaki, M. (2014, November). Economic inequality and population health. In *142nd APHA annual meeting and exposition (November 15–November 19, 2014)*, APHA.

Theoharis, G. (2007). Social justice educational leaders and resistance: Toward a theory of social justice leadership. *Education Administration Quarterly, 43*(2), 221–258.

Thorn, H. (2009). The meaning(s) of solidarity: Narratives of anti-apartheid activism. *Journal of Southern African Studies, 35*(2), 417–436.

United Nations. (2006). *The international forum for social development: Social justice in an open world – The role of the United Nations*. Retrieved from http://www.un.org/esa/socdev/documents/ifsd/SocialJustice.pdf

United Nations (UN) Global Education Initiative. (n.d.). Retrieved from http://www.globaleducationfirst.org/about.html

United Nations Department of Economic and Social Affairs [UNDESA]. (2014). Retrieved from http://www.un.org/waterforlifedecade/scarcity.shtml

Valocchi, S. (2005). Collective action frames in the gay liberation movement, 1969–1973. In J. A. Noakes & H. Johnston (Eds.), *Frames of protest: Social movements and the framing perspective* (pp. 53–67). Lanham, MD: Rowman and Littlefield Publishers, Inc.

van der Hoeven, R. (2010). *Labour markets trends, financial globalization and the current crisis in developing countries*. United Nations Department of Economic and Social Affairs. Retrieved from http://www.un.org/esa/desa/papers/2010/wp99_2010.pdf

Waldman, D. A., & Galvin, B. M. (2008). Alternative perspective of responsible leadership. *Organizational Dynamics, 37*(4), 327–341.

Walraven, G. (2011). *Health and poverty: Global health problems and solutions*. London: Earthscan.

World Health Organization [WHO] (2010). Bulletin of the world health organization. Retrieved from http://www.who.int/bulletin/volumes/88/4/10-010410/en/

World Health Organization [WHO]. (2012). *Interesting facts about aging*. Retrieved from http://www.who.int/ageing/about/facts/en/

Yukl, G. (2013). *Leadership in organizations* (8th ed.). Upper Saddle River, NJ: Prentice Hall.

Leadership for Sustainability and Peace: Responding to the Wicked Challenges of the Future

Rian Satterwhite, Whitney McIntyre Miller
and Kate Sheridan

> The separateness we thought we were creating melts into the unending dance of coadaptation and change as we become ever more aware of those from whom we cannot be separate.
>
> Wheatley and Kellner-Rogers (1996, p. 52)

In the past century our understanding of leadership has changed as the contexts in which leadership occurs evolve. Today, constructs of leadership that do not incorporate concepts such as systems thinking no longer match the realities of the world in which leadership is exercised and the challenges we seek to address. The challenges we face as a global community have increased in complexity, size, scope, and consequence. As a result of this contextual evolution, our definition of effective leadership is evolving as well.

These global challenges can be categorized as social, complex adaptive challenges, or wicked problems; those which, while familiar, are in some way new and have no prescribed solutions. Defined further, Rittel and Webber (1973) detail 10 distinguishing characteristics of wicked problems, including that they have no definitive formulation; that solutions are beneficial or harmful (as opposed to true or false) but have no immediate tests; and that each wicked problem is — while a symptom of other problems — also essentially unique. Grint (2010) expands upon this notion of wicked problems and usefully and explicitly links them to modern leadership challenges by arguing that "wicked problems require the transfer of authority from individual to collective because only collective engagement can hope to address the problem" and that leadership is then "the art of engaging a community in facing up to complex collective problems" (p. 18). Effectively responding to wicked problems requires the best collective responses that communities can generate, and a commitment that we learn our way through them together — finding the most beneficial responses. We believe that crafting these responses, while increasing the resilient capacity of our communities and systems, is the crucial leadership challenge of the next several decades.

Two of the most pressing wicked problems impacting current and future generations are the issues of sustainability and peace. This chapter will outline the interconnectedness of these two challenges; discuss how emerging leadership theories are contributing to the understanding of these wicked problems; and imagine how leadership theory, practice, education, and development will evolve in the next 35 years in order to meet these and other such challenges.

Sustainability

In order to effectively make the case that sustainability and peace represent the two most significant leadership challenges in the next 35 years, we must proceed with a set of assumptions, evidenced by the research of countless others. These basic assumptions in terms of sustainability are that (1) anthropogenic climate change is real; our industry, transportation, consumption habits — and to a mixed degree our population growth (Satterwhite, 2012) — are the primary generators of artificially high greenhouse gas concentrations in the atmosphere and oceans; (2) climate change is happening now and is not some hypothetical future state; (3) we are precipitating the 6th major global extinction; (4) in our ingenuity, love, and greed we have created a new geological epoch, the Anthropocene, where a majority of the earth's ecological systems are directly impacted by one species; and (5) we do not know as much as we would like, but we know enough to make informed predictions about future states of the global climate that are sufficiently strange and disruptive so as to inspire both fear and action. Let us together help ensure that action prevails.

The concept of sustainability often summons to mind visions of protecting the Amazon rainforest, or of preserving aesthetically pleasing natural areas. In fact, it refers in a holistic manner to two perspective shifts in how we understand the world: (1) timescales ranging from multiple generations to much longer – sometimes called deep time – while ensuring that our actions are consistent with the priorities of such timelines and (2) challenging ourselves to think ecocentrically; that is, to operate from ecocentric rather than anthropocentric value systems. Ecology – coined by German biologist Ernst Haeckel in 1866 from the Greek word *oikos* ("household") – is perhaps best described as the study of biological systems and their relationships. What has become increasingly clear is that we require an ecologically literate perspective to thrive in this time of the Anthropocene.

Natural systems surround and define our lives. We are active participants in them. Indeed, any sense of separation from them is false; we *are* them and they *are* us. Changing watersheds and precipitation patterns, ocean acidification, desertification, the decline of pollinators, dramatic loss in biodiversity, the increase in extreme weather events, declining fishery yields – these are all issues that should cause existential concern in and of themselves, but they also directly impact jobs, the cost of items in the grocery store, where we will choose to live and travel, the welfare of our children, and countless other daily considerations. This is our new lived experience. We must become more literate in understanding complex adaptive systems, and our role as active participants in them, if we wish to ensure that our grandchildren's grandchildren are able to thrive in the world that they inherit. What we seek in effective leadership, and how we craft leadership education and development experiences, must now reflect this goal.

An emerging and powerful message in the sustainability literature is that in order to effectively address environmental challenges you must simultaneously pursue economic, social, and educational justice. One of the most hopeful books in recent memory, Paul Hawken's *Blessed Unrest* (2008), brings to the fore the as of yet under recognized groundswell of global energy that is organically weaving these elements together through civil, economic, and political initiatives. The clear lesson is that ecological and social justice are both necessary to advance the other. Yet there has been a temptation to compete for priority among all of these urgent issues, which masks the truly interconnected nature of the challenge. For years, an artificial divide existed between activists in environmental justice and ecological justice communities. These areas have at times been antagonistic in that the former pursues justice in the human, or anthropocentric, domain (i.e., the disproportionate burden of environmental degradation and pollution that communities of color and low socioeconomic status typically bear) and the latter pursues justice in the biological, or ecocentric, domain (i.e., the preservation of natural ecosystems and endangered species). Both are essential, but bridging them conceptually as well as in practice has been a challenge, creating an artificial competition over prioritization.

Schlosberg and Carruthers (2010) bring the theory of environmental justice in line with its multidimensional practice by introducing a "pluralistic discourse of justice" utilizing the capabilities theory approach of Amartya Sen, advancing Schlosberg's claim (2007) that "we can draw parallels between the application of notions of justice as distribution, recognition, capability, and participation in both the human and non-human realms" (p. 6). By introducing a more nuanced and less rigid conception of environmental justice as a practice concerned with multiple discourses of justice, Schlosberg and Carruthers (2010) provide a dynamic framework within which to work and collaborate across the anthropocentric and ecocentric domains.

Constructing additional bridges between the artificially divided eco- and anthropocentric worlds, Edwards (2005) succinctly expands the discourse of sustainability to include the "four Es": environment, equity, education, and economy. In doing so, he links together many complex global challenges and helps us better understand them as facets of a broader movement. We will make a similar case in this chapter, arguing that (1) sustainability and peace represent two sides of the same coin, a currency of global wicked problems, (2) that they each offer important insights into how we will define leadership in the future, and (3) that when taken together they have the potential to alter leadership theory, practice, education, and development in the coming decades.

Peace

Our ability to see the interconnected nature of social and environmental justice offers an important entree into discussing peace. Indeed, sustainability and peace may be seen as intrinsically linked, as issues of sustainability may result in challenges to peace, and vice versa. Despite difficulties in establishing causal relationships between environment and conflict, researchers are trying to fully understand the potential role environmental challenges have on challenges to peace (Libiszewski, 1991; Gleditsch, 1998; Deligiannis, 2012). Libiszewski (1991) quotes the Environment and Conflicts Project defining environmental conflicts as those that "… manifest themselves as political, social, economic, ethnic, religious, or territorial conflicts, or conflicts over resources or national interests, or any other type of conflict. They are traditional conflicts induced by an environmental degradation" (p. 14).

Some research has documented the role that conflict – frequently resulting in population migration – has on the environment, particularly in Western Africa (Aning & Atta-Asamoah, 2011). Amster (2014), however, presents a more positive view, believing that as more adaptations are needed to survive climate change, societies may find new and more horizontal ways to work together in order to build both peaceful and sustainable communities. He charges us to "collectively articulate and implement a way of being in the world that does not make us the enemies of each other and the balance of life on the planet" (p. 478). Perhaps Amster's (2014) hope is reflected in the global movement, documented by Hawken (2008), discussed above.

Amster (2014) and Hawken (2008) are not alone in calling attention to the positive movement afoot. The world has gotten increasingly more peaceful, particularly since the two World Wars, with a 40% decrease in armed conflict since 1992 (Institute for Economics and Peace, 2014). This does not mean the world is lessening in violence, however. There has been a sharp rise in terrorist attacks around the world, and many countries have an increasing homicide rate (Institute for Economics and Peace, 2014). These statistics might encourage us to question whether we are any closer to achieving peace if the violence may not be decreasing, only shifting. Despite society's historical and modern predilection for violence and conflict, however, there is convincing evidence that humanity is actually better constructed for peace than violence (Chappell, 2013). In fact, Chenoweth and Stephan (2011) find that nonviolent resistance movements are over twice as effective as violent movements in enacting social change. Discussions of future leadership education and development must move away from a tradition of focusing solely on managing conflict to include an understanding and appreciation of the creation of peace.

There are numerous definitions and understandings of peace both in academic literature and in practice. One of the most meaningful and clear definitions of peace comes from Galtung (1996), who discusses two types of peace – positive and negative. It is these distinctions between positive and negative peace that are currently shaping and informing the field of peace studies. Positive peace is that which is built upon positive relationships and interactions of all human society. These are structural conditions that serve to develop the world as a place built on positive interactions and engagements. Negative peace, on the other hand, is the focus on the reduction of violence, or efforts to solve current problems of conflict and discord. In many ways, it is essential to focus both on building the structures and practices that instill a positive peace in our society while also focusing on solving the problems that lead to violence and conflict, as they exist today. This duality in timescales seen within the peace arena may very well exist in most wicked problems; it certainly does with sustainability. Complex challenges demand both immediate responses and longer-term systemic change, and successful leaders must have the nurtured capacity to operate in both simultaneously.

It stands to reason, then, that as we develop the leaders of the future, we must focus on this duality and determine how we might both resolve existing problems of violence while simultaneously creating space for current and future peaceful societal and institutional relationships. In the past 20 years, researchers have begun to study the efforts of leaders engaged in the work of both positive and negative peace. Those who have studied the phenomenon to date have tended to focus on individual leaders and their roles in developing peaceful organizations, nations, and societies. However, some are now making broader arguments about the concepts of peace leadership rather than individual leaders of peace.

The most common examples in the literature are those who discuss the work of negative peace- or leaders who are working to challenge violence and conflict. Much of this literature points to characteristics and practices embodied by leaders who work to minimize violence and conflict (Boyer, 1986; Ganz, 2010; Hermann & Gerard, 2009; Lieberfeld, 2009, 2011; Reychler & Stellamans, 2005). Several authors, however, discuss positive aspects of peace leadership. Global PeaceWorks (n.d.) are leader-focused as well, but center their leadership model on looking within, building trust, serving others, creating the future, and modeling peace. Other authors writing on positive peace leadership discuss a shift from an individual leader focus to a broader more inclusive focus on leadership for the building of peaceful communities, which includes utilizing dialogue, participatory leadership, empowerment, and the inclusion of women (Adler, 1998; Ledbetter, 2012; Spreitzer, 2007).

There is a need now, however, to think about peace leadership that bridges the gap between negative and positive peace, as for the foreseeable future, leadership will need to incorporate work for both forms of peace. Sarsar (2008) begins this work by suggesting that leaders tend to favor working in one domain over the other, and true peace movements would take leaders from both segments working together. Perhaps the goal is not to take leaders from each movement and put them together, but to develop peace leadership that embraces the work in both positive and negative peace as a way to manage the duality inherent in these wicked problems. In order to create these complex and multifaceted systems of leadership, we must understand, respond to, and indeed actively shape the emerging notions of leadership to embrace new possibilities of creating peace in both forms. McIntyre Miller and Green (2015) aim to do this in their new integral perspective of peace leadership. Built with a peace leadership focus around Wilber's (2000) integral theory, the framework looks at the intersections of innerwork, theories and processes, communities and practices, and the globality of the field of peace leadership.

Effective leadership in the next few decades must simultaneously work toward sustainability and peace. Sustainability allows us to adopt long-time perspectives and recognize the role that we play within broader natural systems. Peace allows us to bridge cultural and societal divides while addressing issues of justice and equity. Both require systems literacy and an authentic life-long learning orientation at both the individual and collectives levels. Nurtured by effective leadership education and development, these new ways of knowing position us to effectively shape the world that we want to create.

Emerging Leadership Discourse

Our wounds are deep, like old bad habits. There is much we need to forget. There is also much we need to remember. Above all, we need to remember the future.

Ausubel (2012, p. 147)

Moving away from the command and control and hero-leader models of the past, newer ways of conceptualizing leadership — such as those presented by Drath (2001), Heifetz (2006), Satterwhite (2010), Scharmer (2009), Scharmer and Kaufer (2013), Senge (2006a, 2006b), Senge, Smith, Kruschwitz, Laur, and Schley (2008), Western (2008), Wheatley (2006), and Wilber (2000) — emphasize the importance of interconnectedness, broadening our spheres of concern, building systemic capacity, and seeing our communities and the organizations in which we function as living, dynamic systems. These themes are not altogether new in the leadership literature; indeed they have informed the work of scholars for several decades, articulated perhaps most notably in Peter Senge's *The Fifth Discipline* (1990) as the model for learning organizations of the future. Yet their influence in shaping our approach to leadership education, leader development, and in our preparation for the future is still unfolding. These emerging leadership discourses reframe the way we think about leadership in order to address the wicked problems now so embedded in our daily lives.

Heifetz (2006) describes leadership as generating "new cultural norms that enable people to meet an ongoing stream of adaptive challenges, realities, and pressures," while going on to say that "... leadership develops an organization or community's adaptive capacity" (p. 76). Heifetz (2006) suggests that leadership is a property of social systems that draws in increasingly more participants and addresses collective challenges. Drath (2001) argues that "leadership effectiveness is related more to the sharing of meaning in a community than it is to any particular style or approach to leadership" (p. 28). Thus, we argue that effective leadership is that which helps communities and organizations make meaning of and effectively adapt to complex adaptive challenges, or wicked problems, such as sustainability and peace.

Senge (2006a, 2006b) and Senge et al. (2008) integrates systems thinking and embraces the web of relationships present within an organization and its surrounding environment, while also introducing the concept of systems citizenship characterized by three learning capabilities for systemic change: seeing systems, collaborating across boundaries, and creating desired futures. Wheatley (2006) embraces systems thinking while learning the lessons of chaos and complexity through examining the natural world. She asserts that it is important for us to embrace the natural flow that exists within our organizations and to look beyond ourselves to understand that we are parts of a larger system in which we must participate to be successful.

Western (2008) observes the emergence of a new eco-leader paradigm, which focuses on distributed leaders working within networks of organizations and larger systems. As we emerge from the "heroic" leadership age, we find that leadership no longer belongs to one person or one entity. Satterwhite (2010) offers an emergent model of leadership that draws from certain biological principles, deep ecology, and a complexity leadership perspective. He suggests that we are all inextricably linked to, and embedded within, larger natural systems, necessarily broadening the "circle of care" that leaders must develop and highlighting a capacity for systems intelligence that must be nurtured. Satterwhite (2010) wrote that, "Leaders help make meaning of adaptive challenges" (p. 241); in other words, leaders help us understand and respond to wicked problems while calling attention to our role within a multitude of complex systems. Perhaps no emerging theory tries better to link all of these pieces than Wilber's (2000) integral theory. Combining work in the interior and exterior with work in the individual and collective spheres, Wilber (2000) outlines a framework for us to fully embrace the complexities of our time.

Taken together, these authors may inform the applied efforts in sustainability and peace leadership. Essential to this work is shared meaning-making around complex problems, embracing distributed leadership throughout organizational levels, and understanding interactions among and between anthropocentric and ecocentric philosophies. From this, we grow to accept that the complexity in the work we do to address these wicked problems requires us to develop innovative, emergent, and boundary-spanning approaches.

Scharmer (2009) offers some guidance we might utilize in order to determine how best to move forward in the next 35 years as we strive to better understand the leadership that helps meet the world's complex challenges, particularly sustainability and peace. Scharmer (2009) believes that we exist at the precipice of individual and collective transformational change and we must break the patterns of the past in order to tune in to our highest potential. Furthermore, Scharmer and Kaufer (2013) suggests that the major fault lines that define the geography of human relationships, the "collective socioeconomic body," can be understood in terms of three primary relationships: "(1) our relationship with nature and our planet; (2) our relationship with one another; and (3) our relationship with ourselves" (p. 36). If one of leadership's primary challenges may be defined as healing these three relationships, we believe that the lenses of peace and sustainability – and the lessons that they teach us – will be central to this work.

These emerging leadership discourses have started us down this path of moving beyond our leadership theories (i.e., patterns) of the past. In the remainder of this chapter, we will dream about the future of leadership education and development, using the lens of the dual wicked problems of sustainability and peace.

A Paradigm Shift in Leadership Education and Development

We need to be prepared to question every single aspect of the old paradigm. Eventually, we will not need to abandon all our old concepts and ideas, but before we know that, we need to be willing to question everything.

Capra and Luisi (2014, p. 13)

We believe that emergent leadership discourses, responding to global challenges such as sustainability and peace, will redefine how we think about, teach, and practice leadership in the future. Shriberg (2012) makes a convincing case that "leadership skills required for sustainability closely mirror the skills needed to address other major challenges of the 21st century" (p. 469). He continues, arguing that "this shift is necessary not only because it would be good for the planet and, therefore, for the natural capital that underlies all wealth but also because this form of leadership would create fundamentally different and higher functioning organizations" (p. 477). Indeed, we suggest that the currency of wicked problems (sustainability and peace, together) will not only come to be central in leadership education and development, but that they are already birthing fundamentally different ways of conceiving what successful leadership is and that this will have a transformative impact on the conception, structure, and function of human organizations.

As we enter into an unfolding future that requires new forms of leadership, the perspectives discussed in this chapter may inform our approach to leadership preparation and education, just as previous theories have informed the leadership preparation of their time. These emerging constructs of leadership implore us to operate from a level of consciousness that sees the world as a dynamic and interdependent system of communities and organizations on which we will all have an impact, yet the prevailing message in leadership education and development is still one of skill development, structure, and positional influence (Wheatley, 2006). We build organizations to defend against chaos and change, yet it is our ability to cope with and exist within these uncertainties that will make us resilient and able to respond to the wicked problems we face.

Prevailing concepts of leadership rely on the leader "… to create stability and control, [for fear that] without human intervention there is not hope for order … [but] as we cling ever more desperately to these false beliefs, we destroy our ability to respond to the major challenges of these times" (Wheatley, 2006, p. 171). We must therefore move beyond old notions of leadership education and development to an approach that emphasizes worldview shaping, greater self and systems consciousness, and the cultivation of a deep respect for all life. As Scharmer (2009) advises, we must release previous ways of thinking in order to find new theories and practices from the future as it emerges. It is vital that leadership education and development continue to evolve in concert with the wicked problems shaping our common future. While the scope of these problems is global, our ability to confront and address them begins with individuals and invested communities.

As we postulate how to educate and equip leadership for the future, it is worth considering two notable questions regarding leadership and adaptive learning in our world today: "What will it be important to know for citizenship in the twenty-first century? [And] are we preparing people for a world that isn't going to be there?" (Daloz Parks, 2011, p. 142). The answer to these questions begins with the meaning-making process, an endeavor that Drath (2001) maintained is inextricably linked to the practice and understanding of effective leadership. "There is an enormous need," Daloz Parks (2011) asserts, "for an understanding and practice of human development that prepares people to become citizen-leaders … to participate in discovering and creating responses to challenges both new and ancient" (p. 15).

In our shared future, new models of leadership education and development will be necessary to prepare our future citizen-leaders to begin addressing the types of problems that Daloz Parks (2011) identified, and those that we have deemed wicked problems. The objective of leadership education is to "expand a person's capacity to be effective in leadership roles and processes" (Riggio, Ciulla, & Sorenson, 2003, p. 227), and should be grounded in the mental models that characterize the emerging leadership zeitgeist. Industrial notions of leadership were concerned primarily with task or relational orientation within an organization and thus, developing tangible skills that promoted task efficiency and relational effectiveness was tantamount to effective leadership (Yukl, 2008). As the context of leadership changes, leadership education and development must continue to evolve to fit the dynamic demands of leadership and its intended outcomes (Heifetz & Linsky, 2002; Komives, Dugan, Owen, Slack, & Wagner, 2011).

In a future defined by the fundamental issues of sustainability and peace, effectiveness in leadership must include the ability to perceive and adhere to long timelines, challenge ourselves to think ecocentrically, cope with difficult dualities, and co-create the future. Leadership, as defined by the emerging theories in this chapter, belongs not to one person or position but to a social system or organization (Heifetz, 2006; Western, 2008; Wheatley, 2006; Satterwhite, 2010); therefore, leadership education and development are not relevant simply for a select few, but rather critical to any individual or group who seeks to contribute to a shared objective or strives for a better future as an active member in a community. When leadership communities engage in creating meaning, it creates ownership for those who must adapt and respond to complex problems (Drath, 2001). As Senge (2006b) and Wheatley (2006) urge, seeing systems, collaborating across boundaries, and examining the natural world for inspiration will all be critical components of the future of leadership education and development.

Formal leadership education seeks to cultivate individuals with a capacity for engaged and informed systems citizenship, while placing important but limited emphasis on the development of a specific set of skills (Komives et al., 2011). Opportunities for cognitive, affective, and behavioral development collectively build an individual's leadership capacity, which includes the potential to purposefully apply skills, but perhaps more importantly, refers to the expansion of one's sense of self through a more holistic, encompassing definition that includes context and connection to community (Komives et al., 2011). Pedagogies that challenge participants to develop new ways of understanding leadership will be at the forefront of developing the capacity of individuals to address the issues of sustainability and peace. Pedagogical practices such as experiential learning, team-based learning, peer education, sociocultural discussions, service-learning, and contemplative practice, create powerful learning environments and transform outdated notions of leadership that no longer serve us (Komives et al., 2011).

Opportunities for dialogue and group interactions that expose participants to different perspectives and lived realities can provide a deeper understanding of the complexity of our world and the nature of living and working in organizations. The challenges of sustainability and peace require an understanding of leadership that acknowledges such complexity and tolerates cognitive dissonance. Many leadership education programs in higher education encourage or require study abroad or community service experiences aimed at providing a broadened perspective, greater empathy, and an appreciation for difference, but more can still be done. Maintaining that difference and "otherness" found in external experiences allows for an illusion of distance; dialogue and perspective-sharing in organizations and communities is essential to uncovering the complexity of lived experiences that is all around us (Komives et al., 2011).

Leadership in this new arena will also require engagement with, and an understanding of, the emerging theories discussed in this chapter: those that implore us to operate from a level of consciousness that sees the world as a dynamic and interdependent system for which we are all responsible. In fact, we believe that by 2050 many of the paradigms of modern life will have more fully completed the dramatic shifts that have already begun, further contributing to this new context for leadership. These paradigm shifts – this shift in collective consciousness – will further shape all aspects of our lives. In Table 1, we have contemplated the potential trajectories for many of these paradigm shifts. Although exploring each shift is beyond the scope of this chapter, many excellent scholars and practitioners driven by the commitment to shape a more peaceful and sustainable world are advancing these transformations. We believe that examining leadership theory and practice using the lenses of sustainability and peace will provide insight into and feed the paradigm shifts listed in Table 1.

The next 35 years require us to embrace the flow and emergent characteristics of the work in both sustainability and peace, and acknowledge the interconnectedness of each, in order to provide the space for collective work and groundbreaking problem solving. To do this, we must let go of old notions of leadership and organizational structure and focus on the future as it emerges after great reflection, sensing (Scharmer, 2009), and true understanding of the human and natural systems that surround us. While approaches to leadership education and development have advanced in this direction in recent years, a deeper shift that provides greater reflections of

Table 1: Contextual Paradigm Shifts.

Orientation	Established/Predominant Paradigms	Emerging (or Re-Emerging) Paradigms
Business	Profit	Triple bottom line; B-corp; social responsibility
Causality	Linearity	Nonlinearity
Civic power	Government and business	Community, government, NGO, and business collaboration
Conception of life	Life as a human-dominated hierarchy	Web of life is interdependent (life creates conditions for life)
Design	Mechanistic	Biomimicry; cradle to cradle
Economy	Growth	Stability and equity
Education	Knowledge retention	Systems and emotional intelligence
Energy sources	Fossil fuels	Renewables (solar and wind)
Food production	Monocropping	Organic
Leadership	Characteristics of the individual	Capacity of the system
Peace	Negative peace	Positive and negative peace
Problem solving	Reactive problem solving and risk avoidance	Creating desired futures
Relationship with nature	We stand apart from nature	We stand as part of nature
Time	Today, tomorrow, and the financial quarter	Multi-generational and deep time
Values focus	What needs to change	What we choose to conserve (allowing all else to shift)
Worldview — collective	Anthropocentric	Integrating anthropocentric and ecocentric perspectives
Worldview — individual	Egocentric/idiocentric	Allocentric

our interconnected systems is essential in order to meet the wicked problems of sustainability, peace, and the other challenges that are shaping our present and future world. Such a shift will likely be advanced on multiple vectors and in different ways as we move to address our collective wicked problems.

Ausubel (2012), referencing David Orr's work around ecological literacy, writes, "What all education is finally about is how we are to live in this interdependent world" (p. 189). It will be the role of leadership scholars and practitioners to further reflect on these notions of emergent leadership for sustainability and peace, and to find unique ways to ensure that leadership education and development effectively meets the needs, goals, and expectations of the future as it emerges.

The future appears alien to us. It differs from the past most notably in that the Earth itself is the relevant unit with which to frame and measure that future. Discriminating issues that shape the future are all fundamentally global. We belong to one inescapable network of mutuality: mutuality of ecosystems; mutuality of freer movement of information, ideas, people, capital, goods and services; and mutuality of peace and security. We are tied, indeed, in a single fabric of destiny on Planet Earth.

Mieko Nishimizu (as cited in Senge, 2006b, p. 21)

References

Adler, N. J. (1998). Societal leadership: The wisdom of peace. In S. Srivastva & D. L. Cooperrider (Eds.), *Organizational change and executive wisdom* (pp. 205−221). San Francisco, CA: The New Lexington Press.

Amster, R. (2014). Toward a climate of peace. *Peace Review: A Journal of Social Justice, 25*(4), 473−479.

Aning, K., & Atta-Asamoah, A. (2011). *Demography, environment, and conflict in West Africa.* KAIPTC Occasional Paper No. 34. Retrieved from http://dspace.africaportal.org/jspui/bitstream/123456789/31687/1/Occasional-Paper-34-Aning-and-Asamoah.pdf?1

Ausubel, K. (2012). *Dreaming the future: Reimagining civilization in the age of nature.* White River Junction, VT: Chelsea Green.

Boyer, P. (1986). Peace leaders, internationalists, and historians: Some reflections. *Peace and Change, 11*(3−4), 93−104.

Capra, F., & Luisi, P. L. (2014). *The systems view of life: A unifying vision.* Cambridge: Cambridge University Press.

Chappell, P. (2013). *The art of waging peace: A strategic approach to improving our lives and the world.* Westport, CT: Prospecta Press.

Chenoweth, E., & Stephan, M. J. (2011). *Why civil resistance works: The strategic logic of nonviolent conflict.* New York, NY: Columbia University Press.

Daloz Parks, S. (2011). *Big questions, worthy dreams.* San Francisco, CA: Jossey-Bass.

Deligiannis, T. (2012). The evolution of environment-conflict research: Toward a livelihood framework. *Global Environmental Politics, 12*(1), 78−100.

Drath, W. (2001). *The deep blue sea: Rethinking the source of leadership.* San Francisco, CA: Jossey-Bass.

Edwards, A. R. (2005). *The sustainability revolution: Portrait of a paradigm shift.* Gabriola Island, British Columbia: New Society Publishers.

Galtung, J. (1996). *Peace by peaceful means: Peace and conflict, development, and civilization.* Los Angeles, CA: Sage.

Ganz, M. (2010). Leading change: Leadership, organization, and social movements. In N. Nohria & R. Khurana (Eds.), *Handbook of leadership theory and practice* (pp. 509−550). Cambridge, MA: Harvard Business Press. Retrieved from http://leadingchangenetwork.com/files/2012/05/Chapter-19-Leading-Change-Leadership-Organization-and-Social-Movements.pdf

Gleditsch, N. P. (1998). Armed conflict and the environment: A critique of the literature. *Journal of Peace Research*, *35*(3), 381–400.

Global Peacworks. (n.d.). *Prinicples of peaceful leaderships*. Retrieved from www.globalpeaceworks.org/principles

Grint, K. (2010). *Leadership: A very short introduction*. Oxford: Oxford Press.

Hawken, P. (2008). *Blessed unrest: How the largest social movement in history is restoring grace, justice, and beauty to the world*. New York, NY: Penguin.

Heifetz, R. (2006). Anchoring leadership in the work of adaptive progress. In F. Hesselbein & M. Goldsmith (Eds.), *The leader of the future 2: Visions, strategies, and practices for the new era* (pp. 73–84). San Francisco, CA: Jossey-Bass.

Heifetz, R., & Linsky, M. (2002). *Leadership on the line*. Boston, MA: Harvard Business Review Press.

Hermann, M. G., & Gerard, C. (2009). The contributions of leadership to the movement from violence to incorporation. In B. W. Dayton & L. Kriesberg (Eds.), *Conflict transformation and peace building: Moving from violence to sustainable peace* (pp. 3–44). Abingdon, Oxon: Routledge.

Institute for Economics and Peace. (2014). *Global peace index*. Retrieved from http://www.visionofhumanity.org/sites/default/files/2014%20Global%20Peace%20Index%20REPORT.pdf

Komives, S., Dugan, J., Owen, J., Slack, S., & Wagner, W. (2011). *The handbook for student leadership development* (2nd ed.). San Francisco, CA: Jossey-Bass.

Ledbetter, B. (2012). Dialectics of leadership for peace: Toward a moral model of resistance. *Journal of Leadership, Accountability, and Ethics*, *9*(5), 11–24. Retrieved from http://www.nabusinesspress.com/JLAE/LedbetterB_Web9_5_.pdf

Libiszewski, S. (1991). What is an environmental conflict? *Journal of Peace Research*, *28*(4), 407–422.

Lieberfeld, D. (2009). Lincoln, Mandela, and qualities of reconciliation-oriented leadership. *Peace and Conflict: Journal of Peace Psychology*, *15*(January), 27–47.

Lieberfeld, D. (2011). Reconciliation-oriented leadership: Chilean President Michelle Bachelet. *Peace and Conflict: Journal of Peace Psychology*, *17*, 303–325.

McIntyre Miller, W., & Green, Z. (2015). An integral perspective of peace leadership. *Integral Leadership Review*, *15*(2). Retrieved from http://integralleadershipreview.com/12903-47-an-integral-perspective-of-peace-leadership/

Reychler, L., & Stellamans, A. (2005). Researching peace building leadership. Cahier of the Center for Peace Research and Strategic Studies (CPRS). Retrieved from http://www.diplomaticthinking.com/diplomaticthinking/wp-content/uploads/2012/11/Cahier71_ReychlerStellamans.pdf

Riggio, R., Ciulla, J., & Sorenson, G. (2003). Leadership education at the undergraduate level: A liberal arts approach. In S. E. Murphy & R. Riggio (Eds.), *The future of leadership development* (pp. 223–236). Mahwah, NJ: Lawrence Erlbaum Associates, Inc.

Rittel, H., & Webber, M. (1973). Dilemmas in a general theory of planning. *Policy Sciences*, *4*, 155–169.

Sarsar, S. (2008). Reconceptualizing peace leadership: The case of Palestinian-Israeli relations. *International Leadership Journal*, *1*, 24–38. Retrieved from http://tesc.innersync.com/documents/ILJ_Nov_2008_final.pdf - page=25

Satterwhite, R. (2010). Deep systems leadership: A model for the 21st century. In B. Redekop (Ed.), *Leadership for environmental sustainability* (pp. 230–247). New York, NY: Routledge.

Satterwhite, R. (2012). Halting the decline: How leadership theory and practice can address global biodiversity loss. In D. Gallagher (Ed.), *Environmental leadership: A reference handbook* (pp. 577–585). Los Angeles, CA: Sage.

Scharmer, O. (2009). *Theory U: Leading from the future as it emerges.* San Francisco, CA: Berrett-Koehler.

Scharmer, O., & Kaufer, K. (2013). *Leading from the emerging future: From eco-system to eco-system economies.* San Francisco, CA: Berrett-Koehler.

Schlosberg, D. (2007). *Defining environmental justice: Theories, movements, and nature.* Oxford: Oxford University Press.

Schlosberg, D., & Carruthers, D. (2010). Indigenous struggles, environmental justice, and community capabilities. *Global Environmental Politics, 10*(4), 12–35.

Senge, P. (2006a). Systems citizenship: The leadership mandate for this millennium. In F. Hesselbein & M. Goldsmith (Eds.), *The leader of the future 2: Visions, strategies, and practices for the new era* (pp. 31–46). San Francisco, CA: Jossey-Bass.

Senge, P. (2006b). *The fifth discipline: The art and practice of the learning organization* (Revised ed.) (Originally Published in 1990). New York, NY: Doubleday.

Senge, P., Smith, B., Kruschwitz, N., Laur, J., & Schley, L. (2008). *The necessary revolution: How individuals and organizations are working together to create a sustainable world.* New York, NY: Doubleday.

Shriberg, M. (2012). Sustainability leadership as 21st century leadership. In D. Gallagher (Ed.), *Environmental leadership: A reference handbook* (pp. 469–478). Los Angeles, CA: Sage.

Spreitzer, G. (2007). Giving peace a chance: Organizational leadership, empowerment, and peace. *Journal of Organizational Behavior, 28*(8), 1077–1095.

Western, S. (2008). *Leadership: A critical text.* Los Angeles, CA: Sage.

Wheatley, M. (2006). *Leadership and the new science* (2nd ed.). San Francisco, CA: Berrett-Koehler.

Wheatley, M., & Kellner-Rogers, M. (1996). *A simpler way.* San Francisco, CA: Berrett-Koehler.

Wilber, K. (2000). *A theory of everything: An integral vision for business, politics, science and spirituality.* Boston, MA: Shambhala Publications.

Yukl, G. (2008). *Leadership in organizations* (8th ed.). Upper Saddle River, NJ: Prentice Hall.

Leadership 2050 – The Call to Shift from Private to Social Reason: Wake Up, Sober Up, and Inquire

Stan Amaladas

> Practice is conducting oneself and acting in solidarity. Solidarity ... is the decisive condition and basis of all social reason. There is a saying of Heraclitus, the "weeping" philosopher: The *logos* is common to all, but people behave as if each had a private reason. Does this have to remain this way? (Italics original).
>
> Gadamer (1981b, p. 87)

The Problem: Dominance of Private Reason

Close to 35 years ago Gadamer[1] (1981b) disturbingly concluded that the consequences of our failure to act on the basis of social reason were no different from Heraclitus' (*ca.* 540–475 BCE)

---

[1]The original article appeared in Gadamer's collection of articles entitled *Vernunft im Zeitalter der Wissenschaft*, 1976, by Suhrkmp Verlag, Frankfurt. The English translation appeared in Gadamer (1981).

observation during his time. In his second fragment (Wheelwright, 1959), Heraclitus suggests that to behave as if each had a private reason, is to live one's life as if it was disconnected from what is common to all (logos). While Heraclitus does not offer us his assessment of the consequences of acting on the basis of private reason, we get a glimpse of this tragic choice through a poem written more than five decades ago by Kinney (2012).

Six men, trapped in happen-stance,

In bleak and bitter cold.

Each man possessed a stick of wood,

Or so the story is told.

Their dying fire in need of logs.

The first man held his back, for of the faces around the fire, he noticed one was black.

The second man looking across the way saw one not of his church

And could not bring himself to give the fire his stick of birch.

The third man, sat in tattered clothes,

He gave his collar a hitch: "Why should his log be put to use to warm the idle rich?"

The rich man sat and thought of all the wealth he had in store,

And how to keep what he had earned from the lazy shiftless poor.

The black man's face bespoke revenge,

As the fire passed from sight.

All he saw in his stick of wood was a chance to spite the white.

The last man of this forlorn group did nought except for gain,

Giving only to those who gave is how he played the game.

Their logs held tight in human hands was proof of human sin,

They did not die from the cold without,

They died from the cold within.

Five decades later, private reason continues to feed our racial prejudices (Augoustinos & Reynolds, 2001), religious beliefs that divide (Haidt, 2012; Hoffer, 1951/2002), stereotypes (Pickering, 2001), spite, and revenge expressed through violence, terrorism, genocide, and ethnic cleansings (Akçam, 2012; Geyer & Rihani, 2010). While our dying fire is in need of logs, these negative beliefs and practices continue to contribute to one tragic result: humanity continues to die from the cold within. As Gadamer (1981b) asks, "Does it have to remain this way?" If social fragmentation and disconnectedness are not going to be our collective fate in the future, then, what specifically can future leaders do to address this challenge? This question takes on both importance and urgency as we look toward 2050 and the many challenges facing the globe. Irrespective of the particular issue, the problem of rationality remains constant. Continuing to respond, on the basis of private reason, to new and different challenges in our modern and post-modern world will only spell disaster. Too many of us are living our lives in a private story that choreographs the dance of our lives. Alternative stories *are* possible. We can empower ourselves to co-construct new stories. The questions that surfaces then include, "What prevents us from constructing these new stories" and "What holds us imprisoned in our old stories?" As we look toward the future, what should leaders do in order to generate conditions for new stories? These questions define the problem, context, and the purpose of this chapter.

Barriers to Co-Constructing New Stories

George (2003) and Heifetz (1994) suggest that there are *no easy answers*. However, as George writes, "that shouldn't keep us from talking about them" (p. 7). In an interview in *Fast Company*, Heifetz reminds us of the danger confronting individuals (leader or not) who courageously choose to take up the challenge of addressing the complex adaptive social challenges of our time, and acknowledges that their efforts will "generate resistance and pain [because] … people are afraid … that they're going to have to give up something that they're comfortable with" (Taylor, 1999). They can also expect to be "marginalized, diverted, attacked, (and) seduced" (Taylor, 1999). One only has to watch the evening news to see examples of this every day.

The Work of Future Leaders

Heifetz notes that future leaders, practicing adaptive leadership, will be called to intentionally focus on "influencing the community to face its problems" (Heifetz, 1994, p. 14) and "mobilize people toward some collective purpose, a purpose that exists beyond [one's own] individual ambition" (Heifetz, 2009, p. 3). This work of leadership is markedly different from the conventional leader-centric or ego-centric models of leadership. In a leader-centric world, "leadership means influencing the community to follow the leader's vision" (Heifetz, 1994, p. 14). In a leader-centric world, if things do not go as planned, the leader is blamed. But, if the role of the leader is to influence the community to face and make progress on its own problems, then everyone accepts responsibility. So, how do leaders go about this new work?

In an interview with Jena McGregor at the *Washington Post*, Vielmetter and Sell speak to the "how" of this new work through their altrocentric model of leadership. "'Altrocentric' means focusing on others. Such a leader doesn't put himself at the very center. He knows he needs to listen to other people. He knows he needs to be intellectually curious and emotionally open. He knows that he needs empathy to do the job, not just in order to be a good person" (McGregor, 2014).

Within the context of the dominance of private reason, Heifetz (1994) and Vielmetter and Sell (2014) offer us a critical formulation of the "what" and the "how" of the work of future leaders. To answer the "what," future leaders will be called to influence and challenge the community to tackle the tough problems of private reason thinking and behaving that continue to contribute to social fragmentation rather than unity (genuine solidarity). They are being called to make progress on the task of acting on the basis of social reason. Future leaders will answer the "how," by being intellectually curious, emotionally open, focusing on others, and listening empathically.

For Heifetz, the success of the "what" and the "how" would require future leaders to be prepared in two ways. First, in concurrence with Schön's (1982) notion of "reflection-in-action" future leaders would need to be equipped with the capacity to engage in a "practical orientation so that [they] can evaluate events and actions in progress, without waiting for outcomes" (Heifetz, 1994, p. 26). This practical reflection-in-action is the capacity to get to the bottom of what is happening in the experiencer's processes, decision-making, and feelings at the time of the event or interaction. Second, in addition to being intellectually curious and emotionally open, Heifetz also suggests, that future leaders will need a "governor" to guide their "tendencies to become arrogant and grandiose in (their) visions" including the temptation "to flee from harsh realities and the dailyness of leadership" (p. 26).

Connecting to the Past: Renewed Call for *Practical Wisdom*

The "what" and the "how" which are attributed to the work of future leaders, as described above, are not entirely new. This line of thinking was already captured in Aristotle's (1941) notion of practical wisdom or phronesis, with a fundamental difference. In his book *Nicomachean Ethics*, Aristotle defines the practical orientation and wisdom of phronetic leaders as an integration of five critical elements. Phronetic leaders (a) entertain remote goals and (b) make them real through enlightened choices. Their enlightened choices are governed by (c) just deliberation, (d) subordinating self under common ends, and (e) holding fast to binding norms. For Aristotle, the intentional integration and governance of all five elements is exemplary of practical wisdom and what it means to act on the basis of social reason. In essence "practical wisdom (is) a reasoned and true state of the capacity to act with regard to human good ... practical wisdom is a virtue ..." (Aristotle, 1941, p. 1027). For Aristotle, a virtue is a human disposition to *act well*. Accordingly, practical wisdom is the capacity to act well with regard to human good.

It is here that we see the similarities and the differences between Aristotle, Heifetz (1994), and Vielmetter and Sell's (2014), notions of leadership. The similarity between all three types of leaders is that they do not put themselves at the center. However, unlike the focus of Vielmetter and Sell's altrocentric leaders, the "other" that Aristotle and Heifetz envision, is more than the "interactional other." For Aristotle and Heifetz, the "other" includes and goes beyond focusing on actual others. From the perspective of acting on the basis of social reason, Aristotle and Heifetz can be heard as introducing a third interlocutor. For them, intentional regard for the human good, and not the interactional other, is the third interlocutor, which acts as the governor and guide for phronetic leaders. In this way, we can understand Heifetz's call for a "governor" as being congruent with Aristotle. We can understand Heifetz as suggesting that the regard for the human good (collective purpose) is the "governor" (third interlocutor) of both our interactions with each other and our tendencies to become arrogant and grandiose. Table 1 summarizes the similarity and differences between these three notions of leadership and their corresponding practices.

Aristotle also notes that practical wisdom involves more than the ability to decide how to instrumentally achieve what one thinks is good and then doing what can be done to achieve it. If *techné*

Table 1:   The Work of Future Leaders.

The Work of Future Leaders	Adaptive Leadership Heifetz (1994, 2009)	Altrocentric Leadership Vielmetter and Sell (2014)	Phronetic Leadership Aristotle (1941)
Action	Influence others to tackle and make progress on the problems confronting them	Acquire digital wisdom and engage employees across cultures and business roles through new mediums	Make remote goals real
Choice	Focus on collective purposes that exist beyond one's own individual ambitions	Focus on others	Make enlightened choices with a view to human good (practical wisdom)
Guide	Need for a "governor" to balance our tendencies to become arrogant and grandiose	Be intellectually curious Open to the emotions of others Listen empathically	Deliberate justly Subordinate self to common ends Hold fast to binding norms

(instrumental rationality) is all there is, he cautions that we can just as easily fall prey to the seduction of sharp operators and con-artists that get what they want by lying, deceiving, brainwashing, or manipulating. Similar to the leader-centric model, *techné* can become a feeding ground for private reason. In our world, where goals have become complex, sometimes even contradictory, where people continue to behave as if they each have their own private reason, and where they get entangled in their "positions," it is important to revisit and renew what is often considered a "no-longer vital tradition of Aristotelian philosophy" (Gadamer, 1981a, p. 88).

Taking this into account, the work of future leaders is defined as practically influencing self and others to confront their current choices, to mobilize self and others to deliberate justly, and to make socially enlightened choices in ways that are guided by a relation to human good.

Setting the Stage

Grounded in the qualitative tradition of narrative inquiry, the remainder of this chapter will focus on the stories of three scholars across three centuries, Rousseau (18th century), Marx (19th century), and Weber (20th century), to "experience the experience" of the problem of private reason in their times of tumultuous change. For Clandinin and Connelly (2000), the phrase "experience the experience" is a "reminder that … narrative inquiry is aimed at understanding and *making meaning* of experience" [Italics original] (p. 80). Clandinin and Connelly believe that narrative inquiry is one way of understanding experience through "collaboration between researcher and participants, over time …. Simply stated … narrative inquiry is stories lived and told" (p. 20). The opinion that people lead storied lives is shared by many others (Bateson, 1979; Berger & Luckmann, 1966; Bruner, 1986, 1991; Carr, 1986; Czarniawska-Joerges, 1998; Geertz, 1986; Heilbrun, 1988; Rorty, 1989; Schwartzman, 1993; Turner, 1986). At the same time, engaging in the stories of Rousseau, Marx, and Weber, provides us an opportunity, to "indirectly" make visible the "threats to social integration" (Habermas, 1984, p. 137) and, as Gadamer (1981b) notes, to face and tackle the challenge of acting decisively on the basis of social reason. The focus on making meaning of Rousseau, Marx, and Weber's experiences provide us an opportunity to better understand, confront, and make progress on the collective task of acting on the basis of social reason.

Jean Jacques Rousseau (18th Century): The Call to Wake Up

Rousseau (1761/1997) shared his experience of change through his romantic novel, *Julie, or the New Heloise*. In an archetypal move that will be representative of millions of people for centuries to come (Berman, 1982), Rousseau's young hero, Saint-Preux moves from the country to the city. Rousseau's reflections on the social-psychological conditions of living in the city, where the "man of the world takes in everything and has time to reflect on nothing" (p. 202), are expressed through Saint-Preux's letters to his love Julie. Two sections of his letters, written at different times, are quoted at length with the primary intent of surfacing Rousseau's understanding of what is calling for our attention.

> You would think that … individuals who are independent would have a mind of their own; not at all: just more machines that do not think …. There are … a small number of men and women who think for all the others … and as each person is mindful of his own interest, no one of the common good, and as individual interests are at odds with each other, there is a perpetual clash of cliques and

> factions .... There is more ... everyone puts himself con-
> stantly in contradiction with himself, without occurring to
> anyone to find this wrong. They have principles for conver-
> sation and others for practice; the contrast scandalizes no
> one .... In a word everything is absurd and nothing shocks.
>   (Rousseau, 1761/1997, pp. 191–192)

After several months in this tumultuous social environment, Saint-Preux describes the psychological effects of being in the middle of this fast-paced-private-reason city life, to his love Julie: "I am beginning to experience the intoxication into which this restless and tumultuous life plunges those who lead it, and I am falling into a dizziness like that felt by a man whose eyes a plethora of objects are rapidly passed. None of those that strike me engages my heart, but taken together they disturb and suspend its affections, so much so that I forget what I am and who I belong to" (Rousseau, 1761/1997, p. 209).

Rousseau could be heard as challenging future leaders to confront their communities to tackle the contradictions of their private choices for the sake of living well. Recall, for instance, that for Aristotle (1941), practical wisdom is a virtue — a human disposition to act and live well. Consequently, we are all (leader or not) called to confront our decisions to (a) have one set of principles for conversation and others for practice; (b) lead intoxicated and restless lives; (c) behave like machines and abdicate our capacity to think for ourselves; (d) feel like the only role we can have is to consume; and (e) orient only to private interest and not the common good. Rousseau is disturbed by what he sees: everything is absurd and nothing shocks. Is Rousseau being overly dramatic in claiming that no one, other than him, is scandalized by these contradictions? Perhaps, this is his way of deliberately shaking his audience (and us) out of their (our) slumber and complacency. It is time to wake up!

Within organizations today, there is an urgent need to wake up to the contradiction and negative effects between having one set of principles for conversation and another for practice (saying one thing and doing another). For example, this contradiction continues to feed high levels of cynicism (Duck, 1998; Kouzes & Posner, 2012; Senge, 2006), anger (Noer, 1993), and change fatigue (Saxena, Scharmer, & Goldman Schuyler, 2014). Change-based programs with their plethora of change techniques, for example, are received as "another management fad in an endless series of management fads" (Duck, 1998, p. 63), as being yet another "flavor of the month program" (Senge, 2006, p. 6), or as another "same old, same old" (Saxena et al., 2014, p. 26). In short there is a lack of trust (Bennis, Goleman, & O'Toole, 2008) that there will be any meaningful change.

What then is the work for future leaders in the midst of these contradictions? While Rousseau does not offer any explicit solutions, there is a hint of the work of future leaders in Rousseau's (1761/1997) observation: the "man of the world takes in everything and has time to reflect on nothing" (p. 202). In the midst of this restless consumption we can understand Rousseau as calling future leaders to create conditions for reflection and not for more action. Today, this call for reflection continues to be echoed in the literature (Carroll, 2007; Göker, 2012; Gonzales, 2012; Pellicer, 2003). The promise of reflection is that it offers men and women the opportunity to deliberate justly (Aristotle, 1941), make sense (Weick, 2009), and make meaning (Clandinin & Connelly, 2000) of their restless activities and contradictions. Moving ahead by about 200 years from Rousseau's time, we notice another scholar Weber (1958), resurfacing the need to inquire into the restless activity of men and women who "are never satisfied with what they have" (p. 70).

Max Weber (20th Century): The Call to Inquire

In his book *The Protestant Ethic and the Spirit of Capitalism*, Weber (1958) inquires and interprets the restless activity of business people as follows.

> If you ask them what is the meaning of their restless activity, why they are never satisfied with what they have ... they would perhaps give the answer, if they know at all: "to provide for my children and grandchildren." But ... since that motive is not peculiar to them, but was just as effective for the traditionalist, more correctly, simply: that business with its continuous work has become a necessary part of their lives ... it at the same time expresses what is ... from the view-point of personal happiness so irrational about this sort of life, where a man exists for the sake of his business, instead of the reverse. (p. 70)

Weber was not convinced that the capitalists of his time were restlessly engaged in their business activities for the altruistic purpose of providing for their children and grandchildren, because such a motive, as he attests, was "not peculiar to them" (p. 70). His interpretive understanding was that the human decision to allow the work of business to become so necessary to their lives moved capitalists to the point that they could not live without it. From the point of view of personal happiness, this intoxicated irrationality can be expressed as follows: humans first created their business and now existed for the sake of their business.

When Weber stopped "to experience the experience" (Clandinin & Connelly, 2000, p. 20) of this excessive attachment to one's business, he could not help but stray away from his intent to provide a purely historical and scientific discussion. In his reflective moment, Weber wondered what the future would be like: "no one knows who will live in this cage in the future or whether ... entirely new prophets will arise or there will be a great rebirth of old ideas and ideals, or, if neither, mechanized petrification, embellished with a sort of convulsive self-importance. For of the last stage of this cultural development it might well be truly said: 'Specialists without spirit, sensualists without heart'; this nullity imagines that it has attained a level of civilization never before achieved" (Weber, 1958, p. 182).

If this is not to become a self-fulfilling prophecy, Weber could be heard as calling future leaders to tackle the tough problem of acting on behalf of the human spirit while being in the midst of people who have privately embellished themselves with a sort of convulsive self-importance, "without occurring to anyone to find this wrong" (Rousseau, 1761/1997, p. 209). Is it a surprise then to hear Heifetz (1994) making the call for a "governor on our tendencies to become arrogant and grandiose? ..." (p. 26).

We notice how close Weber is to reviving an old ideal that was expressed by his predecessor, Rousseau. For Rousseau's hero Saint-Preux, for example, while a plethora of objects rapidly passed through his eyes, nothing engaged his heart. Here again, 200 years later, we find Weber calling future leaders to lead in ways that engages the spirit and the heart. While there are no easy answers (George, 2003; Heifetz, 1994), Weber offers us a starting place and a governing model. We could hear Weber as calling future leaders to mobilize self and others to purposefully inquire into the meaning of their (our) restless activities and intentionally lead in ways that engages the human spirit. His message continues to ring true today. For example, as reflected in Renesch and Defoore's (1996) edited book, *The New Bottom Line: Bringing Heart and Soul to Business*, we find numerous authors once again appealing for the need to bring spirit, heart, and soul back to business. More recently, we see other authors being "very worried" (Speth, 2008, p. x) about the relentless drive for profit and growth which is simply spinning out of control (Mander, 2012; Speth, 2008). Is it a surprise to hear George (2003), making this observation: "Capitalism (has become) the victim of its own success?" (p. 3).

Karl Marx (19th Century): The Call to Sober Up

In between Rousseau and Weber's time, another writer, Marx (1978b) shares his experience of social change wrought by industrialization through his question: "But although the atmosphere in which we live weighs upon everyone like a 20,000 lb. force, do you feel it?" (p. 577). Like the Parisians in Rousseau's (1761/1997) story, it appears as if many of Marx's contemporaries were oblivious to feeling the weight of this 20,000 lb. force. The drastic results of industrialization at this time are reflected below.

> On the one hand, there have started into life, industrial and scientific forces, which no epoch of human history had ever suspected. On the other hand, there exist symptoms of decay, far surpassing the horrors of the latter times of the Roman Empire. In our days, everything seems pregnant with its contrary: Machinery, gifted with the wonderful power of shortening and fructifying human labor, we behold starving and overworking it. The newfangled sources of wealth, by some strange weird spell, are turned into sources of want; the victories of art seem bought by the loss of character.
>
> (Marx, 1978b, p. 577)

Marx (1978b) was troubled by what he saw occurring in his day, namely, that while "everything seems pregnant with its contrary" (p. 577) many did not feel the weight of this contradiction. Unlike Rousseau, for Marx, it was not a question of complacency. Marx argued that it was the bourgeoisie's total addiction to their own successes that caused them to lose touch and become disconnected with the contradictions that they were constructed. What were the successes of the bourgeois-industrialists that were so intoxicating and how were they achieved? "The bourgeoisie ... has created more massive and more colossal productive powers than have all preceding generations together. Subjection of nature's forces to man, machinery, application of chemistry to industry and agriculture, steam navigation, railways, electric telegraphs, clearing of whole continents for cultivation, canalization of rivers .... What earlier century had even a presentiment that such productive forces slumbered in the lap of social labor?" (Marx, 1978c, p. 477).

It is as if Marx did not come to bury the bourgeois-industrialists but to praise and celebrate their success. In less than a 100 years, through their laboring and economic activity, they produced a compelling image of the good life as being the life of labor and production (Arendt, 1958). The laboring activity of industrialists was exhilarating because it enabled the production of more than what was sufficient to one's needs. In so doing, the bourgeois-industrialists were able to distinguish themselves from, as Adam Smith described it, menial servants who, like "idle guests ... leave nothing behind them in return for their consumption" (as cited in Arendt, 1958, p. 86). For the industrialist, it was simply invigorating to instrumentally apply the principles of machinery and chemistry in the creation of a world of surplus. However, their addiction to creating surplus and their absolute control over nature moved them to subject everything to their will. We notice the grandiose tendency to embellish oneself with a "sort of convulsive sense of self-importance" (Weber, 1958, p. 182) fully in display. Their success was also very damaging. For example, instead of shortening and fructifying human labor, there was a starving and overworking of it; sources of wealth are turned into sources of want; victories of art are bought by the loss of character (Marx, 1978a). Today, the addiction for more, has led to recent corporate and banking scandals like Enron, Arthur Anderson, Bear Stearns Companies, Inc., Tyco Ltd., and Parmalat (HR World, 2008). The recent movie, *The Wolf of Wall Street*, directed by Martin Scorsese, is yet another dark example of the extent of modern day addiction for more.

In the midst of our socially addicted conditions, Marx could be heard as making a practical plea: that it is time for all to sober-up, and "face with sober senses his real conditions of life, and his real relations with his kind" (Marx, 1978c, p. 476). For Marx, individuals who are addicted are incapable of understanding the real conditions of their lives because they are too busy being intoxicated. In their intoxicated stupor and *hubris* they comfort themselves in ways that deny them the opportunity to confront the real conditions of their private decisions and choices. Marx could be heard as saying that the integration of all five elements of practical wisdom, as formulated by Aristotle (1941), and the capacity to act on the basis of social reason, would first require future leaders to construct conditions for sobriety. Isn't it revealing to hear the Philippine Centre for Islam and Democracy (PCID) calling for "sobriety and peaceful resolution" in 2013, amidst violent clashes between the forces of the Moro National Liberation Front and government forces?

Closing Thoughts

As we look toward 2050, with seismic social, economic, and political changes that will continue to avalanche upon our heads, there is an important and urgent need to keep the conversation between acting on the basis of private reason and social reason alive. Given our current realities, there is a greater need for phronetic leadership and practical wisdom to guide us along the path of acting and living well. There is a greater need to orient to human choices with a view to both the collective and human good.

Rather than being asleep at the wheel with their social contradictions (Rousseau: the call to wake up), or being intoxicated with the addictions of their time (Marx: the call to sober-up), or being driven by restless activity (Weber: the call to inquire into the meaning of one's restless activities), a key leadership characteristic that defined the stories of these scholars was that they were deeply disturbed by the erosion of the social character and soul of their communities. As we look toward 2050, what would occur if individuals (leader or not) choose *not* to be disturbed by what they see? What would occur if leaders choose *not* to influence and mobilize their communities to tackle the problem of private reason and make progress on the challenge of acting on the basis of social reason? Would we not be justified in predicting that we will continue to have the same social fragmentation (dying from the cold within) that we are witnessing today and have witnessed since the 18th century? Brown (1983) paraphrased it well, "insanity is doing the same thing over and over again but expecting different results" (p. 68). Is it not time to end this madness?

Acknowledgment

I want to personally thank Ms. Diane Kristjanson, MA, Dr. Dennis Silvestrone, Dr. Michelle Gallant, and Dr. Mindy McNutt for their thoughtful comments and feedback.

References

Akçam, T. (2012). *The young Turks' crime again humanity: The Armenian genocide and ethnic cleansing in the Ottoman Empire*. Princeton, NJ: Princeton University Press.

Arendt, H. (1958). *The human condition*. Chicago, IL: The University of Chicago Press.

Aristotle. (1941). Nicomachean ethics. In R. McKeon (Ed.), *The basic works of aristotle* (pp. 935–1112). New York, NY: Random House.

Augoustinos, M., & Reynolds, K. J. (2001). *Understanding prejudice, racism, and social conflict*. Thousand Oaks, CA: Sage.

Bateson, G. (1979). *Mind and nature: A necessary unity*. New York, NY: E. P. Dutton.

Bennis, W., Goleman, D., & O'Toole, J. (2008). *Transparency: How leaders create a culture of candor*. San Francisco, CA: Jossey-Bass.

Berger, P., & Luckmann, T. (1966). *The social construction of reality: A treatise on the sociology of knowledge*. New York, NY: Doubleday.

Berman, M. (1982). *All that is solid, melts into air: The experience of modernity*. New York, NY: Penguin Books.

Brown, R.-M. (1983). *Sudden death*. New York, NY: Bantam Books.

Bruner, J. (1986). Ethnography as narrative. In V. W. Turner & E. M. Bruner (Eds.), *The anthropology of experience* (pp. 139–155). Chicago, IL: University of Illinois Press.

Bruner, J. (1991). The narrative construction of reality. *Critical Inquiry, 18*, 1–21.

Carr, E. (1986). *Time, narrative, and history*. Bloomington, IN: Indiana University Press.

Carroll, M. (2007). *The mindful leader: Ten principles for bringing out the best in ourselves and others*. Boston, MA: Trumpeter Books.

Clandinin, D., & Connelly, F. (2000). *Narrative inquiry: Experience and story in qualitative research*. San Francisco, CA: Jossey-Bass.

Czarniawska-Joerges, B. (1998). *A narrative approach to organization studies*. Thousand Oaks, CA: Sage.

Duck, J. (1998). Managing change: The art of balancing. In *On change* (pp. 55–81). Boston, MA: Harvard Business School Press.

Gadamer, H. G. (1981a). Hermeneutics as practical philosophy In Reason in the age of science *(F. G. Lawrence, Trans.)* (pp. 88–112). Cambridge, MA: The MIT Press.

Gadamer, H. G. (1981b). What is practice? In Reason in the age of science *(F. G. Lawrence, Trans.)* (pp. 69–87). Cambridge, MA: The MIT Press.

Geertz, C. (1986). Making experiences, authoring selves. In V. W. Turner & E. M. Bruner (Eds.), *The anthropology of experience* (pp. 373–380). Chicago, IL: University of Illinois Press.

George, B. (2003). *Authentic leadership: Rediscovering the secrets to creating lasting value*. San Francisco, CA: Jossey-Bass.

Geyer, R., & Rihani, S. (2010). *Complexity and public policy: A new approach to 21st century politics, policy, and society*. New York, NY: Routledge.

Gonzales, M. (2012). *Mindful leadership: The 9 ways to self-awareness, transforming yourself, and inspiring others*. Mississauga: John Wiley & Sons.

Göker, S. D. (2012). Reflective leadership in EFL. *Theory and Practice in Language Studies, 2*(7), 1335.

Habermas, J. (1984). *The theory of communicative action* (Vol. 2). Boston, MA: The Beacon Press.

Haidt, J. (2012). *The righteous mind: Why good people are divided by politics and religion*. Toronto: Random House.

Heifetz, R. (1994). *Leadership without easy answers*. Cambridge, MA: Harvard University Press.

Heifetz, R. (2009). *The practice of adaptive leadership: Tools and tactics for changing your organization and the world*. Boston, MA: Harvard Business Press.

Heilbrun, C. (1988). *Writing a woman's life*. New York, NY: W. W. Norton.

Hoffer, E. (1951/2002). *The true believer: Thoughts on the nature of mass movements*. New York, NY: Harper Collins Publishers Inc.

HR World. (2008). *The 33 biggest corporate implosions. Ever.* Retrieved from http://www.hrworld.com/features/33-biggest-corporate-implosions-042808/

Kinney, J. P. (2012). The cold within. In Hawkins, S. (2012, March 14). *The Cold Within by James Patrick Kinney: Poem, Purpose. Progress.* Retrieved from http://www.allthingsif.org/archives/1405

Kouzes, J. M., & Posner, B. Z. (2012). *The leadership challenge: How to make extraordinary things happen in organizations*. San Francisco, CA: Jossey-Bass.

Mander, J. (2012). *The capitalism papers: Fatal flaws of an obsolete system*. Berkeley, CA: Counterpoint Press.

Marx, K. (1978a). For a ruthless criticism of everything existing. In R. C. Tucker (Ed.), *The Marx-Engels Reader* (pp. 12–15). New York, NY: W.W. Norton & Company, Inc.

Marx, K. (1978b). Speech at the anniversary of the people's power. In R. C. Tucker (Ed.), *The Marx-Engels reader* (pp. 577–578). New York, NY: W.W. Norton & Company, Inc.

Marx, K. (1978c). Manifesto of the communist party. In R. C. Tucker (Ed.), *The Marx-Engels reader* (pp. 469–500). New York, NY: W.W. Norton & Company, Inc.

McGregor, J. (2014). Leadership skills for the year 2030. *The Washington Post.* Retrieved from http://www.washingtonpost.com/blogs/on-leadership/wp/2014/02/25/leadership-skills-for-the-year-2030

Noer, D. M. (1993). *Healing the wounds*. San Francisco, CA: Jossey-Bass.

PCID. *PCID calls for sobriety and peaceful resolution to Zamboanga standoff.* Retrieved from http://www.luwaran.com/index.php/welcome/item/554-pcid-calls-for-sobriety-and-peaceful-resolution-to-zamboanga-standoff. Accessed on July 13, 2014.

Pellicer, L. O. (2003). *Caring enough to lead: How reflective practice leads to moral leadership*. Thousand Oaks, CA: Corwin Press.

Pickering, M. (2001). *Stereotyping: The politics of representation*. New York, NY: Palgrave.

Renesch, J., & Defoore, B. (1996). *The new bottom line: Bringing heart and soul to business*. San Francisco, CA: New Leaders Press/Sterling & Stone, Inc.

Rorty, R. (1989). *Contingency, irony, and solidarity*. New York, NY: Cambridge University Press.

Rousseau, J. J. (1997). Julie or the new heloise: Letter of two lovers who live in a small town at the foot of the Alps. In *The collected writings of rousseau (P. Stewart and J. Vaché, Trans.)* (Vol. 6). Hanover: University Press of England. (Originally published in 1761).

Saxena, S., Scharmer, O., & Goldman Schuyler, K. (2014). Connecting inner transformation as a leader to corporate and societal change. In K. G. Schuyler (Ed.), *Leading with spirit, presence & authenticity* (pp. 13–37). San Francisco, CA: Jossey-Bass.

Schön, D. A. (1982). *The reflective practitioner: How professionals think in action*. New York, NY: Basic Books.

Schwartzman, H. B. (1993). *Ethnography in organizations*. Newbury Park, CA: Sage.

Senge, P. M. (2006). *The fifth discipline*. New York, NY: Doubleday.

Speth, J. G. (2008). *The bridge at the edge of the world: Capitalism, the environment, and crossing from crisis to sustainability*. Devon, PA: Duke & Company.

Taylor, W. C. (1999). The leader of the future: Harvard's Ronald Heifetz offers a short course on the future of leadership. *Fast Company*, May 31. Retrieved from http://www.fastcompany.com/37229/leader-future

Turner, V. (1986). Dewey, dilthey, and drama: An essay in the anthropology of experience. In V. W. Turner & E. M. Bruner (Eds.), *The anthropology of experience* (pp. 33–44). Chicago, IL: University of Illinois Press.

Vielmetter, G., & Sell, Y. (2014). *Leadership 2030: The six megatrends you need to understand to lead your company into the future*. New York, NY: the Hay Holdings Group, Inc.

Weber, M. (1958). *The protestant ethic and the spirit of capitalism*. New York, NY: Charles Scribner's Sons.

Weick, K. (2009). *Making sense of the organization: The impermanent organization* (Vol. 2). West Sussex: John Wiley & Sons.

Wheelwright, P. (1959). *Heraclitus*. Princeton, NJ: Princeton University Press.

CHAPTER

6

Geopolitical Citizenship 2050: From Totalitarian Statism to Polyarchical Ideologies

Icarbord Tshabangu

The world has in the last two decades experienced media and technological advances that have consequently unsettled the paternalistic leadership ideologies and witnessed citizens agitating for diversified and distributed forms of leadership. To understand these current and future trends, this chapter gives an overview of past regimes, how they shaped the present and to some extent predestined future trajectories in geopolitics and citizenship.

The Historical, the Present and the Future

Difficult and imperfect as it may be, the science of prediction cannot be avoided since the human spirit always strives to discover as to what the future holds for the human race. This peering into the future has been enhanced by technology, scientific research, historical and current trends. In this chapter, we observe that both current and historical trends give strong indices as to the future possibilities. From time immemorial there has been an unparalleled human desire to break free from centralised regimes and create multiple centres of power as this will be explained in the discussion on historical trends section below. These polyarchical and liberal democratic trends that have emerged strongly in the last few decades are set to continue to surge into 2050. The current and future advances in technology, which have helped increase the spirit of individualism, are likely to aid and sustain such liberal trends (Future Timeline, 2014). In our endeavour to predict the future possibilities in mid-21st century, this chapter presents a historical perspective based on the notion *'show me a people who don't know their history and I will show you a people who don't know where they are going'*. The world's future is inextricably interlinked to its past. Further trends in politics, economics and education are then analysed in terms of changing contexts and the leadership implications for the future posited. It is further noted that strategies for leadership development, particularly the role of democratic education in educational contexts may be instrumental for a sustainable liberal democratic polity, thereby help address global challenges and meet future needs of citizens.

Methodology

In seeking to project into the political future in 2050, we have predicated our predictions on the historical and recent trends in democracy, economics and education. A review of global historical trends in political systems indicates a sustained trend of growth from totalitarian regimes to democracy and to some extent towards liberal democracy, also referred to as polyarchy. An analytical review of existing literature and unpublished data on contemporary contexts in leadership was also conducted to show the emerging trends particularly in economics and education so as to offer insights for the future. In using World Bank GDP data and population growth indices and other secondary sources of data, we have been able to make fair predictions into 2050.

Trends – The Historical: From Totalitarianism to Democracy

The most commonly known political systems in the world have been the monarchy, feudalism, absolutism, imperialism, democracy and communism (Okey, 1986). Some of the political systems linked to the above have included an oligarchy, a theocracy and an aristocracy. It should be borne in mind that each of the political systems developed out of the needs and associated struggles of the people at the time and thus shaped the nature of citizenship in each epoch. These historical trends help to explain the present as well as paint a picture as to how far political systems have changed over the years and the possible impact as we look further ahead.

TOTALITARIAN REGIMES IN HISTORY – A WORLDVIEW

One of the most common political systems to exist in Europe and Japan was feudalism. Feudalism developed after the fall and disintegration of the Roman Empire about 500 CE. Feudalism rose out of the need to repel Germanic invaders who raided weakened western European cities. The king who owned a lot of land would allocate some of that land to powerful Lords in exchange of their loyalty. The lords became vassals of the king. In turn, these lords would issue some of the land to lesser lords, who in turn would allocate some of the knights who became in direct control of the land, the peasants and the town folk in a given area. Under this system everyone had a defined place in society (Okey, 1986). The feudal system strikes resemblance with some African political systems especially in the manner in which they developed. Stronger tribes often absorbed the weaker tribes so as to be protected from other hostile invading armies. The weaker tribes would be given land and cattle in exchange of their loyalty. Kings who followed this method often became very powerful and were often the last kings to stand against the invading colonial settlers in the 1800s. For his advisers, the king surrounded himself with chiefs who came from nobility. Senior males often came from commoners. The military consisted of all able males (Tyrell & Jurgens, 1983).

MONARCHIES

The political system of monarchy is one of the earliest, and still survives in some parts of the world, but with far diminished powers. A monarchy, in which the government is under the control of one powerful leader is known to have developed strongly as a political system in Europe, some parts of China, India, Africa and South America (Kishlansky, 1996; Okey, 1986). In the old civilisations the strongest military man often became the king. It can be noted that some kings and queens played a dual role by performing religious duties, thereby earning themselves the divine right to govern (Crick, 2002). After the enlightenment age culminating in the search for democratic political systems, most monarchs across the globe saw their power diminish or taken over in a political struggle with the nation's citizens. Despite the monarchy's diminishing state, it can be observed that the existence of one political party system in some countries covertly served well the place of absolutist monarchies. The emergence of 'life presidents' in some countries bore resemblance to covert absolutist monarchies.

In China, their emperors claimed the divine right of rule. It is said that a dynasty would last longer as far as there is good governance. When the dynasty abused its power and its influence faced decline, the citizens translated this as lack of heavenly mandate and thus another strong leader will rise to set up a new dynasty. Throughout Indian history, the Mauryan Empire is a good example of a monarchical system. It had a rigid centralised government and an efficient bureaucracy run by government officials (Anderson & Chase-Dunn, 2005).

In Rome, the Roman Empire ruled the whole of Italy, had conquered southern Europe and Asia Minor but culminated in civil wars leading to Julius Caesar's murder in 48 BC. In the middle Ages, European kings and nobles battled with the Roman Catholic Church's supremacy. In England and France, kings began to strengthen and centralise their power and restrict the church. The fighting which also included the appointment of bishops in some countries led to the formation of nation states under different political systems. In Spain, England, France, Austria and Russia, absolute monarchs were established (Okey, 1986). Spain in the 1500s emerged as a powerful state because of two successive absolutist monarchs, namely Charles V and his son Phillip II. In Russia, Peter the Great and Catherine the Great used autocratic means to expand Russia's influence. In the 1600s Charles I of England was an absolutist monarch who ruled by decree. Charles I was later dethroned by the parliament led by Cromwell. The 1688 English bill of rights was to ensure parliament's supremacy over the monarchy (Crick, 2002). In France, Protestants and Catholics tore the country apart in the late 1500s through fighting and in the 1640s Cardinal Richelieu helped King Louis XIV to assume absolutist power. He ruled for many years and was known as the 'Sun King' and was said to be God's representative on earth by Jacques Bousset (Okey, 1986). In the Islamic world, a good example of an absolutist monarchy was that of Ottoman sultan Suleiman who was often seen as a perfect ruler with knowledge of justice. His contemporary was the third Nughal, emperor of India Akbar the Great who ascended the throne in 1556. Akbar won the admiration of both Hindus and Muslims through his efficient institutionalisation of bureaucracy (Crick, 2002; Okey, 1986). In Africa Tshaka the Zulu can be regarded as one of the absolutist monarchies of the 17th century Africa (Tyrell & Jurgens, 1983).

IMPERIALISM

Modern imperialism developed after the industrial revolution and its root cause was to open new markets as well as to satisfy demands for raw materials (Mbah & Igariwey, 2001). Imperialism manifested itself where strong nations conquered weaker ones and dominated their economic, political and cultural life. Imperialism in the 1800s manifested itself in the colonisation of Africa, India and the

Americas by some European countries. Apart from seeking raw materials and new markets, some of the reasons for colonisation were born out of national pride, as some European powers sought to exert their power and prestige (Fulcher, 2004; Okey, 1986). One of the notable resultants of colonialism was the fusion of cultures. The enlightenment ideas of social justice and liberty later rejuvenated the colonies and this resulted in political revolutions, finally overthrowing colonialism throughout the occupied regions. It is also noted that the industrialisation efforts in colonial states later gave birth to radical unionisms buoyed by Marxist and Leninist socialist ideals as workers agitated for justice, equality and political change.

COMMUNISM

In Russia, Vladimir I. Lenin and L. Trotsky led the Bolsheviks known as socialist revolutionaries, against Czar Nicholas II and prevailed. However, it is alleged that power appropriated from the monarchy later became concentrated in the communist party and citizens were as a result brutalised so as to adhere to a one-party state system. Under Joseph Stalin, Russia became even more totalitarian. The government controlled everything in what was to be described as a command economy (Okey, 1986).

Most African revolutions against colonialism were supported by Russia both ideologically and militarily, a situation which manifested itself in the formation of one-party statism after independence reminiscent of the political systems in Russia. It can be noted that communist revolution in Africa was not necessarily the working class rising up against the bourgeoisie but the people against a repressive imperialistic government. Although socialism was used as the rallying point, it was nationalism that confronted and led to the demise of colonialism. In China it was also the same where the poor peasants fought against an imperial state, which led to the establishment of communist China under the Chinese communist party led by Mao Zedong (Anderson & Chase-Dunn, 2005; Maoist International Movement, 2005). It can be observed that under communism and consequentially under a command economy, the state executed absolutism in most instances and the citizens' rights to self-determination, equality and justice were overlooked. Most colonies who used socialism and communism as the rallying point found themselves stumbling into the same experience of totalitarian rule, where the state sought to control every aspect of a citizen's life.

THE RISE OF DEMOCRACY

Democracy started making inroads far early in Europe though it was not until 1215 CE in England, for example where the nobility compelled King John to sign a Great Charter which was to be known as Magna Carta, some form of constitutional law, recognising their rights as land owners, citizens of England and subjects of the king (Crick, 2002). It was not until after the enlightenment age, that Glorious Revolution of England took place in 1688 and moved towards a partial democracy. In 1776 the American colonies declared their independence from England and quickly modelled their democratic ideals after the enlightenment thinkers. The French Revolution followed in 1789 and that of Latin America in the 1790s and early 1800s. Democracy continued to be partially practised. After the Second World War, most parts of Japan, Europe and the Americas continued to practise some form of democracy. In Africa, the 20th century witnessed the liberation of all countries from imperial colonial rule. Since then the continent has witnessed partial and fluctuating democracies (Potter, Goldplatt, Kiloh, & Lewis, 1997).

It is noted that during the latter part of the 20th century, democracy became a global phenomenon. The numbers of world's populations living under democracy have steadily increased with successive waves of democracy, some associated with wars. The fall of the Soviet Union followed by its independent republics seeking to liberalise and democratise their governance systems in the 1990s undoubtedly added to the number of countries classed as democratic. It is noted, therefore, that there has also been a general acceptance by liberal democratic countries of illiberal democracies (Dahl, 1989). As depicted by Freedom House (2014), the wider acceptance of free and partially free countries that are seen as belonging to a democratic community of nations has in itself broadened the concept of democracy.

Trends in democracy continue to show a steady rise of liberal democracies, and this increase is bound to substantially increase by 2050, particularly in view of advances in technology and will drastically affect citizens' perceptions as to what constitutes moral and effective leadership. In the next section we discuss the notion of polyarchy as the most probable and moral way to govern.

POLYARCHY AS THE 21ST CENTURY ALTERNATIVE

As noted above, the rise in the number of democracies (quantity), will in turn give rise to polyarchy, as citizens seek quality in democratic governance. Guided by 'choice' as its mantra, polyarchy is a democratic paradigm that seeks the empowerment of individuals and communities in a way that neither they (individuals or communities) nor the state dominate the other. One of the compelling arguments for democratisation is found in democratic peace theory or democratic pacifism (Ceadel, 1980). This Kantian theory claims that liberal democracies almost never go to war with one another. It is generally believed that liberal democracies often tend to use democracy and arbitration with each other, and others also believe that the accountability of democratic states often compels leaders to be less likely to use force. This assertion may be problematic for some in view of the wars that have been led by some democracies in the Middle East, sometimes against wider public opinion within their polity. Since liberal democracy is seen as likely to bring peace, its ideology has found favour in many revolutions as seen in the last quarter of the 20th century (Dahl, 1989; Potter et al., 1997), leading to the reduction of countries classed as not free. The nation states that are classed as free and partly free are more liberal and also projected to have increased to a total of 85% by 2050.

Reinhold Niebuhr cited in Crick (2002) once said that, 'man's inclination to justice makes democracy possible; but man's capacity for injustice makes it necessary' (p. 120). In most parts of the world, democracy is seen as the only ethical way to govern and any deviation is likely to be perceived as lacking both in legitimacy and standard form of human society (Ceadel, 1980; Crick, 2002; Harber, 1995). With projected increase in the number of 'free' states by 2050, the main trend among emerging and fluctuating democracies will witness more effort to establish sound democratic institutions ahead of putting faith in party politics and in persons of power. True to the polyarchical ideologies, the nature of freedom will mean more in terms of individual liberties than mere holding of free and fair elections once in four or five years.

Trends – The Political: Citizens Claiming Their Rights

Most nation states have had long histories of poor and oppressed people organising to claim their rights (Fanon, 1965) or living under failing states and fluctuating democracies (Potter et al., 1997). Totalitarian democracy often takes root under forms of illegitimacy, where the state, under the guise of sovereignty or tyrannical majority, brutalises the minority and the individual. Such democracy becomes characterised as 'everything for the state, from the state and by the state' (Polyarchy Organisation, 2003). Despite gross violation of human rights, such nation states still claim to be democratic. For much of the developing world, citizens have remained stuck with an empty word 'democracy'.

The late 20th and early 21st century has witnessed a gradual departure from leadership approaches that tended to rely heavily on the 'Strongman' or the 'Bigman' of the nation, modelled after unquestioning deference (Harber, 1995), to forms of a polyarchical nature (Dahl, 1989). Polyarchy could be the best alternative for most communities who are largely divided by ethnicity (Salih, 2001). In most nation states downward economically and politically slides can largely be linked to a non-polyarchical order (Babu, 1981; Rodney, 1981; Stiff, 2002) and surrender to irrationality or blind obedience to others' decisions, which often invites all the brutalities of totalitarian regimes (Popper, 1945 cited in Bailey, 2000).

Many citizens of the world who have lived under failed and failing states would readily identify with Kropotkin's words, which, though appearing as an anarchist, are a classic indicator of the exasperation at the excesses of the state under totalitarian statism. Kropotkin cited in Freedom Press (1897) commented thus: 'Either the State for ever, crushing individual and local life, taking over in all fields of human ... or the destruction of States, and new life starting again in thousands of centres on the principle of the lively initiative of the individual and groups and that of free agreement, the choice lies with you' (p. 60). The assertion by Kropotkin advances a strong view in favour of individual liberties and these are projected to rise further going into the middle of the 21st century due to technological advances, as stated earlier. The following section considers the current trends in citizenship and how these may impact leadership practices leading up to 2050.

THE FUTURE CITIZEN

Centuries ago, citizens were largely uneducated. Rulers often had a monopoly of information and leaders often demanded or enforced obedience without question (Tolstoy, 1894). In the 21st century where the media and technology have revolutionised modern democracy, such forms of leadership at every level have become obsolete and a greater demand for shared leadership has taken root. The world in the last decade has experienced media and technological advances consequently unsettling the paternalistic leadership ideologies resulting in a greater desire for diversified and distributed forms of leadership (Harris, 2008; Spillane & Diamond, 2007). These emerging trends have been in part, precipitated by global and local community demands both in the political and in the business world. In technology, the ability to access vital information online and the ability to use various technological tools has meant that most citizens can position themselves as producers of information and of products in ways that make them influential over the *status quo*. Notable examples can be found in photography, free-lance journalism, private investigation and intelligence sharing, political commentary and blogging and tools for self-diagnosis in the medical world. The diversified use of technology in the future would have risen exponentially in 2050 with most citizens capable even of accessing hand-held CT scans (Future Timeline, 2014).

DEMOGRAPHICS

Despite notable decline in fertility rates over the last 60 years, it is estimated that in 2050 the planet will have about 9.4 billion people, which is over 30% more than today and the majority of these people will live in cities and urban areas (World Bank, 2014). In the drive towards liberal democratisation processes in contemporary Africa, Ake (1996) observed that this phenomenon is a largely urban one. Taking into consideration that the larger population in Africa, for example, are situated in the rural areas this creates a problem for the development of democratic citizenship where rural people are often cowed to submission by state terror as evidenced in some countries during elections campaigns (Department for International Development, 2008; Freedom House, 2012). The global trend which predicts more people living in towns and cities by 2050 implies more political awareness and activism among citizens. It is further estimated that in 2050, countries such as Nigeria will be as populated as the United States, with some developing countries such as Ethiopia surpassing Europe's developed nations such as Germany and the United Kingdom. Despite remaining relatively poor on per capita basis, the doubling of some populations in most developing countries is likely to increase their economies in competitive terms in view of Europe's largely ageing population (HSBC Global Research, 2013). For example Russia and Japan's working populations are forecast to contract by 31% and 37%, respectively by 2050. Germany will see a decline of 24% while most other parts of Europe are forecast at 29% decline. In the United States evidence depicts boomers on the verge of retirement and also in a poorer state of health than their predecessors (Bridgette, Perrotta, Augustine, & Perrotta, 2008). Such trends will have far reaching implications on sovereign debt, economic and competitiveness and will undoubtedly witness marginal to significant power shifts in view of emerging economies (PricewaterhouseCoopers Economics, 2013).

The geopolitical picture, which is often sustained by economic clout, will likely shift towards a diversified outlook where previously poor economies emerge to exert some influence or will break loose to form multiple regional blocks to reflect these new developments. With China expected to be the world's largest economy in 2050, and a host of other obscure economies gaining economic clout (Foure, Benassy – Quere, & Fontagne, 2010; HSBC Global Research, 2013), future leaders of Organisations such as the UN and its Security Council, the IMF and the World Bank, will find themselves under immense pressure from other global citizens to reform their political constitutions going into the middle of the 21st century. This would be largely driven by demographic changes, technological revolutions and the shifting economic realities as discussed above (HSBC Global Research, 2013; The Carnegie Endowment for International Peace, 2010).

MULTICULTURALISM

The authoritarian values in citizenship often seek to homogenise the heterogeneous masses (Hersh, Miller, & Fielding, 1980), while the democratic approach often seeks to be multicultural, inclusive and tolerant of other views (Osler & Starkey, 2005). The mid-21st century will witness a greater embrace of pluralism in ideas. It is noted that most democratisation efforts, particularly in the developing countries have failed due in large part to citizens' lack of experience with public discourse and traditional reliance on state paternalism. This is a *status quo* where everything becomes for the state, from the state and by the state (Polyarchy Organisation, 2003). With projected increased levels of education forecast in these economies by 2050 and a higher level of participation in politics by mostly urban populations, a more liberal democratic dispensation buoyed also by empowerment through technology is likely to have developed. The traditional media will be fragmented and diversified by 2050 (Future Timeline, 2014). The traditional role of the intelligentsia and political elite of seeking to suppress citizens into 'see no evil hear no evil and speak no evil' culture will diminish and prove difficult to enforce as citizens, particularly in developing countries use technology to good effect and also shift from trusting political persons of power to seeking the establishment of stronger institutions that may hold leaders to account.

In our present world of nation states citizenship is readily understood in reference to status (Isin & Wood, 1999; Osler & Starkey, 2005). The influence of globalisation and population movements across the globe will render connections between the individual and the nation state much more problematic, with obvious implications for the construction of multiple identities and multicultural notions of belonging will be much more common.

TRENDS – THE ECONOMICAL: SHIFTING GROWTH AND POWER OF INFLUENCE

The emerging economies of mostly Africa and Asia are projected to substantially increase their GDPs as they continue to show a stronger potential for growth compared to advanced economies of Europe and America (Foure et al., 2010). In the 1970s, the average growth in the developed markets was over 3% and has stagnated to around 1% going into 2014 and is projected to remain so into the 2040s, while the emerging markets have experienced a steady rise from 1% growth on average in the 1970s to around 2% currently and is projected to be over 2.5% in the 2040s (HSBC Global Research, 2013). Economic global growth in the 2050s is projected to be powered by emerging economies. These predictions are likely to be manifest if there are no debilitating wars due in part to pacifist ideals in view of increased liberal democracies as discussed above and that these emerging economies continue to pursue friendly policies beneficial to both local and international investors.

It is noted that most of the economic activity in the emerging markets will be powered mostly by new technologies which have not been available to these economies until recently. Democracy as an enabler of peace and the rule of law will also prove pivotal for sustained growth into the 2050s, implying that leaders of nations who continue to pursue illiberal and totalitarian policies on their citizens, will not only ensue depreciation of their economies but will also most likely face moral isolation from a largely liberal global leadership. The traditional ways of working will drastically change as more and more employers and governments find ways to access offshore expertise otherwise unavailable before due to poor technologies. Such trends are more likely to further benefit infrastructural, capital and knowledge growth in emerging economies. The income per capita growth will in turn improve households spending powers and spur further growth in key areas such as education and health.

As shown in the global trends of average GDP growth per capita against average population growth (PricewaterhouseCoopers Economics, 2013), it is noted that despite population growth in emerging economies their GDP growth is focused to be substantial and therefore likely to offset the negatives related to population growth. Such trajectories in economic development will help further improve the quality of democracy in these regions (Bhagwati, 1995). The advances in democratic governance will witness a shift from largely republican forms of democracy which encourage participation and the voice, to a more polyarchical dispensation, which promotes individual liberties and choice. Africa with its current share of fastest growing countries will gradually emerge from its obscure past to become a competitive economic region.

TRENDS – THE EDUCATIONAL: DEVELOPING DEMOCRATIC LEADERS FOR THE FUTURE

Aristotle cited in Harber (1995) once observed that 'it is useless to have the most beneficial rules of society fully agreed on by all who are members of the polity if individuals are not going to be trained and have their habits formed for that polity' (p. 1).

It is noted that some of the world's failing states have liberal constitutions on paper yet citizens have not been prepared adequately to appreciate the constitutional arrangements so as to bring to account those that govern. In light of the above, educational institutions have a moral imperative to prepare their learners and students in the appreciation of democratic values and effective political participation in the life of their nation states as citizens. The United Nations Education for all agenda has witnessed remarkable successes in most countries leading to significant rising enrolments particularly in developing economies and also matched by higher completion rates at both primary and secondary education (Dorius, 2012; UNESCO, 2013). Such accomplishments in knowledge and skills development would do well if educators not only taught democratic education but also provided opportunities to their students to exercise their voice and choice in a variety of educational practices and processes. The UNESCO's post 2015 development agenda in education places emphasis on rights and equity while expanding further the vision of access to quality education at all levels (UNESCO, 2014). Such a trajectory future focus will further embed polyarchical values among future learners and citizens.

A further projection between 2005 and 2050 on 120 countries in all regions of the world also shows improved completion rates in education particularly in developing economies of Africa, Asia and Latin America, thereby contributing huge numbers of highly qualified people to their working-age population (Samir et al., 2010). In view of the projected changes ahead in the 21st century, the educational institutions from primary to higher education should provide opportunities and a fertile ground not just for teaching democratic leadership values but designing for its practice within the wider confines of their institutions. The U.N. Convention on the Rights of the Child Article 12.1 states that 'a child shall be entitled to participate once he or she is capable of forming his or her opinions' (UNICEF, 2014). In tandem with a polyarchical dispensation that is set to rise, educators face the challenge of socializing learners into active 'namers of the world' and not let others name the world for them (Freire, 1970). Since those who will govern in the future and those who should make them accountable are in educational institutions today, the schools and universities, without limiting themselves to being a mirror of society (Bernstein, 1970; Gould, 1993) have an opportunity and a nobler influential role to develop leadership traits that will promote a tolerant and a polyarchical culture projected to gain prominence as the world move closer to the middle of this century.

IMPLICATIONS FOR FUTURE LEADERSHIP

It is observed that in most parts of the world, organisations and governments have been built and studied on the basis of the concept of leaders directing subordinates to accomplish a vision designed by them (Jackson as cited in Wepman, 1985). This paradigm has been challenged particularly in the western world but recently more so in the southern hemisphere (Northouse, 2010). New leadership ideologies are emerging providing for a gradual shift towards emphasis on distributed forms of leadership (Spillane, 2005; Spillane & Diamond, 2007). Leadership practice continues to witness a growing emphasis on the capacity to influence rather than the exercise of authority (Bush, Bell, & Middlewood, 2009; Harris, 2008). Such distributive forms of leadership provide for the loosening of formal roles within an organisation coupled with devolution of power from the centre, thereby allowing followers to exercise some level of power and influence, either individually, through teams or as local communities. The following is a summation of some leadership challenges in 2050.

WISDOM

The leaders of the future will have to adapt more and more to the realisation that they will have no monopoly over the knowledge economy due to technological revolution and the strengthening of polyarchical ideologies. Even though everyone might not be a decision-maker, the expertise of many will be valued in the decision-making process. Leaders who excel will be those who can broaden their horizon and allow it to merge in the multicultural, thereby providing a stronger foundation for a vision within their organisations, governments and wider communities. With future planetary and environmental challenges set to grow as evidenced in climate change (World Economic Forum, 2013), distributed leadership approaches to a shared global village will require a shared visionary leadership and these attributes will prove indispensable.

QUALITY

The benchmark of effective leadership will be determined by the leader's ability to influence a multiple of autonomous power bases within organisations, governments or globally. The new mid-21st century leader will need to radically adapt to emerging realities of a new world order where information flows within organisations and governments and around the world would become harder to manage and the traditional hierarchies upon which statism and totalitarianism survived, will prove harder to sustain. Quality in leadership will emerge to be seen largely in terms of the leader's influence rather than authority. This will mean being pragmatic by tapping the expert ideas of everyone involved (Colander, 2000).

THE MORAL

As indicated in earlier discussions, the rise of liberal nations in the world will as a consequence diminish autocracies and statism among the community of nations. The mantra of 'Strongman' or 'Bigman' of a country as has been challenged during the revolutions in the Arab world, dubbed the 'Arab spring' will be shunned upon as rooted in moral pariah in mid-21st century. Those leaders who practice autocratic and tyrannical ways of leadership will face moral isolation from a largely liberal global leadership and citizenry. The 20th century democracy in general quickly became a conceptual and an ideological-mediating artifact and a perceived standard of governance within geopolitical affairs. In most parts of the world today, democracy became seen as the only ethical and moral way to govern and any deviation perceived as lacking both in legitimacy and standard form of human society (Crick, 2002; Harber, 1995). In the mid-21st century, liberal democracy will emerge as the moral yardstick on governance and will influence international relations, public policy and private entities.

WORK PLACE

To be successful in change management most organisations will not only encourage sharing of ideas but will also demand it to survive. Traditional ways of working and managing will change in many ways as physical presence and geography becomes less significant coupled with redefined boundaries in education and economics (Colander, 2000). The advances in virtual learning environments, for example will radically change how educational institutions operate, rendering some systems, processes and practices redundant. In business, the diminishing importance of geography and presence in the work place will mean fluid loyalties and eroded hierarchies. The successful leaders of the future are those who will be courageous enough to adapt and thus remodel their institutions, breaking from the norm to stay relevant and afloat. Being multilingual, flexible, internationally mobile, adaptable and culturally sensitive (Hay Group, 2011), will prove critical for leaders in view of strengthened emerging markets and doing business in largely diverse environments.

DEALING WITH THREATS

With advances in technology, military and business solutions will be undertaken not with a 'boots on the ground' mentality of seeking to deploy multiple physical resources, but effective reconnaissance, discovering new approaches and testing of these through controlled and reasoned risk. There will be more of partnering against adversity and less of 'going it alone' as a norm. Some of these approaches have already taken root in the United States's war or terror despite opposition from conservative ideologies (The White House, 2011). The United Nations Security Council would have reformed and will largely oversee peace and security with a greater global acceptance than prior. Non-state actors, largely mobile in nature, will prove to be a great challenge on the 'war on terror' (World Economic Forum, 2013), and the efforts to securing peace and global stability will demand distributed leadership approaches and broader international cooperation than what exists at present.

LEGISLATION

The regulation of business, migration, labour, law and order and surveillance will have changed dramatically to respond to news ways of working; doing business; protecting the public from crime and proliferation of weapons of mass destruction among non-state actors; regulating easily accessible technological tools and health instruments. Under labour, for example the law will have to adapt to more and more contractual and fluid arrangements as opposed to long-term employer − employee relations. The ageing populations of Europe coupled with the burgeoning middle class in emerging markets and rising populations, point to challenges and opportunities which will necessitate legislative changes particularly on immigration, business and employment law.

THE SPIRIT

Guided by the polyarchical ideology, most leaders will be rooted on the notion of 'everybody matters' in their individual capacity, giving rise to greater inclusivity amidst diversity. Despite current failed attempts to break away from the centre as evidenced in Scotland of United Kingdom, Catalonia of Spain, Tibet of China and many other regions of the world seeking independence from their governments, these pressures for independence will ironically fuel more devolution of power as evidenced in the United Kingdom (British Broadcasting Corporation, 2014), thereby advancing further and sustaining polyarchical ideologies into the future.

CONCLUSION

We have explored the historical and current trends in geopolitical citizenship and what these may mean for the future. Current socio-economic trends and secondary sources of data have been used to make fair projections into 2050. Both historical and current trends point to a polyarchical future in many spheres of life and this will be enhanced by advances in technology. The implications for future leadership challenges were noted as wide-ranging and will require diversified and distributed leadership approaches.

References

Ake, C. (1996). *Democracy and development in Africa*. Washington, DC: Brookings Institution.

Anderson, E. N., & Chase-Dunn, C. (2005). *The historical evolution of world-systems evolutionary processes in world politics*. New York, NY: Palgrave Macmillan.

Babu, A. M. (1981). *African socialism or socialist Africa?* Harare: Zimbabwe Publishing House.

Bailey, R. (2000). *Teaching values and citizenship*. London: Sage.

Bernstein, B. (1970). Education cannot compensate for society. *New Society, 15*(387), 344–347.

Bhagwati, J. (1995). New thinking on development. *Journal of Democracy, 6*(4), 50–64.

Bridgette, L., Perrotta, M. U. P., Augustine, L., & Perrotta, D. O. (2008). Access to state-of-the-art healthcare: A missing dynamic in consumer selection of a retirement community. *The Journal of the American Osteopathic Association, 108*(6), 297–305.

British Broadcasting Corporation. (2014). *Scottish referendum: Miliband queries English powers plan*. Retrieved from http://www.bbc.co.uk/news/uk-politics-29281819

Bush, T., Bell, L., & Middlewood, D. (Eds.). (2009). *The principles of educational leadership and management*. London: Sage.

Ceadel, M. (1980). *Pacifism in Britain, 1914–1945: The defining of a faith*. Oxford: Clarendon Press.

Colander, D. (2000). New millennium economics: How did it get this way and what way is it? *The Journal of Economic Perspectives, 14*(1), 121–132.

Crick, B. (2002). *Democracy: A very short introduction*. Oxford: Oxford University Press.

Dadush, U., & Stancil, B. (2010). *The world order in 2050. The Carnegie Endowment for International Peace*. Retrieved from http://carnegieendowment.org/files/World_Order_in_2050.pdf

Dahl, R. A. (1989). *Democracy and its critics*. New Haven, CT: Yale University Press.

Department for International Development. (2008). *Elections in Kenya in 2007*. Retrieved from https://www.gov.uk/government/uploads/system/uploads/attachment_data/file/67654/elections-ke-2007.pdf

Dorius, S. F. (2012). *The rise and fall of worldwide education inequality from 1870 to 2010: Measurement and trends*. London: Sage.

Fanon, F. (1965). *Wretched of the earth*. London: Penguin.

Foure, J., Benassy – Quere, A., & Fontagne, L. (2010). *The world economy in 2050: A tentative picture*. CEPII Working Paper No. 2010-27. Retrieved from http://www.cepii.fr/anglaisgraph/bdd/baseline.htm

Freedom House. (2012). *Freedom in the world: Zimbabwe*. Retrieved from https://freedomhouse.org/report/freedom-world/2012/zimbabwe#.VIr0Tz_ROSo

Freedom House. (2014). *Country status and ratings overview: Freedom in the World 1973–2014.* Retrieved from http://www.freedomhouse.org/report-types/freedom-world

Freire, P. (1970). *Pedagogy of the oppressed.* London: Penguin.

Fulcher, J. (2004). *Capitalism: A very short introduction.* New York, NY: Oxford University Press.

Future Timeline. (2014). *2050–2059 timeline contents.* Retrieved from http://www.futuretimeline.net/21stcentury/2050-2059.htm#.VB8CxxaRq1c

Gould, W. T. S. (1993). *People and education in the third world.* New York, NY: Longman.

Harber, C. (1995). *Developing democratic education.* Derby: Education Now Books.

Harris, A. (2008). *Distributed school leadership: Developing tomorrow's leaders.* London: Routledge.

Hay Group. (2011). *Leadership 2030.* Retrieved from http://www.haygroup.com/leadership2030/

Hersh, R. H., Miller, J. P., & Fielding, G. D. (1980). *Models of moral education: An appraisal.* New York, NY: Longman.

HSBC Global Research. (2013). *The world in 2050.* Retrieved from http://www.research.hsbc.com

Isin, E. F., & Wood, P. K. (1999). *Citizenship and identity.* London: Sage.

Kishlansky, M. (1996). *A monarchy transformed: Britain 1603–1714.* London: Penguin.

Kropotkin, P. (1897). *The state.* London: Freedom Press.

Maoist International Movement. (2005). *What is the difference between communism and socialism?* [Online]. Retrieved from http://www.etext.org/Politics/MIM/faq/commievssoc.html

Mbah, S., & Igariwey, I. E. (2001). *African anarchism: The history of a movement.* Tucson, AZ: Sharp Press.

Northouse, P. G. (2010). *Leadership.* London: Sage.

Okey, R. (1986). *Eastern Europe 1740–1985: Feudalism to communism.* London: Hutchinson Education.

Osler, A., & Starkey, H. (2005). *Changing citizenship: Democracy and inclusion in education.* Maidenhead: Open University Press.

Polyarchy Organisation. (2003). *Polyarchy: a paradigm.* Retrieved from http://www.polyarchy.org/paradigm/english/democracy.html

Potter, D., Goldplatt, D., Kiloh, M., & Lewis, P. (1997). *Democracy: From classical times to the present.* Abingdon: Polity Press.

PricewaterhouseCoopers Economics. (2013). *World in 2050 – The BRICs and beyond: Prospects, challenges and opportunities.* Retrieved from http://www.pwc.com/en_GX/gx/world-2050/assets/pwc-world-in-2050-report-january-2013.pdf

Rodney, W. (1981). *How Europe underdeveloped Africa.* New York, NY: Harvard University Press.

Salih, M. M. A. (2001). *African democracies and African politics.* New York, NY: Pluto Press.

Samir, K. C., Barakat, B., Goujon, A., Skirbekk, V., Sanderson, W., & Lutz, W. (2010). *Projection of populations by level of educational attainment, age, and sex for 120 countries for 2005–2050.* Retrieved from http://www.demographic%20research.org/Volumes/Vol22/15/. doi:10.4054/DemRes.2010.22.15

Spillane, J. P. (2005). Distributed leadership. *The Educational Forum, 69,* 143.

Spillane, J. P., & Diamond, J. B. (Eds.). (2007). *Distributed leadership in practice.* New York, NY: Teachers College Press.

Stiff, P. (2002). *Cry Zimbabwe: Independence – Twenty years on.* London: Galago Publishing.

The White House. (2011). *The national strategy for counterterrorism.* Retrieved from http://www.whitehouse.gov/sites/default/files/counterterrorism_strategy.pdf

Tolstoy, L. N. (1894). *On patriotism, in Panarchy.Org (2001–2007).* Retrieved from http://www.panarchy.org/tolstoy/189

Tyrell, P., & Jurgens, B. (1983). *African heritage.* London: Macmillan Press.

UNESCO. (2013). *Summary of progress towards education for all.* Retrieved from http://www.unesco.org/new/fileadmin/MULTIMEDIA/HQ/ED/ED_new/pdf/Summary%20of%20progress%20towards%20EFA-colors.pdf

UNESCO. (2014). *Position paper on education post – 2015.* Retrieved from http://unesdoc.unesco.org/images/0022/002273/227336E.pdf

UNICEF. (2014). *The UN convention on the rights of the child.* Retrieved from http://www.unicef.org.uk/UNICEFs-Work/UN-Convention/

Wepman, D. (1985). *Jomo Kenyatta.* London: Burke Publishing.

World Bank. (2014). *Population estimates and projections.* Retrieved from http://datatopics.worldbank.org/hnp/popestimates

World Economic Forum. (2013). *Young global leaders – what the world will look like in 2030?* Retrieved from http://www.weforum.org/news/young-global-leaders-%E2%80%93-what-world-will-look-2030

Healthcare 2050: Anticipatory Leadership, Physician Shortages, and Patient-Centered Care

Barry A. Doublestein, Walter T. Lee and Richard M. Pfohl

The practice of leadership has matured beyond the level of simply using certain skills to gain follower buy-in to the use of those skills focused on taking followers into uncertain futures using anticipatory strategy development processes. Wayne Gretzky said, "A *good hockey player plays where the puck is. A great hockey player plays where the puck is going to be*" (Gretzky, 2014). Leaders of many entrenched industries like education, energy, and transportation find themselves struggling to anticipate where trends are driving their futures instead of proactively engaging with these trends to create favorable futures. The healthcare industry currently finds itself in a similar position, for it must also change its leadership focus from "playing where the puck is," to "playing where it is going to be." If left to its own devices, the profession will continue to slide toward irrelevancy through benign neglect and stagnation. Too often over the last few decades, healthcare leadership has settled on strategies that are reactive to disruptions instead of taking proactive steps to create futures of its own determination. It is time for today's healthcare leaders to shed old models of thinking and move toward models that include innovation and foresight (Petrie, 2014).

If healthcare leadership hopes to assure relevance in 2050, it will not necessarily need to revise or change the content of the practice; rather it will be necessary to change its context. Future leaders will need to be prepared to broaden their personal perspectives and practice strategic foresight skills which will help them to devise strategies which anticipate trends playing themselves out as time moves forward and use the developed strategies to innovate.

Supporting this need for healthcare leaders having a future-focused mindset is Sandeep Jauhar, MD's newly minted memoir, *Doctored: The Disillusionment of an American Physician*, which uncovers the ugly underbelly of what happens when leaders fail to practice foresight skills that would confront the rapid rise of uncertainty in their profession. He writes: "Today medicine is just another profession, and doctors have become like everybody else: insecure, discontented and anxious about the future (Jauhar, 2014, p. 6)." Unfortunately, this attitude is found too often in organizations, both inside and outside of healthcare, with roots established in benign neglect, willful disregard of attention to driving trends, exhaustion associated with reacting to constant change, or simple ignorance of skills that could help to determine a future of one's own choosing. Whatever the reason behind this present rampant physician insecurity, discontentment, and anxiety, it need not be. In fact, the time has come for healthcare, as a profession, to apply the principles of anticipatory leadership, which when applied correctly, removes insecurity, discontentment, anxiety, and uncertainty associated with uncertain futures.

This chapter describes a methodology for healthcare leaders to implement within their strategy development processes which will help them to remain relevant as they move into uncertain futures. The principles outlined in this chapter are not unique to healthcare and can benefit leaders on any level within any organization; however, the authors have chosen to focus on anticipatory leadership practices within the healthcare industry in this chapter for it stands to most significantly and directly impact people, for better or worse, on a global scale. The chapter begins with a definition of anticipatory leadership and distinguishes it from other leadership and management practices current being utilized by industry leaders. Next, the authors provide a broad, yet simplified list of six principles that are necessary for the anticipatory leader to practice as they attempt to deal with uncertainty. Finally, the chapter unfolds examples of two significant problems facing healthcare, which must be faced with anticipatory leadership skills if the profession hopes to remain relevant in 2050; address physician shortages and the move toward patient-centered care.

Anticipatory Leadership

To respond to the present healthcare leadership challenge, today's organizations must integrate anticipatory leadership practice into their daily strategic development processes. Since anticipatory leadership is not a commonly used term within the leadership community, it is necessary to define it and the principles used to accomplish successful outcomes. Anticipatory leadership is about seeing, aligning, and changing an organization. It is the combination of the disciplines of *strategic thinking,* through the use of strategic foresight, *strategic alignment,* by utilizing strategic leadership, and *strategic action,* through the use of strategic management. Anticipatory leadership creates a conceptual model of the future by utilizing foresight, practicing strategic leadership to create a logical model of the future, and finally utilizing strategic management to create the actual physical strategic model.

Leaders apply anticipatory foresight as they begin to navigate the future through understanding ideas, social change, worldviews, and cultural patterns. By doing this, anticipatory leaders will be well equipped in their understanding of external forces, the influences behind these forces, and their impact on the internal organization. Anticipatory leadership is about taking people to a place they would not go on their own, disrupting the core, upsetting the *status quo,* and possessing and utilizing the proper skills to envision a preferred future (Doublestein, 2010).

Applying anticipatory leadership within industries or organizations is a process of understanding how decisions are made by those entities. In those organizations which adhere to traditional leadership practices, decisions are made on "what can be seen (visible future)." In organizations utilizing strategic leadership practices, decisions are made on "what cannot be seen but can be predicted (predictable future)." On the other hand, in organizations practicing strategic leadership, with a focus on foresight, decisions are made on "what cannot be seen (invisible future)." But, for those organizations committed to anticipatory leadership practices, decisions are made based on "what can and cannot be seen nor predicted, but can be anticipated (anticipated future) (Table 1)."

In this sense, anticipatory leadership takes a holistic, non-fragmented view of the future so that the organization is not just predicting but anticipating the future in its decision-making practices. If organizations, or for that matter entire industries, want to create sustainable competitive advantage over others, they must ensure their vision is not just what they see "above the surface" but "below the surface" as well. Anticipatory leadership focuses right at

Table 1:   Leadership Practices and the Type of Future
upon which Strategic Decisions Are Made.

Leadership Practice	Decisions Based On
Traditional	Visible future
Strategic	Predictable future
Strategic with foresight	Invisible future
Anticipatory	Anticipated future

the heart of the leadership challenge by making sense of a turbulent and complex future.

Anticipatory leadership ties together concepts of strategic leadership, strategic management, anticipatory management, futures studies, innovation, and foresight. According to William Ashley, how anticipatory management is introduced to an organization determines its success (Ashley & Morrison, 1995). He believes it should be presented as an extension of strategic management and as a method for discovering forces in the external world which affect decision-making at all levels of an organization with significant bottom-line consequences (Ashley & Morrison, 1995). Anticipatory leadership is based on aligning the gaps identified by anticipatory management and the disciplines which are necessary to fill these gaps. Strategic leadership is based on decision-support, not decision-making which links the external environment to the internal organization (Ashley & Morrison, 1995). Anticipatory management aids in seeing that strategic direction happens before and in harmony with strategic planning (Ashley & Morrison, 1995). Since strategic planning is a subset of strategic management the strategic direction happens after foresight is applied but before strategic management through the use of strategic leadership. Without question, one of the most significant and important aspects of anticipatory leadership is that it drives strategy deeply into an organization.

Strategic Foresight

If strategic leaders utilize the foresight necessary to address healthcare's leadership challenges, it is important to assess its value in building a future of its own making. Strategic foresight is of direct use to organizational policy development and practice on a day-to-day basis (Slaughter, 1999). While organizations must eventually face long-term issues, their first priority must be to remain in business for the immediate- and near-term future. This is where strategic foresight can bring into play a new range of factors and possibilities.

By utilizing environmental scanning techniques, an organization can receive signals in its operating environment that herald challenges to its business, new opportunities, and the identification of new products and services (Slaughter, 1999). Likewise, scenario planning, another strategic foresight tool, can provide organizations with a range of high quality insights into the near-future environment (Slaughter, 1999). With appropriate foresight, organizations can use strategies which can be explored utilizing different assumptions and conditions. As such, an organization is not only alert to "signals of change," it can grasp opportunities to develop a range of possible responses which reduces an organization's reaction time and improves their response time (Slaughter, 1999). Therefore, decisions can be made in a broader context and with greater confidence because the near-term future ceases to be an abstraction; it becomes a highly significant part of the immediate operating environment (Slaughter, 1999).

Another value that strategic foresight provides is that it can be developed to the point where it opens up, what Hamel and Prahalad have called "future competitive space"; in which organizations do not have to wait for the promptings of competitors or the mythical call of market demand (Hamel & Prahalad, 1994, p. 22). Alternatively, they can decide to move forward in a manner of their own determination. Organizations with this forward view are better equipped to see the many novel and unconventional possibilities for them to target. A forward view is where insights into new industries, new ways of solving old problems, new sources of impact-free wealth creation, and new business and civic cultures can be found (Slaughter, 1999). A forward view is a significant capability which can contribute to the strategic leadership and foresight of an organization. The poet Rainer Maria Rilke suggests there are signs, which indicate the future enters us, in order to be transformed in us, long before it happens (Rilke, 2001). The anticipatory leader recognizes that he/she becomes part of the future before he/she realizes it and guides the transformation process by serving as the change agent within the organization (Pfohl, 2009).

Finally the greatest value foresight offers is based not only on the amount of change but the velocity of that change present in today's global marketplace. In a time characterized by continuous, unpredictable change and where there is no indication of an end in sight, organizations need to practice anticipatory leadership. In such times, a host of challenges and complexities have risen without warning (O'Hara-Devereaux, 2004). These challenges and changes include: rising healthcare costs, the stratification of healthcare, the growing number of elderly with healthcare concerns, the uninsured, new technologies, new and emerging infectious diseases, the threat of terrorism, and rediscovery of lifestyle-related health issues; all reinforcing the need for a new type of leadership (Blendon & Desroches, 2003). Anticipatory leaders are the forward thinkers who look externally to the signals, trends, and patterns and strongly influence their organizations through the practice of foresight skills (Pfohl, 2009). They also are skilled at aligning their organizations internally with the uncovered external forces and aligning their specific organizational cultures with an anticipatory mindset at all leadership levels; creating an atmosphere that is intentionally dedicated and equipped for the future (Pfohl, 2009). The risk of operating without anticipatory leadership forces organizations to a place where the main components and resources of foresight, leadership, and management are disconnected. However, by incorporating anticipatory leadership, an organization maintains fluidity to effectively align and apply global forces within its internal organizational systems.

Healthcare faces increased complexity with a host of new challenges and may not be appropriately equipped to handle or respond to these changes. These challenges demand new ways of thinking and implementation of radical strategies to keep the industry moving forward. In a time such as this, global healthcare leaders need to become anticipatory in order to keep their global competitive advantage intact. The challenge for healthcare becomes how to invoke anticipatory leadership within this changing global context.

Six Principles of Anticipatory Leadership

For purposes of this chapter, the concept of anticipatory leadership in healthcare involves the application of six simplified principles which, when applied to the practice of strategic leadership, provides leaders with a way to affirmatively deal with uncertain futures (Table 2). Anticipatory leadership begins with a process of scanning the horizon for trends that are driving medicine to unknown and uncertain futures. Once trends are identified, the strategic leader begins to interpret/forecast the ends derived from these driving trends if left to their own conclusion. The astute leader develops strategies that would take their organization toward preferable futures or away from those futures determined to be detrimental to them. This process requires leaders to place themselves into the future and backcast step-by-step strategies that would enhance the likelihood of them achieving the outcomes of their choice.

Next the leader would create a vision around the overall developed foresight process such that organizational members can join in helping to bring about the future of their own choosing. Once the organizational members have firm grasps on the strategic vision, leadership needs to enable followers to implement the predetermined

Table 2:   Six Simplified Principles of
Anticipatory Leadership.

- Strategic foresight
  - Scanning for trends
  - Interpretation/forecasting trends
- Strategic leadership
  - Strategy development/backcasting
  - Visioneering
- Strategic management
  - Strategy implementation
  - Evaluation

strategies. Finally, the astute anticipatory leader evaluates the success of each strategy implementation as it relates to moving the organization toward their preferable future, being careful to consider possible "wild card" actions which could render strategic initiatives irrelevant. This principle offers feedback to adjust the backcasting stage to keep the process honed, as much as possible, on reaching the preferable end.

In order to properly discuss the concept of anticipatory leadership in healthcare, it will be necessary to consider two examples that appear to be causing some of the uncertainty found in the profession: physician shortages and the move toward patient-centered care. It is important to consider that these examples are merely representative of a host of issues that have been impacting healthcare of late. Clearly, it is not possible to place proper attention on all of the issues relevant to healthcare today in this chapter, however, assessment of these two examples can provide the healthcare leader tools that can be used to corral uncertainty. Such is the substance of anticipatory leadership.

Physician Shortage

Primary care access helps to prevent illness and death, lowers costs, and reduces inequities in the population's health (Starfield, Shi, Grover, & Macinko, 2005). If global health is to improve equitably, a concerted effort must be made to educate primary care physicians where the need is the greatest. In order to accomplish this, tomorrow's healthcare leaders will need to go beyond the limits of the systems within which they operate today to perceive what those systems might become (WEF, 2013).

While there are 2409 recognized and operating medical schools in the world as of 2014 (FAIMER, 2014), very few are designed structurally and academically to create primary care physicians. In the United States, a nation that is known for having one of the most advanced healthcare systems in the world, the need for primary care services are pronounced (FAIMER, 2014). With the passing of the Patient Protection and Affordable Care Act (PPACA) in 2010, upon full enactment, it is expected that an additional 32 million patients will have greater access to the US healthcare system, yet at present there is an insufficient number of candidates in the physician pipeline to accommodate the expected influx of patients.

Currently, primary care physicians comprise 32 percent of the US physician population, of which 12.7 percent are family physicians, 10.9 percent are general internists, 6.8 percent are general pediatricians, and 1.6 percent are in general practice; in rough numbers, this equates to 256,000 of the 800,000 total population (COGME, 2010). The Council on Graduate Medical Education (COGME) estimates that the US healthcare system will experience a shortage of between 85,000 and 200,000 physicians by 2020 (COGME, 2005; Cooper, Getzen, McKee, & Laud, 2002; Dill & Salsberg, 2008). Annually, all 157 US medical and osteopathic medical schools graduate approximately 23,000 physicians, a number that is woefully inadequate to meet expectations (AACOM, 2014; AAMC, 2014).

The looming crisis is amplified when these staggering statistics are seen in the light of the aging physician population, with an average age of 47, and 47 percent of the total physician workforce over the age of 50, and 25 percent of the primary care workforce over the age of 55 (COGME, 2010; MHA, 2007). Equally disturbing are the results of a 2009 Investor's Business Daily survey which found that 45 percent of practicing physicians would consider leaving the practice of medicine if the then-debated PPACA was passed (Jones, 2009) or the 2013 Deloitte Survey of US Physicians which found that 62 percent of respondents say that it is likely that more physicians will retire earlier than planned or cut back on practice hours (Deloitte, 2013). Although the reasons surrounding early retirement vary from the physician perspective (less time with patients, longer hours with less pay, dealing with government regulations, and insurance companies) (Deloitte, 2013), if the percentage of physicians retiring equals the Investor's Business Daily survey results and medical schools roughly continue to produce only 23,000 graduates each year, it will take 15.7 years just to cover the losses associated with this new law's enactment and the changes it brings to the practice of medicine. The US healthcare system is in a major crisis regarding a physician shortage.

Closely coupled to the physician shortage concern, is how the current medical education model does not adequately prepare graduates for careers in modern medicine. Medical schools (undergraduate medical education), residencies (graduate medical education), and lifelong learning programs (continuing medical education) have not kept pace with patients' needs, public expectations, technological advances, and changing organizational requirements and financing (IOM, 2003). In addition, it has failed to be adequately patient-centered, team-oriented, and evidence-based (IOM, 2003). Is it any wonder that physicians have become more disillusioned when their preparation has demonstrated itself to be so inadequate?

The present model of medical education at the undergraduate and graduate levels is being reformed from its century-long fixation on corrections made by Abraham Flexner in his famous 1910 report: *Medical Education in the United States and Canada*. These reforms, however, are not keeping pace with driving trends (Cooke, Irby, & O'Brien, 2010). Even Flexner himself, never intended that his reforms would serve to solve medicine's problems permanently; yet medicine has found comfort in looking at solving today's educational needs through the prism of Flexner's reforms (Cooke et al., 2010).

Two current trends accentuate this point: As stated earlier, the need to create more primary care physicians has never been as critical as it is at present. It is known that professionals are likely to practice in environments to which they have been exposed in training (Markle, Fisher, & Smego, 2007). Unfortunately, primary care specialty training mostly occurs in academic health centers not in ambulatory health centers in community settings where these professionals will spend the majority of their time seeing patients (Markle et al., 2007). Research also demonstrates that selection of primary care specialties is predicated upon connection to early primary care role models, early primary care rotations, and administrative support for the specialty; all of which are not seen as priorities in most academic educational programs (Campos-Outcalt, Senf, & Kutob, 2004; Osborn, 1993; Senf, Campos-Outcalt, & Kutob, 2003). Current academic structure is not producing the needed number of primary care physicians because its infrastructure is not designed to reinforce its stated ends.

The second driving trend is found occurring at all levels of education today; knowledge acquisition moving rapidly from traditionally focused teacher-centric models to those that are student-centric or autonomous. By 2018, it is expected that 75 percent of all elementary and secondary coursework will be delivered in an on-line format, within school classrooms, with teachers moving from teaching to a facilitation role with students (Christensen, Horn, & Johnson, 2008). Medical schools must reassess their pedagogical systems to assure that they complement these new models which resemble earlier student experiences (Christensen & Eyring, 2011; Christensen, Grossman, & Hwang, 2009). Clearly, there has been little to no anticipatory leadership practiced by medical education leaders that exposes the need to modify systems to meet current student expectations in a technologically advanced world.

It is quite plausible that if anticipatory leadership principles had been implemented in the past, the state of medical education would be different today. Fortunately, anticipatory leadership principles can be implemented at any point in time offering organizational leaders the chance to "begin anew" at any moment. If medical education leaders had scanned their horizons about 20 years ago, they would have seen the need to direct more resources into the development of more primary care physicians. With the limited numbers of graduates deciding to enter primary care medicine, more specialists were created; ultimately responsible for some healthcare cost increases, since highly structured specialty care is expensive and not necessarily associated with better health outcomes for patients (Starfield, Shi, & Macinko, 2005). As such, an astute anticipatory healthcare leader would have seen the trend of decreasing physicians entering primary care specialties as a call to develop an educational system entirely focused on primary care medicine; something that does not exist in today's medical education paradigm.

Equally concerning is the trend driving education from teacher-centric to student-centric learning models. An astute anticipatory medicine leader would realize that his/her medical education delivery model is not keeping pace with the change being driven at the elementary, secondary, and post-secondary levels. In order to maintain relevancy, medical education leaders must begin to backcast strategies that will bring about structural changes that match students' earlier experiences and skill levels.

Patient-Centered Care

Although the concept of patient-centered care has been around for many decades, its prominence in the literature of late finds its roots in the Institute of Medicine's 2001 seminal report: *Crossing the Quality Chasm* (Millenson & Macri, 2012; Planetree, 2014). This report identified a number of ways to improve quality of care, but none were as prominent as their recommendation that patient-centeredness become one of the driving methods of bringing about quality and patient safety (IOM, 2001). The report elevated patient-centeredness from a peripheral aim to prominence in that the way in which care is delivered is now as equally important as the care itself (Frampton et al., 2008). Additionally, the prominence of late with respect to the focus on patient-centered care is found at the foundation of the PPACA (GPO, 2010). Many of the provisions outlined in the PPACA support patient-centered care over traditional curative-care services (Cogan, 2011).

When the concept of patient-centered care is discussed, it is necessary to carefully define its meaning. There are five attributes which define patient-centered care, they include: (1) whole-person care, (2) coordination and communication, (3) patient support and empowerment, (4) ready access, and (5) autonomy (Bechtel, 2010). These five attributes place the patient at the center of their care, and any efforts to shift that focus away from them back to providers, jeopardizes the opportunity for improved care outcomes (Bechtel, 2010). In fact, any innovative models designed to meet patient-centered care expectations, including patient-centered medical homes and accountable care organizations, may be rejected by patients if they do not include these attributes (Bechtel, 2010). One such successful model, P4 Medicine, appears to be situated appropriately to meld technology enhancement with patient-centeredness.

According to Leroy Hood, MD, PhD, President of the Institute for Systems Biology, and inventor of the automated DNA sequencer:

> The convergence of systems biology, the digital revolution and consumer-driven healthcare is transforming medicine from its current reactive mode, which is focused on treating disease, to a P4 Medicine mode, which is medicine that is predictive, preventive, personalized and participatory. P4 Medicine will improve the quality of care delivered to patients through better diagnoses and targeted therapies. These advances facilitate new forms of active participation by patients and consumers in the collection of personal health data that will accelerate discovery science. Soon a virtual data cloud of billions of health-relevant data points will surround each individual. Through P4 Medicine, we will be able to reduce this complex data to simple hypotheses about how to optimize wellness and minimize disease for each individual.
>
> Hood (2014)

Dr. Hood describes his view of the future of medicine at the intersection of system biology, digital technology, and consumer-driven healthcare. With the ability to identify genomic conditions found in specific individuals that manifest themselves in certain diseases, medicine moves from group generalizations to precise disease management/prevention that is individual-specific. This innovation provides healthcare practitioners with more accurate classification of diseases and ultimately enhancement of diagnoses and treatment (National Research Council, 2011).

The P4 Medicine model affords practitioners with ways to address patient-centered care in ways that were previously unused. Each of the components of P4 Medicine, which include: (1) predictive, (2) preventive, (3) personalized, and (4) participatory, places the patient at the center of care. Once the human genome data cloud reaches sufficient size, it will be possible to connect certain genetic variations with certain diseases enabling practitioners to predict that certain outcomes will most likely occur unless concerted efforts are made to prevent their early onset. With this knowledge, the physician and patient will be able to develop personalized-prevention strategies (e.g., exercise, nutrition, certain behavior avoidance, and pharmaceuticals/nutraceuticals) that would help to avoid early-onset of diseases or conditions. Finally, this model calls for a commitment from both the patient and the physician to mutual participatory acts to assure adherence to predetermined preventive strategies.

If the anticipatory leader accepts the P4 Medicine model, he/she considers structural changes that must be implemented in order to promote the model's components and utilization. One such necessary change is to consider how physicians interact with patients as this interaction determines the level of a patient's satisfaction, their feelings of loss of control, greater symptom burden, and the use of more health service resources (Little et al., 2001). For decades, the power relationship in patient care has been tilted toward the provider-side of the exchange (Brody, 1992). In order for a healthy balance to ensue, providers must gain knowledge, skills, and needed attitudes as to their role and responsibilities in the physician-patient relationship (Door-Goold & Lipkin, 1999). Improved patient outcomes require a commitment to more than just paying attention to improved technical skills by providers or from improved information technologies such as electronic medical records. Improvement comes when providers exhibit patient-focused behaviors that arise from a balanced well-developed cognitive, emotional, and behavioral intelligence (Doublestein, Lee, & Pfohl, 2014) and utilize certain "soft skills" demonstrated in excellent patient interactions (e.g., communication and interpersonal skills) (Murphy, Putter, & Johnson, 2014). Anticipatory leaders would begin to integrate cognitive, emotional and behavioral intelligence, and "soft skills" training into the continuum of medical education; from undergraduate to continuing medical education.

The power of bringing awareness to practitioners of a well-developed cognitive, emotional, and behavioral intelligence and its relationship to improved patient care was uncovered during a pilot project at the Duke University Medical Center, Division of Otolaryngology – Head and Neck Surgery (OHNS) in 2013–2014. The Division leadership identified a need to awaken healthcare team members to their cognitive, emotional, and behavioral "blind spots" as they interact with patients and team members on a day-to-day basis. The project referred to as "Leadership Lived Out" was designed to assess participant operational limits within the three domains and aligned toward the core virtues and ethical principles identified within the Division. These virtues and principles, as identified by the Division, included: initiative, integrity, self-discipline, responsibility, and accountability (Doublestein et al., 2014; Lee, 2013). Once identified, participants were coached to identify and implement strategies that would overcome their newly discovered "blind spots." One of the most pronounced results of the project was the realization that once a provider was made aware of their cognitive, emotional, and behavioral intelligence "blind spots," they were unable to continue expressing themselves as they had in the past. In fact, awareness of their "blind spots" caused them to constantly and mindfully consider how their interactions may need to be modified so that they would present themselves in a more professional manner with others. These "blind spots" were exposed in a 360-degree assessment by co-workers, peers, and managers and demonstrated how factors, such as self-regard, empathy, stress tolerance, impulse control, assertiveness, decision-making, modeling, and empowerment impact how the participant and the healthcare team provide care to patients. The project demonstrated how the power of cognitive, emotional, and behavioral intelligence training positively impacts the level of professionalism practiced (Doublestein et al., 2014).

Another result of the pilot project was that, although effective in bringing about personal change in physicians, residents, and other healthcare team members, earlier intervention (bringing awareness of professionalism to undergraduate medical education) would accelerate professionalism practice in individuals along the "novice-to-mastery" medical education continuum. As such, common sense dictates that earlier professionalism intervention (e.g., beginning in the first year of medical school) is the optimum time and place to introduce the process of professionalism development (Doublestein et al., 2014). In fact; support for this earlier intervention is born out in a study that finds professionalism lapses in medical school and residency training correlate with lapses in professionalism later in practice (Papadakis et al., 2005).

Many professionalism lapses occur simply because physicians are unaware of "blind spots" in their make-up that could be changed/modified/enhanced if they only knew what they were. Self-awareness, as a practiced skill is a hallmark of effective leadership (Goleman, 1998) and directly translates into better professional and personal choices (Zes & Landis, 2013). Certainly, self-awareness is foundational to the demonstration of professionalism in the physician but self-awareness alone cannot transform one without an equally strong commitment to self-betterment. Although the specifics of professionalism development are different for each individual, it is the lifelong pursuit of excellence in the physician-patient relationship that unites all efforts in professionalism training. This is reminiscent of Albert Schweitzer, the Nobel Peace Prize Laureate, who was not concerned about attainment of perfection, but about the pursuit of perfection, and well known for his commitment to lifelong self-betterment (Cousins, 1985). Even those, of whom it might be said that they have achieved the highest level of professionalism, still find room for betterment as they pursue excellence. Thus, the anticipatory leader would devise strategies to integrate professionalism development and encourage self-betterment practices throughout the medical education continuum.

The drive for wellness- or prevention-centered care as opposed to curative- or diseased-focused care is accelerating. US healthcare costs continue to rise and will, according to the US Congressional Budget Office, reach 20 percent of the gross domestic product by 2050; up from just 5 percent five years ago. This portion of the gross domestic product will equal the share of the economy now accounted for by the entire federal government budget (Orszag & Ellis, 2007). Clearly, the US healthcare system cannot sustain itself under such a financial burden. The anticipatory leader would realize that a shift of focus from disease management to prevention would be one key solution to help keep costs from bankrupting the system. Leaders practicing these principles could establish financial and system models that emphasize wellness delivery with foresight instead of relying on reactive policies brought on by other industries like government, insurance, or the legal profession.

Inattention to anticipatory leadership practices has the potential to inflict unnecessary damage on the US healthcare industry. Ignoring trend signals that pepper the horizon on a daily basis alone can cause leaders to miss significant events that can render even the most advanced organization irrelevant. Unfortunately, healthcare has done little to establish a foresight infrastructure that could aid them in designing a future of their own choosing. For decades, healthcare has remained committed to reactionary practices which respond to the actions of other industries that proactively analyze trends and make strategic decisions that would advance the probability of them achieving preferable futures of their own choosing. As such, healthcare's choices are limited and confined by the actions of others. Healthcare cannot afford to sit back idly and wait for others to determine the parameters associated with their strategic decisions. The present trajectory of reactionary leadership in healthcare paints a very dim and unsustainable future.

As presented in this chapter, anticipatory leaders are those who look for trends on the horizon and have the ability of determining their impact on their organizations years in advance. They assess the overall consequences of the resulting futures and develop strategies to either enhance attainment of a particular future or strategies that would steer an organization away from a detrimental one. They develop a vision around their strategies that energizes members to pursue the future through a determined set of strategies with earnestness. Finally, the anticipatory leader evaluates the success or lack thereof of the strategies in moving toward a preferable future. Healthcare leaders must dedicate themselves to establishing, promoting, and developing an anticipatory culture in order for the industry to remain relevant and vibrant beyond 2050. The nation's health depends upon it.

So for the reader two questions remain: Are you satisfied with healthcare's current fixation on reactionary strategy development practices, or are you ready to begin the process of proactively creating preferable futures of your own choosing? There is no middleground in response to this query for on one side strategies are framed within the limits imposed by others, and on the other, there are no limits, except those that one purposely sets. Healthcare is crying out for a new form of leadership that is purposeful, intentional, innovative, and committed for the long haul. Anticipatory leadership provides the infrastructure in which the healthcare industry's future can become more certain and better for all in the run-up to 2050 and beyond.

References

AACOM [American Association of Colleges of Osteopathic Medicine]. (2014). *Trends in osteopathic medical school applicants, enrollment, and graduates.* Chevy Chase, MD: American Association of Colleges of Osteopathic Medicine. Retrieved from http://www.aacom.org/docs/default-source/data-and-trends/2014-trends-COM-AEG-PDF.pdf

AAMC [Association of American Medical Colleges]. (2014). *U.S. medical applicants and students 1982–83 to 2010–11.* Washington, DC: American Association of Medical Colleges. Retrieved from https://www.aamc.org/download/153708/data/

Ashley, W. C., & Morrison, J. L. (1995). *Anticipatory management: 10 power tools for achieving excellence into the 21st century* (1st ed.). Leesburg, VA: Issue Action Publications, Inc.

Bechtel, C. (2010). If you build it, will they come? Designing truly patient-centered health care. *Health Affairs, 29*(5), 914–920.

Blendon, R. J., & Desroches, C. (2003). Future health care challenges. *Issues in Science and Technology, XIX*(4). Retrieved from http://issues.org/19-4/blendon/

Brody, H. (1992). *The healer's power.* New Haven, CT: Yale University Press.

Campos-Outcalt, D., Senf, J., & Kutob, R. (2004). A comparison of primary care graduates from schools with increasing production of family physicians to those from schools with decreasing production. *Family Medicine, 36*(4), 260–264.

Christensen, C., & Eyring, H. J. (2011). *The innovative university: Changing the DNA of higher education.* San Francisco, CA: Jossey-Bass.

Christensen, C., Grossman, J., & Hwang, J. (2009). *The innovator's prescription: A disruptive solution for health care.* New York, NY: McGraw-Hill.

Christensen, C., Horn, M. B., & Johnson, C. (2008). *Disrupting class: How disruptive innovation will change the way the world learns.* New York, NY: McGraw-Hill.

Cogan, J. A. (2011). The affordable care act's preventive service mandate: Breaking down the barriers to nationwide access to preventive services. *Journal of Law, Medicine, & Ethics, 39*(3), 355–365.

COGME [Council on Graduate Medical Education]. (2005). *Physician Workforce Policy Guidelines for the United States, 2000–2020, Sixteenth Report*. Health Resources and Services Administration, U.S. Department of Health and Human Resources.

COGME [Council on Graduate Medical Education]. (2010). *Advancing Primary Care, 20th Report*. Health Resources and Services Administration, U.S. Department of Health and Human Resources.

Cooke, M., Irby, D. M., & O'Brien, B. C. (2010). *Educating physicians: A call for reform of medical school and residency*. San Francisco, CA: Jossey-Bass. The Carnegie Foundation for the Advancement of Teaching.

Cooper, R., Getzen, T., McKee, H., & Laud, P. (2002). Economic and demographic trends signal an impending physician shortage. *Health Affairs, 21*(1), 140–154.

Cousins, N. (1985). *Albert Schweitzer's mission: Healing and peace*. Ontario: Penguin Books.

Deloitte Center for Health Solutions. (2013). *Deloitte 2013 Survey of U.S. Physicians: Physician perspectives about health care reform and the future of the medical profession*. Retrieved from http://www2.deloitte.com/content/dam/Deloitte/us/Documents/life-sciences-health-care/us-lshc-deloitte-2013-physician-survey-10012014.pdf

Dill, M., & Salsberg, E. (2008). *The complexities of physician supply and demand: Projections through 2025*. Washington, DC: Association of American Medical Colleges.

Door-Goold, S., & Lipkin, M. (1999). The doctor-patient relationship: Challenges, opportunities, and strategies. *Journal of General Internal Medicine, 14*(Suppl. 1), S26–S33.

Doublestein, B. A. (2010). Response to "Turning doctors into leaders". *Harvard Business Review*, June, pp. 18–19. Harvard Business Review, Boston, MA.

Doublestein, B. A., Lee, W. T., & Pfohl, R. M. (2014). *Leadership lived out: An initiative to develop a new generation of virtuous physician-professionals*. Academy for Professionalism in Health Care 2nd Annual Meeting. Presentation.

FAIMER [The Foundation for Advancement of International Medical Education and Research]. (2014). *Mapping the World's Medical Schools* [International Medical Education Directory (IMED)]. Retrieved from http://www.faimer.org/resources/mapping.html

Frampton, S., Guastello, S., Brady, C., Hale, M., Horowitz, S., Bennett-Smith, S., & Stone, S. (2008). *Patient-centered care improvement guide*. Derby, CT: Planetree. Retrieved from http://planetree.org/wp-content/uploads/2012/01/Patient-Centered-Care-Improvement-Guide-10-28-09-Final.pdf

Goleman, D. (1998). What makes a leader? *Harvard Business Review*. (November-December), 82–91. Retrieved from http://www.undp.org/content/dam/samoa/docs/UNDP_WS_TLDP2_Whatmakesaleader.pdf

GPO [Government Printing Office]. (2010). *Patient Protection and Affordable Care Act (PPACA) Pub. L. No. 111–148*, §2702, 124 Stat. 119, 318–319. U.S. Government Printing Office, Washington, DC. Retrieved from www.gpo.gov/fdsys/pkg/PLAW-111publ148/pdf/PLAW-111publ148.pdf

Gretzky, W. (2014). *Wayne Gretzky Quotes* [Famous Quotes and Quotations at BrainyQuote]. Retrieved from http://www.brainyquote.com/quotes/quotes/w/waynegretz131510.html

Hamel, G., & Prahalad, C. K. (1994). *Competing for the future.* Boston, MA: Harvard Business Review Press.

Hood, L. (2014). *P4Medicine.* Seattle, WA: P4 Medicine Institute. Retrieved from http://p4mi.org/p4medicine

IOM [Institute of Medicine]. (2001). *Crossing the quality chasm: A new health system for the 21st century.* Washington, DC: National Academy Press.

IOM [Institute of Medicine]. (2003). *Academic health centers: Leading change in the 21st century.* Washington, DC: Institute of Medicine Report, National Academy of Sciences. Retrieved from http://www.iom.edu/~/media/Files/Report%20Files/2003/Academic-Health-Centers-Leading-Change-in-the-21st-Century/AHC8pgFINAL.pdf

Jauhar, S. (2014). *Doctored: The disillusionment of an American physician* (1st ed.). New York, NY: Farrar, Straus and Giroux.

Jones, T. (2009). 45 percent of doctors would consider quitting if congress passes health care overhaul. *Investor's Business Daily,* Los Angeles, CA. Retrieved from http://news.investors.com/091509-506199-45-of-doctors-would-consider-quitting-if-congress-passes-health-care-overhaul.htm

Lee, W. T. (2013). Measuring the immeasurable core competency of professionalism. *JAMA Otolaryngology Head Neck Surgery, 139*(1), 12−13.

Little, P., Everitt, H., Williamson, I., Warner, G., Moore, M., Gould, C., et al. (2001). Observational study of effect of patient centeredness and positive approach on outcomes of general practice consultations. *BMJ, 323,* 908.

Markle, W., Fisher, M., & Smego, R. (2007). Understanding global health *(LANGE Clinical Medicine).* New York, NY: McGraw-Hill.

MHA [Merritt Hawkins and Associates]. (2007). *2007 survey of physicians 50 to 65 years old.* Irving, TX: Merritt Hawkins & Associates. Retrieved from http://www.kintera.org/atf/cf/%7BFFD8DCB6-670B-4F3B-99A4-45C1CE493CC5%7D/mha2007olderdocsurvey.pdf

Millenson, M., & Macri, J. (2012). *Will the affordable care act move patient-centeredness to center stage?* Urban Institute. Retrieved from http://www.urban.org/UploadedPDF/412524-will-the-affordable-care-act.pdf

Murphy, S., Putter, S., & Johnson, S. (2014). In R. Riggio & S. Tan (Eds.), *Soft skills training: Best practices in industry and higher education* (pp. 276−308). New York, NY: Routledge.

National Research Council. (2011). Toward precision medicine: Building a knowledge network for biomedical research and a new taxonomy of disease. In *Committee on a framework for development a new taxonomy of disease.* Washington, DC: The National Academies Press.

O'Hara-Devereaux, M. (2004). *Navigating the badlands: Thriving in the decade of radical transformation* (1st ed.). San Francisco, CA: Jossey-Bass.

Orszag, P., & Ellis, P. (2007). Addressing rising health care costs: A view from the congressional budget office. *New England Journal of Medicine, 357,* 1885−1887.

Osborn, E. (1993). Factors influencing students' choices of primary care or other specialties. *Academic Medicine, 68*(7), 572−574.

Papadakis, M., Teherani, A., Banach, M., Knettler, T., Rattner, S., Stern, D., et al. (2005). Disciplinary action by medical boards and prior behavior in medical school. *New England Journal of Medicine, 353*(25), 2673−2682.

Petrie, N. (2014). *Future trends in leadership development.* Center for Creative Leadership, Colorado Springs, CO. Retrieved from http://www.ccl.org/Leadership/pdf/research/futureTrends.pdf

Pfohl, R. M. (2009). *Anticipatory leadership: The role of foresight in navigating images of the future*. Virginia Beach, VA: Regent University.

Planetree. (2014). *About us*. Retrieved from http://planetree.org/about-planetree/

Rilke, R. M. (2001). Letters to a young poet (*S. Mitchell, Trans.*). New York, NY: Modern Library.

Senf, J., Campos-Outcalt, D., & Kutob, R. (2003). Factors related to the choice of family medicine: A reassessment and literature review. *Journal of the American Board of Family Practice, 16*, 502−512.

Slaughter, R. A. (1999). Futures for the third millennium: Enabling the forward view *[Towards a Wise Culture CD-ROM]*. Indooroopilly: Foresight International.

Starfield, B., Shi, L., Grover, A., & Macinko, J. (2005). The effects of specialist supply on populations' health: Assessing the evidence. *Health Affairs*, Web Exclusive: W5-97−W5-107. Retrieved from http://content.healthaffairs.org/content/early/2005/03/15/hlthaff.w5.97/suppl/DC1

Starfield, B., Shi, L., & Macinko, J. (2005). Contribution of primary care to health systems and to health. *Milbank Quarterly, 83*(3), 457−502.

WEF [World Economic Forum]. (2013). *Global agenda council on new models of leadership 2012−2014*. Retrieved from http://www3.weforum.org/docs/GAC/2013/Connect/WEF_GAC_New_Models_of_Leadership_2012-2014_Connect.pdf

Zes, D., & Landis, D. (2013). *A better return on self-awareness*. Korn/Ferry Institute. Whitepaper. Retrieved from http://www.kornferryinstitute.com/sites/all/files//documents/briefings-magazine-download/KFI-SelfAwareness-ProofPoint-6.pdf

Leadership Education 2050: Changing the Spaces and Faces of Experience

Daniel M. Jenkins, Lisa Endersby and
Kathy L. Guthrie

Introduction

The language, theories, and pedagogies typically associated with leadership development will take on new meaning, and present new challenges, with the emergent changes of technological advancement. Tools once only used to display and promote information have raised critical questions concerning the creation and ownership of knowledge. The flattening of our pedagogical playing field runs counter to the more traditional, dualistic model of leadership in which those who possess and create information reign. The digital age has opened a larger, multifaceted space where a plurality of ideas, opinions, and answers coexist. In the same way, the physical places and virtual spaces where we work are more so interchangeable than ever before. As a result, the truths about *where* leadership happens and experience is gained have changed. The Internet and other learning technologies, then, manifest a digital multiplicity, extending Perry's (1970) Scheme of Intellectual and Ethical Development.

The praxis of leadership education is also impacted by the near infinite reach and scope of the digital landscape. The myriad perspectives and data that serve as building blocks for a highly personal, yet deeply interconnected understanding of the self as a leader, will influence leadership identity and its complex development (Komives, Owen, Longerbeam, Mainella, & Osteen, 2005). The application of this identity in cocurricular practice is also extended beyond place-based activity as we reexamine the definition of being "present" in our leadership development activities. The signature pedagogies of leadership education, discussion, and reflection, have been and continue to be impacted by the highly connected, rapidly changing digital space (see Jenkins, 2012). Because leadership in 2050 will demand navigating through increased challenges in technology and distance, a similar demand will require that educators push beyond perceived boundaries of knowledge and discourse to create new definitions, spaces, and places for leadership development.

A futuristic view of the workplace and workplace culture envisions a more interconnected and mobile employee, employer, and organization. As Groth and Nisen (2013) argue, "freedom, autonomy, and flexibility define the future of the workplace." A 2013 Deloitte Report calls this the "elastic workplace," emphasizing the mandatory need for flexibility in both vision creation and execution (Haugen, 2013). In many cases, the workforce, and the leaders who will work within it, must balance a myriad of multiple and competing priorities that will constantly evolve and change with the rapid decline of conceptual boundaries to knowledge, ideas, and individuals. The Deloitte report, for example, argues that leaders in the future workplace must balance their peoples' needs with their business needs, particularly as their employees demonstrate an increased desire for autonomy and transparency. Mobile technologies allow workers to be more flexible with their modes of productivity, reducing the need for fixed and physical offices. Remote working will therefore require that leaders in 2050 balance the demand for productivity with an increased call for work-life balance. With increased competition for top talent and a concurrent rise in internal pressures and consumer demands, the traditional leadership model of setting high expectations to encourage meaningful development will be stretched across physical space and individual managers to become a global and interconnected process. The workplace in 2050 will cater to leaders who can remain firm in their vision, but flexible in its execution.

Moreover, success in the workplace of the future will demand leadership skills that allow for quick and frequent adaptation to change while balancing a deeply held and constant set of values to achieve big picture goals. Far from the sequential, instructor-led, in-person learning common in current educational practices, leaders will acquire much of their training and experience in spaces and places with heavily permeable barriers between the physical and virtual. In an interview with *The Futurist* (2010), Janna Anderson discussed the interlacing of work and leisure hours, extending the typical discussion of work-life balance to include the heightened importance of self-directed learning. An institutionally granted degree of proof of competence, while still relevant, will come to represent a mere fraction of the scholarship and experience gained by leaders in the future. In a 2010 report, *EDUCAUSE* aptly notes, "The digital environment is a 'place' for social interaction and community exchange. Although the value of the campus as a physical place continues, an increasing number of interactions are online, including the emergence of virtual, multinational research organizations" (p. 2).

Surrounded by nearly infinite choices for where, how, when, and what to learn, leaders in the future must employ exceptional analytic skills to consider their options and choose an appropriate vision, while also remaining flexible in their approaches and processes in the face of the inevitable challenges contained in a hyperconnected and dynamic environment. An institution capable of teaching these competing yet intricately connected skills is "inherently big picture, interdisciplinary, and systems-oriented" (Groff, 2014, p. 29). Higher education will shift to competency-based models, moving away from time spent in the physical classroom to learning that "reverse[s] the traditional equation … hold[ing] the learning constant and let[ting] the time vary" (Kelly & Hess, 2013, p. 12). Credentials for leadership education, then, will not be measured by time spent but, rather, by lessons learned, experiences gained, and competencies mastered. Leadership skills of the future will be cyclical and constantly in flux, demanding leaders maintain sensitivity to changes and challenges presented in a broadened and vastly interconnected space that overlaps notions of community, dialogue and privilege in a multidirectional yet flattened context for learning, development, and progress.

Discussion and Review of the Literature

The future of higher education will be increasingly globalized and virtual. Accordingly, educating leaders to succeed in these progressively complex environments will require teaching, learning, and assessment strategies that transcend space and bring together learners in creative ways. Leadership educators will need to look beyond their programs and courses' physical or virtual — in the case of online or blended courses — space to the myriad platforms where leadership will be needed. These platforms will include, but certainly not limited by, social media (Yates & Paquette, 2011), virtual working groups and teams (Verburg, Bosch-Sijtsema, & Vartiainen, 2013), and online work environments we cannot yet imagine (e.g., Johns & Gratton, 2013; Kittur et al., 2013; Sud & Pickering, 2011).

Correspondingly, the leaders of 2050 will work within the aforementioned environments, providing impetus for the necessitated knowledge acquisition, practice, and reflection (see Harvey & Jenkins, 2014) for progressive, meaningful leadership and identity development (see Guthrie, Bertrand Jones, Osteen, & Hu, 2013) across these spaces. Yet, to date only a few studies have explored instructional strategy use in online leadership education generally (e.g., Boyd & Murphrey, 2001; Cini, 1998; Jenkins, 2014; McCotter, 2008; Newberry, Culbertson, & Carter, 2013; Phelps, 2012; Saks, 2009) or with respect to specific online or web-based instructional techniques such as discussion boards (Dollisso, 2011), blogs (Gifford, 2010; Giraud, Cain, Stedman, & Gifford, 2011), service-learning (Guthrie & McCracken, 2010), social media (Odom, Jarvis, Sandlin, & Peek, 2013; Steves et al., 2011), and simulation (Weeks, 2013). In order to facilitate leadership development in rapidly changing learning environments, leadership educators will need to maintain a key focus on the effects of globalization on constructivism in leadership and the process within which virtual teams function. As pedagogical platforms, leadership educators can look toward assignments and activities that integrate and demand process-oriented competency and evaluation/assessment in social media, virtual teams, online gaming, MOOCs, mobile apps, and eLearning Technology (e.g., Blackboard, Canvas). The projected increase in the creation and use of digital technologies and platforms for leadership will advance the field toward more highly interconnected and collaborative learning environments.

Discussion and Implications

The pedagogies discussed here provide a platform for instructional experimentation and are grounded in experiential education. Experiential education is a pedagogy leadership educators rely on for knowledge acquisition and skill development (e.g., Conine, 2014). Kolb (1984) constructs a theoretical relationship between experience and the interpretation of learning. Focusing on how meaning is made from experiences is another critical component of experiential education as pedagogy (e.g., Dewey, 1933) for leadership development. We still do experiential learning, but the sources of experience have broadened. Who we have experiences with and "where" we have them will continuously evolve. In the same way, we still share goals, but how me meet and work together toward those goals is changing.

A review of the literature on virtual experiential learning is ripe with accounts of experiences in virtual worlds, but shallow in transferable skills and dispositions. Arguably, we are less likely to work in a virtual world (e.g., Second Life), but what happens in the virtual realm can and does impact leadership development. Lessons from intentional and meaningfully constructed educational experiences will emerge from new and changing digital laboratories, populated by individuals and ideas that only recently were inaccessible by conventional pedagogies. Technology at all stages of the experiential learning cycle will be crucial for learning, from creating an impactful experience to using social media (e.g., Twitter) to facilitate individual and group reflection.

Likewise, social media differs extensively from virtual worlds in that the latter is an extension of us in our real worlds and the former is a created self in a virtual world. Nonetheless, parallel leadership challenges are present in both real and virtual worlds. However, the barrier between these two worlds has become increasingly permeable, such that the lessons learned virtually can influence behaviors outside the digital space. Leaders in 2050, then, must be adept at existing and communicating in both realms, often traveling between two distinct yet interconnected lands while being fluent in both. While these goals for leadership and leadership education have not changed, how we pursue them will be significantly altered in 2050.

As mentioned prior, Harvey and Jenkins (2014) found a common tripartite model evident in all leadership programs, regardless of discipline: (a) knowledge acquisition; (b) practice; and (c) reflection. In the knowledge economy, the acquisition of information has become as valuable as other, more common resources for survival. Technology has exponentially expanded the fields in which knowledge can be sowed, cultivated, and harvested, ensuring unprecedented access to a much wider array of ideas and opinions that may influence an emerging leader's mindset and practice. Facilitated experiences that provide opportunities for practice, application, and decision-making, as well as their reflective counterpart, live also among limitless boundaries, but still within social constructs. The sections that follow describe several salient opportunities for leadership education that, arguably, will remain near constant fixtures in leadership pedagogy, even when faced with ongoing advances in technology. These technological tools and platforms offer opportunities to learn in the purely online realm, while also acting in supporting roles to augment leadership development in the physical, campus environment.

EXCLUSIVELY ONLINE PEDAGOGY

As a potential tool for leadership education, game-oriented virtual worlds are rapidly emerging opportunities. From a rich history of simulations in leadership education — and the use of virtual worlds in general education environments – the appeal of virtual worlds aligns well with the experiential framework of leadership education. Application of virtual environments in classrooms to teach specific skills sets already occur, from students learning economic principles by studying virtual world economies to applying different social science principles in a simulated online environment to see the effects. Incorporating these same principles from a leadership perspective could follow a multitude of options; from using avatars to explore perceived personality and authenticity related to self-awareness skills to using virtual environments as an arena for trust-building and communication in a groups and teams course for students of all ages (Guthrie, Phelps, & Downey, 2011). In addition, real-life based leadership interventions such as retreats and team-building activities could have interesting discussion points and topics when moved to a virtual environment as a complement to more traditional experiential learning activities. With considerations of the type of leadership development desired appropriately matched with virtual space, utilizing virtual worlds and massively multiplayer online role-playing games (MMORPGs), as a tool in leadership development is appropriate and rife with potential.

An example of how utilizing virtual worlds and MMORPGs could look in the future is the virtual world game *World of Warcraft* (WOW). This online game is focused on group-based content that exists in the form of "instance" dungeons. These instances are the virtual world equivalent of adventure obstacle courses. These adventures are specifically designed for groups ranging from 5- to 40-person teams. For teams to be successful, their leaders must develop and demonstrate proficiency in leadership knowledge and skills. This knowledge and skill base may include technical comprehension, problem-solving, environment mastery, organizational skills, instructional skills, and facilitation. In fact, while teaching a course at the University of South Florida, one of the authors had an undergraduate student who stayed after class to explain his predicament about an upcoming assignment. The student explained that he could not reflect on an organizational issue he had experienced because he was not a part of an organization and had not held a leadership position prior. A few more minutes of dialogue between the student and instructor uncovered the time the student spent playing WOW. And, that the student was not a passive gamer, but instead had organized a clan of virtual warriors, created a virtual web-space where issues were vetted, goals set, and conflicts handled. Ironically enough, the student was experiencing much of the same challenges and successes of his peers in non-virtual organizations.

VIRTUAL LEADERSHIP IN ORGANIZATIONS AND TEAMS

It is estimated that 60% of professional employees currently work in virtual teams (Kanawattanachai & Yoo, 2012). And this number is expected to rise. Ipsos (2012) — a global independent market research company — surveyed a total of 11,383 online connected employees from 24 countries via online survey methodology between October 7 and 20, 2011. The results indicated that one in five (17%) employees who can be connected online to their workplace report they "telecommute" on a "frequent basis." Additionally, a 2012 American Community Survey, 2.6% of the U.S. employee workforce (3.3 million people, not including the self-employed or unpaid volunteers), telecommutes. Moreover, telework grew nearly 80% from 2005 and growth of multiple days per week employee teleworkers (not including self-employed) telecommuting increased 79.7% from 2005 to 2012 though the rate of growth slowed during the recession (http://www.globalworkplaceanalytics.com/telecommuting-statistics).

Alas, a worker who experiences the flexibility of a virtual workplace might have a similar story as one who takes an online college course for the first time. While the content, goals, and expectations may be strikingly similar, the communication channels and access to one's peers/coworkers or instructor/boss have changed. Principally, the process for meeting goals and working with others has and will continuously change. Accordingly, leadership programs that effectively simulate the challenges and successes experienced in such environments will lead the pack. Opportunities for facilitating this type of learning include simulation and role-play, wikis, and eLearning technologies that allow for instructor moderation and "tracking" of team progress.

Assessing Virtual Teamwork with eLearning Technologies

Virtual teams, defined as a group of people working together across time and space, using electronic communication technology (Brandt, England, & Ward, 2011), have their own set of challenges beyond those working in environments who regularly physically interact. Research suggests that communication (Altschuller & Benbunan-Fich, 2010; Gilliam & Oppenheim, 2006) and trust (Kanawattanachai & Yoo, 2012) are the most salient concerns for members of virtual teams. Thus, virtual environments that provide the structure for communication channels (e.g., e-mail, discussion boards, wikis), encourage dialogue through these and synchronous channels (e.g., Skype, Google Hangouts, chat), and allow for file sharing and other content management tools (e.g., DropBox, Google's Drive suite), will also provide the most developmental forum for team-based learning. Moreover, eLearning technologies that provide instructors virtual "footprints" or "timestamps" of students' interactions in the aforementioned will be priceless variables for the facilitation, assessment, and evaluation of learning.

Online Service-Learning

Service-learning is a specific pedagogy based in experience that intentionally connects "academic learning with efforts to address issues of societal concern" (Molee, Henry, Sessa, & McKinney-Prupis, 2010, p. 252). This type of pedagogy has several similarities to leadership education and has been offered in online course formats for many years. The service-learning field has historically endorsed the use of instructional methods that enable critical reflection as integral to experiential learning (Molee et al., 2010); when combined with methods that utilize technologies, such as asynchronous discussion forums, these opportunities will provide a rich depth and breadth within which to cultivate transferrable skills. The future of leadership education will be teaching at the intersection of leadership and service-learning, while providing and capitalizing on the opportunity of it being accessible online.

Use of Mobile Applications

Florida State University (FSU) recently launched a mobile application to educate students of complex leadership concepts. It provides undergraduate students an accessible way to gain information on leadership in a user-friendly manner through their smart phone or on the web. FSU's Leadership Mobile Application, LEAD, will reach students at the exact point in time they are ready to learn how to work with others, create change, make values-based decisions, and lead their organizations, families, and communities forward (Guthrie, Shields, & Zernick, 2014). The LEAD Mobile App has several goals: (a) enhance instruction in leadership-related courses; (b) reach new students by breaking down the barriers of time demands, schedule conflicts, an geographic location, to learning leadership knowledge, skills, and values; and (c) increase students' meaningful conversations around the topic of leadership. While most campuses have several resources on campus relating to leadership, bringing them together by additional instructional activities through a mobile application is beneficial to the campus community and culture of the university.

Simulation and Role Play

In a recent study, Howard, McClannon, and Wallace (2014) facilitated a project-based learning scenario set in a 3-D virtual world, where graduate students in school administration and instructional technology worked together in simulated school teams to develop proposals for integrating technology into a fictitious school. Accordingly, the simulation offered opportunities to develop shared leadership and skills in collaboration outside the usual comfort zone of graduate school classes. Two major themes emerged from the open-ended exit surveys of participating students as strengths of the assignment: (a) opportunity for collaboration and (b) development of leadership skills. As noted by the researchers, "The overarching goal of the project was to prepare students for work in twenty-first-century schools grounded in shared leadership and collaboration" (2014, p. 60). Additionally, "Most students tended to recognize the value in participating in a realistic simulation and focused on the dynamics of the group work and process rather than the product" (2014, p. 60). Correspondingly, the simulation allowed students the freedom to work together and discover their own skills in leadership. Arguably, the facilitated level of interaction has the potential to transform students' thinking, allowing for opportunities to construct one's own meaning of leadership.

OPEN SOURCE LEADERSHIP

As knowledge and access to information quickly becomes the currency of the future, technology and the Internet provide powerful economic tools to facilitate the buying, selling, and trading of this abundant commodity. As a tool for accessibility, online eLearning technologies can facilitate the rapid and frequent exchange of information, providing new opportunities for individual development as well as disrupting common cultural ideas and ideals of community. As we near 2050, the push for social change and positive action through inclusive, collaborative leadership will only increase, and the online platform will take the place of the wooden lectern for activists, authors, teachers, and students to rally their community to voice concerns, pool resources, and mobilize for change as a single, unified voice.

Stern, Adams, and Elasser (2009) found a strong correlation between Internet use and civic involvement, as well as community participation. Social networking tools, including Facebook and Twitter, will be the leader's tools of the trade for creating, engaging, and supporting community. Porter and Umbach (2006) found that social networking can aid in students' feelings of attachment and engagement, and Acosta (2014) noted that "the microblogging phenomenon has the potential for increased networking, connections, and social mobility through community building and conversation" (p. 12). Acosta further argues that participation in social networking can help increase social capital for historically marginalized groups by providing opportunities to participate and engage in these online communities.

This variation on open source technology highlights the need for leaders in 2050 who are able to bring together ideas, information, and individuals from disparate backgrounds and places to create a coherent and meaningful final product. Collaboration, then, will become the key to innovation, with all members of a community having a visible and important role to play. As West and Gallagher (2006) describe, open source is an "exemplar of open innovation because of the shared rights to use the resulting technology as well as the collaborative development of the technology" (p. 322). Replacing "technology" with any desirable learning outcome showcases the powerful potential of these virtual communities to create tangible progress and authentic leaders both within and outside the digital platform.

FACILITATING LEADERSHIP IN OPEN SPACE

The transient, permeable lines between and around spaces for leadership and leadership education anticipated for 2050 will bring new opportunities for knowledge sharing, creation, and analysis. No longer confined to only the boardroom, physical classroom, or digital landscape, leadership will become a ubiquitous phenomenon, where leaders and leadership educators must move between different and ever-changing spaces, each with their own context, knowledge, and culture. The near infinite access to opinions, ideas, and modes of collaboration will greatly influence the creation and dissemination of broad social constructs and the formation of uniquely individual leadership identities. Yet, the process-orientation, vision, and working toward common goals necessary for successful leadership in 2014 and 2050 will remain constant across space and time.

Conclusion

In 2050, Leadership Identity Development (Komives et al., 2005) will be impacted by more permeable barriers for accessing information and ideas, where a broadening view of leadership and group influences is no longer limited to the narrow, physical space of experience and connections. As the future of leadership education continues to be heavily influenced by technology and the digital landscape, leadership development in 2050 will transcend physical and virtual boundaries to incorporate a blend of in-person, online, and hybrid models for discussion and reflection. The leadership educators of the future will have a pedagogical imperative to teach students to be future-oriented with respect to *where* leadership is needed, *when* their skills will be called upon, and in what contexts future leaders can facilitate change. Hence, the simplistic and socially constructed leadership mantra, "meet people where they are," will remain tantamount in leadership education.

References

Acosta, D. M. (2014). Tweet up? Examining twitter's impact on social capital and digital citizenship in higher education. *About Campus, 18*(6), 10–17.

Altschuller, S., & Benbunan-Fich, R. (2010). Trust, performance and the communication process in ad hoc decision making virtual teams. *Journal of Computer-Mediated Communication, 16*, 27–47.

Boyd, B. L., & Murphrey, T. P. (2001). Interest in online leadership education and implications for instructional design strategies. *Journal of Agricultural Education, 42*(1), 29–38.

Brandt, V., England, W., & Ward, S. (2011). Virtual teams. *Research Technology Management, 54*(6), 62–63.

Cini, M. A. (1998). Learning leadership online: A synergy of the medium and the message. *The Journal of Leadership Studies, 5*(2), 103–115.

Conine, T. E. (2014). The virtual simulation: A tool for leadership education in global corporations. *Global Business and Organizational Excellence, 33*(5), 17–28.

Dewey, J. (1933). *How we think: A restatement of reflective thinking to the educative process.* Boston, MA: D. C. Heath.

Dollisso, A. D. (2011). Using an online threaded discussions model for leadership case study: Implications for student engagement and learning in an asynchronous environment. *Proceedings of the 2011 association of leadership educators conference,* 247–254. Retrieved from http://leadershipeducators.org/Resources/Documents/2011%20ALE%20Conference%20Proceedings.pdf

EDUCAUSE. (2010, January). *The future of higher education: Beyond the campus.* Retrieved from http://net.educause.edu/ir/library/pdf/PUB9008.pdf

Gifford, G. T. (2010). A modern technology in the leadership classroom: Using blogs for critical thinking development. *Journal of Leadership Education, 9*(1), 165–172. Retrieved from http://leadershipeducators.org/Resources/Documents/jole/2010_winter/JOLE_9_1_Gifford.pdf

Gilliam, C., & Oppenheim, C. (2006). Reviewing the impact of virtual teams in the information age. *Journal of Information Science, 32*(2), 160–175.

Giraud, V., Cain, H., Stedman, N., & Gifford, G. (2011). Critical thinking skills evidenced in graduate student blogs. *Proceedings of the 2011 association of leadership educators conference,* 238–246. Retrieved from http://leadershipeducators.org/Resources/Documents/2011%20ALE%20Conference%20Proceedings.pdf

Groff, L. (2014, September–October). *Challenges for futures studies in the university.* Retrieved from http://www.wfs.org/futurist/2014-issues-futurist/september-october-2014-vol-48-no-5/futures-education-teaching-and-le-0#2

Groth, A., & Nisen, M. (2013, February). A revolution is happening in offices everywhere. *Business Insider.* Retrieved from http://www.businessinsider.com/the-future-of-the-workplace-slide-deck-2013-2?op=1

Guthrie, K. L., Bertrand Jones, T., Osteen, L., & Hu, S. (2013). *Cultivating leader identity and capacity in students from diverse backgrounds.* (ASHE Higher Education Report, Vol. 39, No. 4). San Francisco, CA: Josser-Bass.

Guthrie, K. L., & McCracken, H. (2010). Making a difference online: Facilitating service-learning through distance education. *The Internet and Higher Education, 13,* 153–157.

Guthrie, K. L., Phelps, K., & Downey, S. (2011). Virtual environments: A developmental tool for leadership education. *Journal of Leadership Studies, 5*(2), 6–13.

Guthrie, K. L., Shields, S., & Zernick, K. (2014). Mobile application: Situating leadership education. *Journal of Leadership Studies, 8*(2), 61–66.

Harvey, M., & Jenkins, D. M. (2014). Knowledge, praxis, and reflection: The three critical elements of effective leadership studies programs. *Journal of Leadership Studies, 7*(4), 76–85.

Haugen, T. (2013). Workplaces of the future: Creating an elastic workplace. Resetting horizons: Human capital trends 2013. Retrieved from https://www2.deloitte. com/content/dam/Deloitte/dk/Documents/technology-media-telecommunications/ Workplaces_of_Future.pdf

Howard, B. B., McClannon, T. W., & Wallace, P. R. (2014). Collaboration through role play among graduate students in educational leadership in distance learning. *American Journal of Distance Education, 28,* 51–61.

Ipsos. (January 23, 2012). *Telecommuting seen to keep talented women in the workplace, reduce stress and support work-life balance.* Retrieved from http://www. ipsos-na.com/news-polls/pressrelease.aspx?id=5486

Jenkins, D. M. (2012). Exploring signature pedagogies in undergraduate leadership education. *Journal of Leadership Education, 11*(1), 1–27. Retrieved from http://leadershipeducators.org/Resources/Documents/jole/2012_Winter/Jenkins.pdf

Jenkins, D. M. (2014). Exploring instructional and assessment strategy use in online leadership education. *Proceedings of the 2013 association of leadership educators conference,* 333–338. Retrieved from http://leadershipeducators.org/Resources/ Documents/2014%20ALE%20Conference%20Proceedings.pdf

Johns, T., & Gratton, L. (January–February, 2013). The third wave of virtual work. *Harvard Business Review.* Retrieved from http://hbr.org/2013/01/the-third-wave-of-virtual-work/ar/1

Kanawattanachai, P., & Yoo, Y. (2012). Dynamic nature of trust in virtual teams. *Journal of Strategic Information Systems, 11,* 187–213.

Kelly, A. P., & Hess, F. M. (2013). *Beyond retrofitting: Innovation in higher education.* Washington, DC: Hudson Institute Initiative on Future Innovation. Retrieved from http://www.hudson.org/content/researchattachments/attachment/1121/beyond_ retrofitting-innovation_in_higher_ed_(kelly-hess,_june_2013).pdf

Kittur, A., Nickerson, J. V., Bernstein, M. S., Gerber, E. M., Shaw, A., Zimmerman, J., ... Horton, J. (2013). *Proceedings from CSCW'13: The 2013 Conference on Computer Supported Cooperative Work.* San Antonio, TX: ACM.

Kittur, A., Nickerson, J. V., Bernstein, M. S. Gerber, E. M., Shaw, A., Zimmerman, J., ... Horton, J. J. (2012, December 18). *The future of crowd work.* Retrieved from http://papers.ssrn.com/sol3/papers.cfm?abstract_id=2190946

Kolb, D. (1984). *Experiential learning: Experience as a source of learning and development.* Upper Saddle River, NJ: Prentice Hall.

Komives, S. R., Owen, J. E., Longerbeam, S., Mainella, F. C., & Osteen, L. (2005). Developing a leadership identity: A grounded theory. *Journal of College Student Development, 6,* 593–611.

McCotter, S. S. (2008). What do they need? Intrinsic motivation and online leadership learning. *Journal of Leadership Education, 7*(1), 92–115. Retrieved from http:// leadershipeducators.org/Resources/Documents/jole/2008_summer/JOLE_7_1_Schwarz-McCotter.pdf

Molee, L. M., Henry, M. E., Sessa, V. I., & McKinney-Prupis, E. R. (2010). Assessing learning in service-learning courses through critical reflection. *Journal of Experiential Education, 33*(3), 239–257.

Newberry, M., Culbertson, A., & Carter, H. S. (2013). Incorporating online learning tools into adult leadership programs. *Proceedings of the 2013 association of leadership educators conference*, 333–338. Retrieved from http://leadershipeducators.org/Resources/Documents/Conferences/2013_ALE_Proceedings.pdf

Odom, S. F., Jarvis, H. D., Sandlin, M. R., & Peek, C. (2013). Social media tools in the leadership classroom: Students' perception of use. *Journal of Leadership Education, 12*(1), 34–53. Retrieved from http://www.leadershipeducators.org/Resources/Documents/jole/2013%20Winter/Odom%20et%20al%202013.pdf

Perry, W. G., Jr. (1970). *Forms of intellectual and ethical development in the college years: A scheme.* New York, NY: Holt, Reinhart and Winston.

Phelps, K. (2012). Leadership online: Expanding the horizon. In K. L. Guthrie & L. Osteen (Eds.), *Developing students' leadership capacity: New directions for student services* (pp. 65–75). San Francisco, CA: Jossey-Bass.

Porter, S. R., & Umbach, P. D. (2006). College major choice: An analysis of person-environment fit. *Research in Higher Education, 47*, 429–448.

Remaking Education for a New Century. (2010). *The Futurist.* Retrieved from http://www.wfs.org/Dec09-Jan10/Anderson.htm

Saks, D. L. (2009). Education at a distance: Best practices and considerations for leadership educators. *Journal of Leadership Education, 8*(1), 137–147.

Stern, M. J., Adams, A. E., & Elasser, S. (2009, November). Digital inequality and place: The effects of technological diffusion on internet proficiency and usage across rural, suburban, and urban counties. *Social Inquiry, 79*, 391–417.

Steves, K., Keene, B. L., Hooker, E., Keane, K., Needles, A., & Fuess, L. (2011). Leadership education: Integrating social media. *Proceedings of the 2011 association of leadership educators conference*, 227–237. Retrieved from http://leadershipeducators.org/Resources/Documents/2011%20ALE%20Conference%20Proceedings.pdf

Sud, S., & Pickering, C. (2011). Computation mobility and virtual worlds – Not just where you work, but how you work. In A. R. Prasad, J. F. Buford, & V. K. Gurbani (Eds.), *Future internet services and service architectures* (pp. 207–226). Aalborg: River Publishers. Retrieved from BLB2015-FinalDraft.docx

Verburg, R. M., Bosch-Sijtsema, P., & Vartiainen, M. (2013). Getting it done: Critical success factors for project managers in virtual work settings. *International Journal of Project Management, 31*(1), 68–79.

Weeks, W. (2013). Teaching leadership concepts using an online simulation. *Proceedings of the 2013 association of leadership educators conference*, 452–456. Retrieved from http://leadershipeducators.org/Resources/Documents/Conferences/2013_ALE_Proceedings.pdf

West, J., & Gallagher, S. (2006). Challenges of open innovation: The paradox of firm investment in open-source software. *R&D Management, 36*(3), 319–331.

Yates, D., & Paquette, S. (2011). Emergency knowledge management and social media technologies: A case study of the 2010 Haitian earthquake. *International Journal of Information Management, 31*(1), 6–13.

Section III
Exploring Integrated Solutions

Plus ça change, plus c'est la même chose – Translation: The more things change the more they stay the same.

Not only will leaders of 2050 face the challenges of a greatly changed world, but they will also be tasked to address many of today's unresolved challenges. Age-old problems of securing resources, addressing inequality, and guaranteeing economic prosperity and peace will continue, but these will exist in concert with new challenges to be solved. We see this when leaders unsuccessfully apply solutions from the past to solve today's problem in an interconnected and interdependent world. Some failures of leadership demonstrate that leaders only know the world of which they are aware, are unaware of what they do not know and therefore, have difficulty seeing these unknowns. Leaders who see the world in its complexity rather than being locked into old mental models will not only find success in their efforts, but they will help others succeed.

The chapters in this section provide examples of future critical challenges, but go further in developing unique ways of viewing these problems and developing the skillsets to solve these problems. Themes of understanding interconnectedness, complexity, and true innovation pervade this section of the volume and underscore the need for theories and general thinking about leadership that moves away from a one-way influence process. Therefore, solutions will come from deeper, expanded thinking and deeper connections with followers and society. The chapters also define the required abilities of future leaders, with a focus on the skills and competencies necessary for leading in an interconnected, complex world. Some of these requirements are familiar, but will be expected to be applied in new ways, while others are more unique to changing circumstances. Many focus on not only the leader's interpersonal influence skills, but also more deeply on leaders' intrapersonal functioning and relational skills. Moreover, those leaders who understand the need to develop followers to work in concert with the leaders, rather than causing followers to become dependent will be prepared to face issues of individualization and digitalization. And finally these chapters provide solutions by focusing on new ways of developing the leaders who will be equipped to meet these new challenges.

The section begins with Nicole L. P. Stedman and Anthony C. Andenoro's enumeration of broad interrelated global challenges facing leaders and underscores the importance of leaders who demonstrate interconnected, adaptive leadership (Chapter 9). The authors focus specifically on how social solutions will be required and describe how leaders who develop emotionally engaged thinking will be better equipped for problem solving in the new environment. Because this enhanced type of thinking can overcome the shortcomings typical in purely rational models of thinking, it is important to understand these emotional aspects that include: foundational awareness, authentic engagement, connective analysis, and empowerment and change.

In Chapter 10, Sebastian Salicru sets the stage for an innovative approach to leadership development as a solution to the shortage of trusted leaders. Additionally, the chapter highlights a number of megatrends that will fundamentally change the types of leaders who will be effective in the future including individual empowerment, global diffusion of power, demographic patterns, and issues of scarcity. Movements to Altrocentric (a focus on others) away from egocentric (focus on self) leadership, collective and shared leadership away from centralized leadership and decision making, and relational leadership away from transactional exchange leadership point to a fundamental change in the psychological contract between followers and their leadership. To move leadership in this direction, five imperatives are presented as well as the Actionable Leadership Model.

Extreme challenges in the continued digital revolution have many implications for the development of leaders. In Chapter 11, Cathleen Clerkin highlights the skillset of leaders in this new era characterized by complexity and volatility. The repercussions of the digital revolution for leadership are explored and questions posed for tomorrow's leaders. The author suggests that the mind as computer analogy locks leaders into receiving the same past-focused leader development, and will not be an effective means to increase leaders' ability to create and innovate, nor to connect socially. This calls for a refocusing of society and leader development programs to help leaders address the implications of the digital revolution including the decreased value of basic information, as well as technological replacement of people through computerization.

In Chapter 12, Susan Cannon, Michael Morrow-Fox, and Maureen Metcalf provide a strategist competency model as an incisive focus on leaders who see must fill the role of a world-centric, and inclusive capacity. These leaders need to show consistent, flexible, holistic, meta-systemic, collaborative, and transformative problem solving. Developmentally these requirements call for leader development grounded in an adult developmental perspective. These leaders are developing what the authors refer to as a Strategist Leader perspective, which includes capabilities that develop their maturity and contribute to their transformative effectiveness through intrapersonal development in thinking and self-awareness, as well as outer focused on inspiration and collaboration. Furthermore, development of these leaders will require the use of "vertical" as compared to "horizontal" development of leadership capabilities.

This mind-expanding chapter by Michael A. Piel and Karen K. Johnson broadens our ideas of the role of leaders and the required skill sets by borrowing from quantum physics (Chapter 13). Current leadership theorizing benefits extensively from the application of science, but the application of quantum physics allows for a fresh look at leadership through the four quantum physics principles of duality, superposition, entanglement, and observation. After a review of the applicable principles of quantum physics, the chapter provides intriguing insight for specific application to leadership and leadership development in a way that highlights important leadership activities such as collaboration, intuition, self-awareness, and the power of connective thought. The chapter shows not only how complexity influences the way we view the world around us, but even more importantly can help leaders develop new ways of thinking to deal with as yet unknown challenges through their design of organizations to meet these challenges.

In Chapter 14, Skye Burn and Jean Houston believe that it is not only imperative for leaders to think differently in the future, but also to incorporate additional leadership capacity that comes from social artistry. By that they mean the ability to connect by incorporating emotion and spirit. The call for social artistry comes from the realization that many changes leaders will face are the result of a "re-patterning" of human nature to one of global citizenry, as well as the "re-genesis" of society through changes in existing social structure, institutions, and governments. This social artistry contains four levels of system change in sensory-physical, psychological-historic, mythic-symbolic, and integral-unitive methods of operating. The chapter offers specific methods for increasing leaders capacities in these areas.

The final Chapter 15 in this section by Bruce H. Jackson concludes with the introduction of Attentional Leadership Theory. This comprehensive leadership theory draws upon many of the concepts introduced in the earlier chapters of this section as it expands intrapersonal dimensions to include also philosophical and spiritual dimensions in addition to emotional, psychological, and physical.

Also, external dimensions for leaders to consider and develop include personal (or full life engagement), interpersonally gifted, as well as a focus on teams, organizations, and communities. And finally a nuanced understanding of dimensionalities of time that are too often overlooked in leadership theories, but make an important contribution to understanding the continuous interaction with leaders and others within their environments. The chapter ends with a focus on leader development within Attentional Leadership Theory.

Susan Elaine Murphy

9

Emotionally Engaged Leadership: Shifting Paradigms and Creating Adaptive Solutions for 2050

Nicole L. P. Stedman and Anthony C. Andenoro

Introduction

The human race is responsible for two things, identifying the problems that we face and solving them. In the last five years, there has been a growing emphasis on what are called the *grand challenges*. These grand challenges, such as climate change or the AIDS pandemic are complex in nature, requiring a different style of problem-solving and leadership.

The White House refers to the 21st century Grand Challenges as, "ambitious but achievable goals that harness science, technology, and innovation to solve important national or global problems and that have the potential to capture the public's imagination" (The White House, 2014, p. 1). The President's strategy for innovation guides the work on four key grand challenges: Brain Initiative, SunShot Grand Challenge, Asteroid Grand Challenge, and Grand Challenges for Development. Each of these challenges threaten some aspect of human livelihood and are positioned to fund more jobs, "Help tackle important problems related to energy, health, education, the environment, national security, and global development;

and serve as a "North Star" for collaboration between the public and private sectors" (The White House, 2014, p. 3).

The White House is not the only organization to purport the development of grand challenges. USAID has a unique set of five including, securing water for food, saving lives at birth, all children reading, powering agriculture, and making all voices count (United States Agency for International Development [USAID], 2014). In fact, a simple Google search produces over 50,000,000 entries for grand challenges across the globe – challenges that require ingenuity and innovative thinking.

Within the scholarly literature, just since the beginning of 2014 there are over 27,000 entries addressing grand challenges representing nearly every discipline, each creating a call to action by scholars and experts. Many of these publications emphasize the challenges as a means to ensure the best future possible. This call often includes what leaders can and should be doing to stimulate this action.

In order for leaders to address this level of action, they must be equipped to synthesize and bring together ideas from a variety of perspectives; this may be one of the grand challenges of leadership education. How can we ensure that leaders are prepared to do this?

The antiquated methods we once used for decision-making are not sufficient to address the problems of the future. An individual leader can no longer bear the responsibility for solving our problems. In today's environment the problems and challenges we face as a society are growing in complexity, requiring better adaptive solutions. The human dynamics of how we operate socially must play a role in how we solve these problems where a singular response is no longer adequate.

Our Grand Challenge

Despite declining global birth rates, Earth's population is rapidly growing. This rapid population growth has the potential to create significant problems for our global community. In fact, of the grand challenges, many theorists believe that population growth will be the greatest problem of our time (Clapp & Cohen, 2009; Ericksen, Ingram, & Liverman, 2009; Food and Agricultural Organization of the United Nations [FAO], 2001, 2008; Rosegrant, Paisner Meijer, & Witcover, 2001; World Bank Group, 2003). Specifically, our challenge is to address and mitigate the problems associated with a global population projected to exceed 9.6 billion by the year 2050. The problems associated with a global population scale fall into five main problems.

The first problem is space. As population increases people migrate to urban areas creating a foundation for two main things to occur – cities expand due to urban sprawl and rural areas decrease in size due to population scarcity and rural flight. This leads to a reduction in the area devoted to agricultural production and the work force necessary for large and small-scale agriculture. Unfortunately, this creates the impetus for our second problem, agriculture production.

Currently, 7.14 billion people reside on our planet. A global population exceeding 9.6 billion will require twice as much agricultural production. Close to 33% of agricultural production is lost in transportation and due to poor preservation techniques (FAO, 2008). This coupled with the rapid growth of population in developing contexts (i.e., Africa and Asia) will require double the agricultural production. This means that we will need to develop innovative ways to reduce waste and increase efficiency to meet the needs of the global population. One of the most difficult pieces of this problem is that the majority of agricultural production requires water, possibly our most prized global commodity. Water Conservation is our third problem.

Approximately, 71% of our planet is covered by water and 96.5% of that water is in our oceans (Brekke et al., 2009). To further exasperate this problem, 68.7% of freshwater is in polar ice caps, glaciers, and permanent snow. This is problematic because we cannot access this water. This means that less than 1% of the world's freshwater is accessible for direct human use (Gleick, 2000). This is the water found in lakes, rivers, reservoirs, and underground sources that are shallow enough to be tapped at an affordable cost. Only this amount is regularly renewed by rain and snowfall and is therefore available on a sustainable basis. Understanding this, water is a finite resource and accessibility to it is becoming more and more of a premium.

The fourth problem is energy. As we increase agricultural production and grow our population we consume more energy. This creates a premium for efficient alternative energies in a world dominated by natural gas, coal, and petroleum. Currently, only 15% of our energy comes from alternative sources and the 85% that comes from natural gas, coal, and petroleum is being depleted at an exponential rate. This coupled with the need to triple our current energy production to meet the needs of 9.6 billion people globally will require massive shifts in energy production and human behavior if sustainability is possible.

Finally, our fifth problem stemming from the cumulative effect of our previously listed problems and their impact on our environment is climate change. Climate change is shifting our ability to be sustainable globally. The Intergovernmental Panel on Climate Change, a United Nations group, reported (Field et al., 2014, p. 20):

Throughout the 21st century, climate-change impacts are projected to slow down economic growth, make poverty reduction more difficult, further erode food security, and prolong existing and create new poverty traps, the latter particularly in urban areas and emerging hotspots of hunger.

In addition to this, the potential exists for natural disasters to happen on a boarder and a more intense scale leading to more areas desperate for humanitarian aid and substandard living conditions. All of these problems create a perfect storm for leaders across the world. Historical leadership strategies will not be adequate and new paths must be forged in order to become a more sustainable world.

The Role of Leadership

In the past, humanity has relied on technology and science to sustain their way of life in times of adversity. However, while technology and science may play a role in how we save our planet, our grand challenge of population growth requires something much greater — massive social and behavioral changes in global populations. This complex adaptive challenge exemplifies the charge and original impetus behind complex adaptive leadership (Heiftez, Grashow, & Linsky, 2009a, 2009b; Lichtenstein, Uhl-Bien, Marion, Seers, & Orton, 2006; Yukl & Mahsud, 2010).

Complex adaptive leadership recognizes that problems are complicated and influenced by various systems replete with countless interactions. This system perspective provides an expanded view of interconnectedness of the problems we face. It brings leadership from an individual perspective to a social perspective, whereby leaders must work together to achieve great things. Leadership resides within the frameworks of the system; it is interactive and dynamic (Lichtenstein et al., 2006).

The greatest benefit of this social perspective of leadership is increases in creativity, influence, and change (Lichtenstein et al., 2006). When each individual can contribute to the leadership whole, there is greater ownership, whereby the formal leaders become less concerned with the right answers and more concerned with the right strategies.

As leaders, we need to be cognizant of these factors and assert strategies grounded in critical perspectives validated by the intersections that exist among people. These strategies require the engagement of our creative processes in an effort to leap beyond traditional approaches to leadership grounded in individual traits and competencies.

Emotionally Engaged Thinking as the Leadership Solution

In the last five years, there has been a growth in the area of neuroscience and leadership (Boyatzis, 2008; Ghadiri, Habermacher, & Peters, 2013; Rock & Schwartz, 2007; Waldman, Balthazard, & Peterson, 2011). This research has led to a greater understanding of how the brain works in key areas of leadership, like decision-making and emotional intelligence and also in important areas, like stress and health. Emotionally Engaged Thinking (EET) was developed from research conducted more than a decade ago, which linked critical thinking and emotional intelligence. This link provided the foundation for how people can use emotion to guide logic. In 2013, Stedman and Andenoro launched EET after refining this connection. Andenoro identified EET as a critical piece of the solution building process during his TED talk (2014). Furthermore, he noted that EET creates a foundation for solving our world's greatest challenges including global population growth, international food security, transnational pandemics, and beyond (2014). EET approaches decision-making using the foundational work in neuroscience to address the use of emotions in a leader's ability to think critically.

EET operates when a leader is challenged with a decision evoking a strong emotional response but which requires a logical reasoned approach. Decision-making has long been understood as one's ability to identify alternatives for a problem and selecting the alternative, which presents the greatest selected utility. In other words, which alternative will one get the most out of, based on underlying desires, motivations, or preferences. It is easy to imagine that this most basic understanding of decision-making often falls short given the complex nature of people. Decision-making would be easy and consistent if it were just a matter of weighing options and going with the best choice. In fact, Holyoak and Morrison (2005) outline six different ways the brain works against the rational theory of choice model, choice of uncertainty, riskless choice, conflict and reasons, processing of attribute weights, and local versus global perspectives. Each of these presents a set of conflicts that the brain has to process in order to complete the decision-making process.

Emotions are central to how many of these principles impact decision-making. From the most basic notion that the loss of something is felt less by an individual in a negative mood versus one in a positive mood to how particular images of recall can influence decision-making. Furthermore, one's current state can influence a decision in the future, which is not directly tied to the current state.

Holyoak and Morrison (2005) describe a situation, in which individuals often use current feelings or emotions to project to a future state. This "myopic decision making" results in an inability to recognize incidental factors as such. These contextual changes have been found to greatly influence the manner, in which people make decisions.

In recognizing the influence of emotion on decision-making, EET sets out to provide a systematic approach for incorporating them into how decisions are made. Our rational selves cannot always take into account situations that are influenced by our emotional selves. Researchers have documented that even the most skilled thinkers often fall victim to biases based upon a dominant thought.

In academia, there has been an effort to address biased thought through the development of critical thinking skills. Critical thinking has long been the standard for rational, purposive, and reflecting thinking (Rudd, Baker, & Hoover, 2000). From the work of Facione, to Ruggiero, to Paul and Elder, critical thinking has a long line of research documenting its development and use across disciplines. Critical thinking has been shown to have a dispositional nature, stylistic preferences, and skill development. Much attention has been focused on how to increase skills, allowing for the greatest opportunity for people to use critical thinking in their daily lives. For leaders this is paramount to their success. Many of the leadership theories that are espoused today incorporate some aspect of decision-making, complex thinking, or problem-solving to their principles. However, few theorists have approached how to make decisions, solve complex problems, or solve problems.

Another fundamental piece to this puzzle is emotional intelligence. EI has become the quintessential approach to assisting leaders better understand their own emotions and those of others around them. Emotional intelligence can be broken down into two areas outlined by Salovey and Sluyter (1997). The areas are the understanding of emotion and the understanding of intelligence, which are concretely united in an effort to delineate the idea of emotional intelligence (Akers, Miller, Fraze, & Haygood, 2002). Thus, educators are forced to explore creative means of delivering curricula, which dispose students to emotional intelligence and develop specific areas of emotional intelligence, much like critical thinking skill. Success in the business world depends on both academic ability and social and emotional skills (Goleman, 1995).

It is important to question if there is a connection between critical thinking and emotional intelligence because both are part of leadership education. Lord and Emrich (2000) surmised there is a direct link between the effects of a social system and the leader's metacognitive processes, which in this case, the researchers would identify the leader's critical thinking ability and the impact on social awareness. This would theorize that these two concepts have an insurmountable impact on organizational learning. Through the examination of these two concepts, one can infer that self-regulation, as a skill of critical thinking, can be likened to certain aspects of the core emotional competencies of emotional intelligence. The four core competencies are as follows (Salovey & Mayer, 1990):

1. The ability to accurately perceive, appraise, and express emotion.
2. The ability to access or generate feelings on demand when they can facilitate understanding of yourself and another person.
3. The ability to understand emotions and the knowledge that derives from them.
4. The ability to regulate emotions to promote emotional and intellectual growth.

Self-awareness emerged from these four core emotional competencies as a governing tenet for the development of emotional intelligence. Self-awareness refers to the ability to recognize a feeling as it happens (Goleman, 1995). This ability is paramount for students exploring service in leadership positions. Goleman noted "the ability to monitor feelings from moment to moment is crucial to psychological insight and self-understanding" (1995, p. 43). He further asserts that if individuals fail to recognize their true feelings, it can be detrimental (Goleman, 1995). "People with greater certainty about their feelings are better pilots of their lives, having a surer sense of how they feel about personal decisions, from who to marry, to what job to take" (1995, p. 43).

At the intersection of critical thinking and emotional intelligence is EET. It promotes the outcomes of critical thinking while capturing the emotions of the leader. As indicated earlier, decisions are often influenced by emotions whether we are cognizant of it or not. The emotions provide a glimpse into inner desire and motive but are overlooked or minimized in an effort to maintain objectivity. EET promotes thinking, which is grounded in emotion providing the leader an opportunity to recognize his/her emotional state or motive with respect to a problem and then logically work through the emotion to arrive at a strategically biased solution.

EET promotes a system's thinking approach that incorporates emotions as the catalyst for positive decision-making. EET is applicable across the spectrum of disciplines, industries, and natural resource areas. The intent of EET is that all individuals involved in decision-making (not just the leader) have some level of emotional investment in challenges and problems facing their particular field.

By engaging in EET all invested parties can actively express their emotions and participate in active dialogue. Using the FACE method, (Foundational awareness, Authentic engagement, Connective analysis, and Empowerment and change) individuals are provided with the tools to think through problems, recognizing their emotion, engaging in dialogue, and promoting shared decision-making. In order to capture this, the example of food security will be used as it evokes a number of human variables (emotion, cognitive, and behavioral).

For the practical purposes of our applied understanding for how the FACE works, the rest of this chapter examines FACE as applied to the second grand challenge identified above – that of food security for 9.6 billion people in 2050. Food security's dynamic human variables and complexity make it a prime example of what Heifetz, Grashow, and Linsky (2009) noted as an adaptive challenge.

Foundational awareness is the first point of reflection in establishing EET. The goal during this phase is for the leader to become aware of his or her emotions related to a problem or decision. Using basic prompts, individuals are asked to consider personal implications of a problem. For the purposes of this piece, the problem of food security and hunger will be used to illustrate these concepts. For some the problem of food security may not be an overt issue ("I have food, so there is no problem"). During this first phase, individuals must come in terms with the problem – understanding that it exists in many contexts and has broad societal implications. This could be applied to any problem or complex situation but is integral in establishing the foundation for moving forward.

The second phase is authentic engagement and is grounded in one's ability to truly relate to the problem. It is how a problem is identified with cognitively. It is often easy to place importance, or value, of a problem elsewhere. In other words one fails to see the personal impact of a problem. In the example above, it may be easy for an individual to not express an understanding of his or her emotional response to food (many people have emotional connections to food beyond the example described here). Authentic engagement relates to how the individual sees him or herself in the scenario (how does this problem connect with who I am, what is my place with respect to the problem). For example, food security elicits a number of emotions depending on an individual's relationship with food and food availability. One could experience the fear of not knowing where the next meal will come from, anxiety over providing food, or excitement of resolving this growing problem. This emotional response is based upon a perceived situation (anticipating what will happen) and can thus influence how the situation is approached. In order to best decide how to approach the situation, one must address how he or she feels about the problem. It provides a level of sincerity in being present in a moment. Key behaviors of authentic engagement include attentive listening, productive dialogue, and reflective thought.

In the third phase leaders are challenged with the big picture. Connective analysis, also a cognitive process, is the means for creating true meaning from an experience or problem. In our scenario, the individual has now embraced an emotional tie to the problem, has fully engaged with experience, and now must relate this experience to others. How can what is experienced provide insight into a future situation? Through the use of connective analysis the 30,000 foot view emerges and one can see how or innermost emotions are often reflected in a number of situations. During this phase, we are also more inclined to be open to other's ideas, emotions, and reactions to the same experience or problem. It is a time of connection within adding depth to who we are and deepening our relationships with others.

Lastly, EET challenges individuals with empowerment and change (behavior). This phase for most is left on the to-do list. At some point, there is a picture of change or a difference being made. For the FACE method this is the phase that creates meaning for the others, it is why the others are so important. If a leader can engage with his/her emotion, be present and authentic, and see the connection with others and the problem, then it only likens that he or she will be empowered to make a difference. While the example to illustrate the FACE method is fairly introductory, imagine the difference this method would make for our leader, but for those staff who will receive feedback in the future.

In reality, the FACE method is a proactive tool to garner productive dialogue, which takes into consideration our emotional connection, seeing the "big picture," and making plans for the future. When it is applied to a complex problem, the FACE method allows for individuals to feel a stronger connection to the problem, but also to one another. For those complex problems will require that everyone is heard, everyone is engaged, and everyone contributes to the solution.

The Model

There have been many recognized models of decision-making, which illustrate how an individual progresses from dilemma or problem to decision. For the purposes of EET, a model shared by Lowenstein and Lerner (2003) is used as the base (Figure 1). Each point in the model represents a number of processes that occur when an individual makes a decision. The process in which EET influences are those between *immediate emotions* and *decision/behavior* and *immediate emotions* and *expected consequence* (starred below). It is in these affective influences where emotion plays the greatest role in determining the decision that is made. The FACE method applies directly to the relationship between *immediate emotion* and *decision/behavior*. When progressing through the phases of the method one can directly influence a decision or behavior. The goal is that as a result of the method we can take greater control over the second part of the model, *expected consequence*. The model depicts the direct relationship between an emotional impulse and the decision or behavior resulting. Within EET leaders are encouraged to

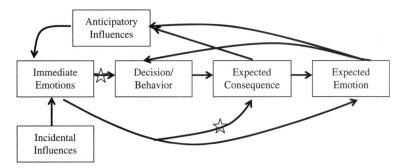

Figure 1.   The Role of EET in the Decision-Making Process.

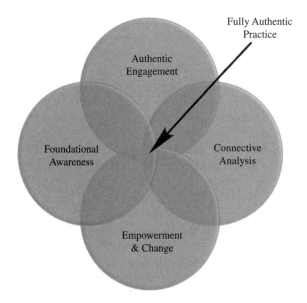

Figure 2.   Fully Authentic Practice through the FACE Method.

acknowledge this emotional impulse, bring attention to it, and logically use it to make decisions. In the current model, without the use of EET, a leader may not fully bring attention to that emotional impulse. The subconscious influence of emotion drives the decision or behavior. EET allows for a conscious recognition of the emotional impulse.

The FACE method actualizes fully authentic practice by encourage individuals to address their emotional response to a particular phenomenon, experience, or problem. It emphasizes the value of authentic engagement by being present, aware, and immersed. Through connective analysis the broader perspectives are realized, bringing into practice empowerment and change (Figure 2).

Conclusion

The proposed model of EET provides a foundation for encouraging a deeper level of thinking, decision-making, and problem-solving. Leaders today must be equipped to address the growing complexity of problems in our world. This can be accomplished by understanding the problems, addressing emotional reactions, connecting with others, and empowering change. By bringing the FACE steps into practice, leaders can venture into Emotionally Engaged Leadership. This shift in leadership allows for leaders to effectively engage their emotions with decision-making. It shifts leadership from an individual phenomenon to one of greater connection, with our problems, with each other and with change. It brings together people, so that we can all take responsibility for providing solutions to change our world.

References

Akers, C., Miller, K., Fraze, S., & Haygood, J. D. (2002). Critical curricular needs of emotional intelligence in agricultural education. *Proceedings of the National Agricultural Education Research Conference*, Las Vegas, NV, 29.

Andenoro, A. C. (2014). The key to saving 9.6 billion. *Proceedings of the TEDxUF 2014*, Gainesville, FL.

Boyatzis, R. E. (2008). Competencies in the 21st century. *Journal of Management Development*, 27(1), 5–12.

Brekke, L. D., Kiang, J. E., Olsen, J. R., Pulwarty, R. S., Raff, D. A., Turnipseed, D. P., ... White, K. D. (2009). *Climate change and water resources management – A federal perspective: U.S. geological survey circular 1331*. Retrieved from http://pubs.usgs.gov/circ/1331/Circ1331.pdf

Clapp, J., & Cohen, M. J. (Eds.). (2009). *The global food crisis: Governance challenges and opportunities*. Waterloo: Wilfrid Laurier University Press.

Ericksen, P. J., Ingram, J. S., & Liverman, D. M. (2009). Food security and global environmental change: Emerging challenges. *Environmental Science & Policy*, 12(4), 373–377.

Field, C. B., Barros, V. R., Dokken, D. J., Mach, K. J., Mastrandrea, M. D., Bilir, T. E., ... Genova, R. C. (2014). *IPCC, 2014: Climate change 2014: Impacts, adaptation, and vulnerability.* Contribution of Working Group II to the Fifth Assessment Report of the Intergovernmental Panel on Climate Change.

Food and Agricultural Organization of the United Nations. (2001). The impact of HIV/AIDS on food security. *Proceedings from Committee on World Food Security*, 27th Session, Rome, Italy.

Food and Agricultural Organization of the United Nations. (2008). *Climate change and food security: A framework document.* Rome: FAO.

Ghadiri, A., Habermacher, A., & Peters, T. (2013). *Neuroleadership.* New York, NY: Springer Publishing.

Gleick, P. H. (2000). A look at twenty-first century water resources development. *Water International*, 25(1), 127–138.

Goleman, D. (1995). *Emotional intelligence: Why it can matter more than IQ.* New York, NY: Bantam Books.

Heifetz, R. A., Grashow, A., & Linsky, M. (2009a). *The practice of adaptive leadership: Tools and tactics for changing your organization and the world.* Cambridge, MA: Harvard Business Press.

Heiftez, R., Grashow, A., & Linsky, M. (2009b). Leadership in a (permanent) crisis. *Harvard Business Review*, 87(7/8), 62–69.

Holyoak, J. K., & Morrison, R. G. (2005). *The Cambridge handbook of thinking and reasoning.* Cambridge, MA: Cambridge Press.

Lichtenstein, B. B., Uhl-Bien, M., Marion, R., Seers, A., & Orton, J. D. (2006). Complexity leadership theory: An interactive perspective on leading in complex adaptive systems. In *Digital commons.* Lincoln, NE: University of Nebraska.

Lord, R. G., & Emrich, C. G. (2000). Thinking outside the box by looking inside the box: Extending the cognitive revolution in leadership research. *The Leadership Quarterly*, 11(4), 551–579.

Lowenstein, G. & Lerner, J. (2003). The role of emotion in decision making. In R. J. Davidson, H. H. Goldsmith, & K. R. Scherer (Eds.), *Handbook of affective science.* Oxford: Oxford University Press.

Rock, D., & Schwartz, J. (2007). The neuroscience of leadership. *Reclaiming Children and Youth*, 16(3), 10.

Rosegrant, M. W., Paisner, M. S., Meijer, S., & Witcover, J. (2001). *2020 global food outlook: Trends, alternatives, and choices* (Vol. 11). Washington, DC: International Food Policy Research Institute.

Rudd, R., Baker, M., & Hoover, T. (2000). Undergraduate agricultural student learning styles and critical thinking abilities: Is there a relationship? *Journal of Agricultural Education*, 41(3), 2–12.

Salovey, P., & Mayer, J. D. (1990). Emotional intelligence. *Imagination, Cognition, and Personality*, 9(3), 185–211.

Salovey, P., & Sluyter, D. J. (1997). *Emotional development and emotional intelligence.* New York, NY: BasicBooks.

The White House. (2014). *Grand-challenges.* Washington, DC. Retrieved from http://www.whitehouse.gov/administration/eop/ostp/grand-challenges. Accessed on April 17, 2015.

United States Agency for International Development. (2014). *Grand challenges.* Washington, DC. Retrieved from http://www.usaid.gov/grandchallenges. Accessed on April 17, 2015.

Waldman, D. A., Balthazard, P. A., & Peterson, S. J. (2011). Leadership and neuroscience: Can we revolutionize the way that inspirational leaders are identified and developed? *Academy of Management Perspective, 25*(1), 60–74.

World Bank Group. (2003). *World development report 2003: Sustainable development in a dynamic world – Transforming institutions, growth, and quality of life.* Washington, DC: World Bank.

Yukl, G., & Mahsud, R. (2010). Why flexible and adaptive leadership is essential. *Consulting Psychology Journal, 62*(2), 81–93.

10

The Global Leadership Psychological Contract Model – Actionable to Shape the Future to 2050

Sebastian Salicru

A map of the world that does not include Utopia is not worth even glancing at, for it leaves out the one country at which Humanity is always landing. And when Humanity lands there, it looks out, and, seeing a better country, sets sail. Progress is the realisation of Utopias.

Oscar Wilde (2015)

The Global Leadership Index published in *Outlook on the Global Agenda 2015* (World Economic Forum, 2014a), which reflects the current thinking of a community of over 1500 of the world's foremost global experts, indicates that 86% of respondents believe that the world is currently experiencing a leadership crisis. Despite the fact that leadership research has produced more models than any other behavioral science (Hunt & Dodge, 2000), and despite 25 years of growth in leadership development programs, the latest research indicates the field is still relatively immature (Day, Fleenor, Atwater, Sturm, & McKee, 2014). Arguably, the failure of most leadership development initiatives can be attributed to four common mistakes: (1) overlooking the context; (2) separating reflection from real work; (3) underestimating the power of mindsets; and (4) failing to measure results (Gurdjian, Halbeisen, & Lane, 2014).

This failure of leadership explains the increasingly negative public perception of national and global economic and political leadership. In 2013, for example, global leaders met at the World Economic Forum in the Swiss mountain resort of Davos. The official theme of the meeting was "Resilient Dynamism" but, according to The Economist (2013), the group's credentials as global leaders looked anything but resilient. There was a big gap between the community's level of trust in the leaders and that of the institutions they led.

If this is the current state of affairs of leadership today, what will it be in 2050? And why does this matter?

Why Is the Future of Leadership between Now and 2050 so Critical?

The world is currently facing major interconnected economic, environmental, geopolitical, societal and technological risks which, when combined, could have a potentially significant impact on the level of trust and mutual obligation between states and their citizens. In turn, this could lead to state collapse, regional and global instability, internal violence, and war. Managing such risks effectively will require great foresight and collaboration between stakeholders across business, government, and civil society (World Economic Forum, 2014b). Underpinning these risks are megatrends that, over the next decades will turn the world and the context for leadership as we know it upside down.

Megatrends are long-term transformational processes with broad scope, dramatic impact, and global reach (Naisbitt, 1984). They are the sustained macroeconomic forces of development that have a pervasive and enduring impact on individuals, businesses, economies, and societies and will re-define an unprecedented pace of change for the future. Four megatrends are expected to progressively gain momentum and cause critical changes in the global environment (National Intelligence Council, 2012) while others are predicted to dramatically impact on organizations (Vielmetter & Sell, 2014) by the year 2030.

1. An increase in individual empowerment. This megatrend will result from significant reductions in poverty and the growth of a global middle class with much greater acquisition power, including greater ownership of property and access to education; wider use of communication and manufacturing

technologies; and advances in health care (National Intelligence Council, 2012). Organizations will face increasing individualization and value pluralism with freedom of choice eroding loyalty; a blurring of boundaries between work and leisure/personal lives; and technological convergence with the greatest technological shifts ever experienced in history on our doorstep (Vielmetter & Sell, 2014).

2. Diffusion of power globally with a shift toward networks and coalitions. As an example, Asia will surpass the combination of North America and Europe in terms of global power based on GDP, population size, military spending, and technological investment. It is envisaged that China alone will have a larger economy than the United States a few years before 2030 (National Intelligence Council, 2012).

3. Demographic patterns. This megatrend predicts that the global population will grow from an estimated 7.1 billion in 2013 to close to 8.3 billion in 2030. Economic growth is likely to decline in countries with aging populations; there will be a decrease in the number of youthful societies; migration will increase; and 60% of the world's population will live in urbanized areas (National Intelligence Council, 2012). In organizations, aging populations will intensify the war for talent (Vielmetter & Sell, 2014).

4. Scarcity of food, water, and energy. The demand for these resources will increase significantly – by approximately 35%, 40%, and 50%, respectively – as a result of the change in demographic patterns (see above). Nearly half the world's population will experience a severe scarcity of such resources (National Intelligence Council, 2012) and predicted environmental crises will make sustainability within organizations paramount (Vielmetter & Sell, 2014).

It is most important to understand that these megatrends are not discrete independent events. In fact, they interact and combine to form a complex "perfect storm," thereby creating new forces that will compound the challenges and complexities to be faced in the future. In this scenario, business leaders will have to grapple with new dilemmas and challenges (Park, 2014).

Appointed leaders will lose power and there will be a massive proliferation of stakeholders. The power of leaders will be compromised by, for example, local managers, environmental concerns, and legislation. Reconceptualization of the conventional notion of what a stakeholder is will result in stakeholder expansion. This new notion of stakeholders within organizations will be far more inclusive including both internal stakeholders (e.g., employees and different groups of employees in multiple locations and cultures) and external stakeholders (society). Hence, leaders will have to decide how to relate to each of their stakeholder groups (Vielmetter & Sell, 2014).

A TRANSFORMED WORLD

The extant literature (National Intelligence Council, 2012) offers four "alternative or potential worlds" for the year 2030 which provide a springboard for potential scenarios describing the world in 2050. The alternative or potential worlds in 2030 are based on the combination of megatrends identified previously and game-changers such as the health of the international economy; global governance; the potential for increased conflict; regional instability; the impact of technological breakthroughs; and the role of the United States: (1) Stalled Engines; (2) Fusion; (3) Gini-Out-of-the-Bottle; and (4) Nonstate World.

Stalled Engines is the worst possible scenario. It entails the United States and Europe stalling by turning inward, as power grows in Asia. Western countries would face extreme levels of tension due to a scarcity of resources, economic depression, and increasing social issues (poverty, crime, and warfare). The best possible scenario is Fusion which depends largely on political leadership and envisages collaboration between the United States, Europe, and China. The Gini-Out-of-the-Bottle scenario represents a world of extremes. It is characterized by inequalities that lead to political and social tensions with distinct winners and losers. In this scenario, the United States ceases to be the "global policeman." The Nonstate World scenario is driven by nonstate agencies such as nongovernmental organizations (NGOs), multinationals, academic institutions, and wealthy individuals taking the lead in confronting global challenges.

The worst case scenario of Stalled Engines could, by 2050, unfold in two possible ways: events could escalate which would represent the collapse of the western world or the Stalled Engines scenario could serve as a wake-up call for affected individuals to become creative and resourceful and focused on survival and further adaptation of the human species.

In considering Fusion — the best possible scenario resulting from collaboration between the major economic powers — two contrasting scenarios could be possible: the Fusion state could be sustained or even improved (the social evolution perspective); or there could be a regression to economic and social collapse (the social cycle perspective) due primarily to complacency resulting from the absence of a major and visible threats or crisis. The first scenario would be consistent with both social evolution theory (Hamilton, 1996) supporting the idea that societies evolve, change, and survive, and sociocultural evolution theory (Lenski, Lenski, & Nolan, 1991), which views technological progress as the most basic factor in the evolution of societies and cultures. The second scenario would be consistent with social cycle theory (Modelski, 1987; Tainter, 1988), which argues that events and stages of society and history generally repeat themselves.

In another scenario in the world of the future, robots are expected to replace or largely eliminate human labor with blurring between industrial and service robots (National Intelligence Council, 2012), and there is speculation about robot technology controlling e-leadership processes and outcomes (Avolio, Sosik, Kahai, & Baker, 2014). As a result, the reliable and safe operation of robots will be paramount. Remote and autonomous vehicles (RAVs) are expected to impact on mining, exploration, and defense, the latter related to interstate conflicts including the enforcement of non-flying zones and national borders. A possible threat will be the use of RAVs by terrorist groups (National Intelligence Council, 2012).

In summary, macro-socio-economic megatrends predict that societies and their leaders will be faced with increasingly adaptive challenges in the future and resolving these challenges will require people to change their ways of doing and being through transformational learning (Heifetz, Linsky, & Grashow, 2009).

Latest Leadership Thinking and Research

In response to these challenges, and as a result of their megatrend analysis, Vielmetter and Sell (2014) predict the emergence of altrocentric leadership which focuses on others rather than on the leaders themselves (egocentric leadership). Altrocentric leadership is based on the assumption that the traditional cliché of the super-hero, or alpha male leader who leads the pack, is no longer relevant in addressing the identified megatrends and consequent challenges and dilemmas of the future. Altrocentric leaders are characterized by the awareness that they cannot achieve success alone; a much higher degree of empathy, maturity, integrity, and openness; skilled strategic and conceptual thinking; the ability to create and empower high-performing teams; and a greater reliance on collaboration and teamwork. Above all, altrocentric leaders know how to create meaning in organizations by generating a collective narrative with all organizational stakeholders. Critical to this is the concept of bounded autonomy — that is, delegating as much power as is effectively possible for others to allow them to thrive within this new context.

This notion of collectivity and inclusiveness is consistent with the latest developments in global leadership in that global leaders are those who build communities through the development of trust in a context involving multiple stakeholders, multiple sources of external authority, and multiple cultures under conditions of temporal, geographical, and cultural complexity (Mendenhall, Reiche, Bird, & Osland, 2012). Global leaders operate in a context of multicultural, paradoxical complexity to achieve results in a diverse world, which is not intrinsically hierarchical (Holt & Seki, 2012). Hence, future leaders will require high levels of cultural intelligence (CQ) to function effectively in an increasingly global and multicultural world (Ng, Dyne, & Ang, 2012). CQ reflects an individual's capability to deal effectively with people from different cultural backgrounds and includes concepts such as global mindset or cross-cultural competence (Earley & Ang, 2003). The latest research in leadership development also identifies an increased focus on collective rather than individual leadership (Petrie, 2014).

Researchers have been advocating for a collective or a shared approach to leadership which views leadership as a social process — the accomplishment of collectives rather than the actions of individuals — for some time (Contractor, DeChurch, Carson, Carter, & Keegan, 2012; Cullen, Palus, Chrobot-Mason, & Appaneal, 2012; Sergi, Denis, & Langley, 2012; Yammarino, Salas, Serban, Shirreffs, & Shuffler, 2012). The notion is not dissimilar from followership theory which views leadership as a relational process that is co-created between people working together (Uhl-Bien, Riggio, Lowe, & Carsten, 2014). Followership shifts the focus from the leader as the main protagonist (the "heroic" or "lone ranger" leader) to post-heroic leadership introducing the possibility that followers have an active influence over leaders in allowing themselves to be influenced (Oc & Bashshur, 2013).

Collective leadership, also referred to as "shared," "distributive," "collaborative," or "emergent" leadership (Bolden, 2011), is a social process that focuses beyond competency-only approaches. In fact, by focusing on the collective environment and strategic collective objectives, collective leadership approaches produce collective outcomes (Cullen et al., 2012). This is line with the concept of shared leadership which views leadership in terms of collaboration between two or more persons (Crevani, Lindgren, & Packendorff, 2007). Interestingly, collective leadership also promotes innovation (Hoch, 2013; Hunter, Cushenbery, Fairchild, & Boatman, 2012). Furthermore, collectivistic approaches to leadership have a greater focus on the social context in which leadership occurs; the creation of social networks; the empowerment of followers; and relationships — including an ongoing and open exchange between leaders and all stakeholders (Mumford, Friedrich, Vessey, & Ruark, 2012). Clearly, the inherent relational nature and shared social influence of collective leadership, as pointed out by Karp and Helgø (2008), reflects the psychologically based process that emerges from the relationships between people and, consequently, the psychological contracts that govern such relationships.

Psychological contract (PC) theory (Guest, 1998; Rousseau, 1989, 1995) has a direct link to collective leadership because it is fundamentally rooted in social exchange relationships and governed by the norm of reciprocity (Conway & Briner, 2005). According to Chang, Hsu, Liou, and Tsai (2013), PCs also contribute to innovative behavior. Recent developments in PC research link PCs to leadership and performance outcomes (McDermott, Conway, Rousseau, & Flood, 2013). Leadership psychological contracts (LPCs) emphasize the need for more relational outcomes measures of leadership, as opposed to leader attributes or competencies, and link a leader's integrity with followers' emotional constructs, extra-role behaviors, and innovation (Salicru & Chelliah, 2014).

The next section examines the leadership imperatives for moving confidently and successfully into the future.

Imperatives for Moving Forward

In moving forward, five key imperatives must be taken into account. First, the strong reliance on leadership approaches that were built to succeed in the past should be discontinued. The premise here is that trying to solve tomorrow's problems with today's methods will not work. Similarly, doing more of the same, or with more intensity, is also unlikely to yield different outcomes. A case in point is the competency movement in leadership development which has been referred to as "a repeating refrain that continues to offer an illusory promise to rationalize and simplify the processes of selecting, measuring and developing leaders, yet only reflects a fragment of the complexity that is leadership" (Bolden & Gosling, 2006, p. 148). In fact, the limitations of the competency movement in leadership development were highlighted some time ago (Zenger & Folkman, 2009) yet, to date, most leadership development frameworks still remain competency-based. Naturally, this does not mean that competencies are irrelevant and should be ignored completely. Competencies will still matter (Hernez-Broome & Hughes, 2004) but will be only part of the way forward. A new way of thinking, combined with an understanding of how we have reached the current situation, is required (Harman & Horman, 1993). This includes paying greater attention to the leader's character and integrity (Hernez-Broome & Hughes, 2004).

The second imperative, which builds on the first, relates to the increasingly extreme contexts in which leaders and their stakeholders will have to operate as a result of the explosive nonlinear growth of future challenges (including globalization, hypercomplexity, and wickedness of problems faced by leaders, aging population, migration, increased access to knowledge and education, urbanization, and new technologies). As a result, as predicted by Heifetz et al. (2009), leaders across sectors and industries around the globe face increasing adaptive challenges. Adaptive challenges are distinct from technical challenges. While technical challenges can be solved by the knowledge of experts, tackling adaptive challenges effectively requires the altering of human dimensions such as pace of adjustment, tolerance for conflict, uncertainty and risks, as well as the resilience of the culture and networks of authority and lateral relationships. All these factors are requirements to successfully negotiate the pain and fear of change (Heifetz & Linsky, 2002). Dealing effectively with such adaptive challenges will require a greater focus on "vertical" development, as opposed "horizontal" development (Petrie, 2014). Horizontal development is related to technical learning and is competency-based, which is useful when problems are clearly defined and techniques for solving them are known. Vertical development, in contrast, refers to the mental and emotional staged process individuals progress through to make sense of the world. Hence, vertical development promotes the transformational learning required to deal with adaptive challenges (Heifetz et al., 2009; Kegan & Lahey, 2009).

The third imperative relates to the fact that the leaders of the future will be increasingly global, as opposed to domestic, leaders. Global leaders will be required to influence individuals and groups (who represent diverse cultural/political/institutional systems) to help achieve their corporation's global ambitions, while managing multiplicities, tackling huge challenges, grappling with instability, and navigating ambiguity (Osland, Bird, & Oddou, 2012). To deal effectively with such complex global challenges, global leaders must develop the capacity to innovate and inspire others (House, Dorfman, Javidan, Hanges, & Sully de Luque, 2014).

The fourth imperative, which builds on the previous one, relates to a greater need for creative thinking and innovation. Innovative behavior has been recognized as paramount in today's uncertain global economy (Janssen, 2001). Leaders facing global challenges must develop the capacity to innovate and perform in such a way that fluency and flexibility will be maintained (House et al., 2014). Leadership has been identified as a chief predictor of creativity – the precursor of all innovation (Amabile, Conti, Coon, Lazenby, & Herron, 1996; Krause, 2004; Volmer, Spurk, & Niessen, 2012; Zhang & Bartol, 2010).

The fifth imperative, which is a strong recurring theme in the literature, is that leadership — as alluded to in the previous section — is, above all, a relational phenomenon. Hence, its effectiveness depends on the quality of relationships (Story, Youssef, Luthans, Barbuto, & Bovaird, 2013) and includes the importance of leaders' ethical behavior (Mayer, Aquino, Greenbaum, & Kuenzi, 2012; Schaubroeck et al., 2012), ability to build trust (Schaubroeck, Peng, & Hannah, 2013), and integrity (Bauman, 2013; Kannan-Narasimhan & Lawrence, 2012).

An Actionable Leadership Model to Shape the Future to 2050

In response to the foregoing discussion of future leadership-related concerns, and drawing on research and practical experience of developing leaders globally, it makes perfect sense to frame the needs of future leadership requirements within a psychological contract framework. Building on Salicru and Chelliah's (2014) LPC model, the Global Leadership Psychological Contract (GLPC) offers a holistic, relational, and global model of future leadership. This model is intended to move beyond competency-only approaches to promote leader accountability, integrity, ethics/fairness, and to inspire trust through building stronger stakeholder engagement. This model also takes into account: the greater need for leaders to promote innovative behavior in an increasingly competitive, complex, and uncertain world (De Jong & Den Hartog, 2007, 2010; Vaccaro, Jansen, Van Den Bosch, & Volberda, 2012); predictions of growth and the need to build global leadership (Bersin & Deloitte, 2013); and findings related to leader expectations across cultures which derive from the GLOBE project — a leadership research project involving 62 cultures across all regions of the world that was first conceived in 1991 and formally began in 1993 (House et al., 2014). In doing so, the GLPC addresses the risks outlined at the beginning of this chapter and assists in dealing with the resulting potential world scenarios also outlined earlier.

The GLPC model comprises the following four components: (1) the leader's promise or nature of the deal; (2) the delivery of the deal or health of the contract; (3) the leader's impact or consequences of the contract; and (4) final outcomes and results. The model is graphically represented in Figure 1.

The first component, the leader's promise to the stakeholders, followers, or constituents, is central to the PC leaders have with their constituents. Consciously or not, leaders convey a promise (expectations of future action) via their espoused principles/values

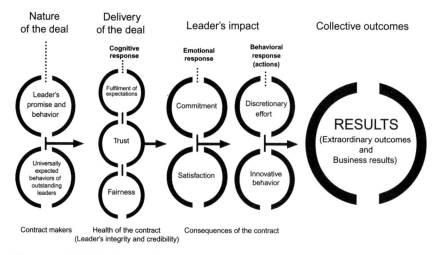

Figure 1.   Global Leadership Psychological Contact (GLPC).

or written statements (the nature of the deal). While most often implicit and unwritten, such expectations, which include universally expected behaviors of outstanding leaders (House et al., 2014), have a strong promissory nature, are pervasive and govern the quality of relationship between leaders and their stakeholders.

The second component, the delivery of the deal, indicates two things: the quality of the delivery of the leader's promise and the health of the contract. This component is determined by the followers' perceptions of congruence between the leaders' promise, espoused principles/values (the nature of the deal), and the leaders' actual behavior or values in action (the delivery of the deal). Followers assess the nature of this gap by asking themselves questions such as: Are our leaders walking their talk? Are they delivering what they promised? Are they transparent, ethical and trustworthy? This component is operationalized using three indicators: fulfillment of expectations; trust – that is, the level of trust followers have in their leader; and fairness – that is, how equitable or impartial followers believe their leader to be. This triple assessment made by followers determines the degree of integrity and credibility they attribute to their leaders.

The third component identifies the impact that leaders have on their followers and determines the consequences of the contract. The impact on followers includes two different types of responses to the previous component (the health of the contract): followers' emotional and behavioral responses. The emotional response is operationalized by measuring the followers' levels of commitment to, and satisfaction with, their leader. The behavioral response is operationalized by measuring the followers' levels of discretionary effort and innovation. Discretionary effort relates to individuals' behaviors that go beyond the call of duty, exceeding standard demands, requirements, or expectations. Innovation refers to creative thinking and innovative behavior which depends on individuals' orientation toward change and likelihood to generate and/or adopt new ideas and/or practices as well as their perseverance in engaging in higher levels of thinking and the promotion and implementation of new and promising ideas.

The fourth component refers to the final collective outcomes which include the specific results achieved by a group, organization, or community. Such results take the form of extraordinary performance, as opposed to mediocre or expected performance, as they relate to accomplishments that are unprecedented. They are attributable to the focused and relentless commitment and creative thinking and innovative actions unleashed by the intense identification with, and emotional bonding between, leaders and followers – the essence of the GLPC. Truly extraordinary outcomes are about "moving mountains." A prerequisite in achieving these spectacular results is that the GLPC is intact – that is, when followers perceive their leaders have upheld or exceeded their promises or obligations. Incidentally, this also creates high levels of follower engagement and low turnover. Conversely, unmet followers' expectations translate into a breach or violation of the GLPC. Perceived violations generate low levels of trust, commitment, satisfaction, effort, and lack of innovation. In turn, this produces low levels of follower engagement, poor performance, unsatisfactory results and, depending on the context, could represent loss of employees, follower support, stakeholder membership, or constituent votes.

In summary, the GLPC aims at balancing the power and diverse interests between leaders and their constituents, followers, or stakeholders within the context of the impending techno-socio-economic revolution. In doing so, this model promotes greater leader accountability, transparency, and integrity; leader-follower emotional connection and satisfaction; collective relentless effort, creative thinking, and innovation.

Conclusion

This chapter has explored the leadership that will be required in 2050 by pondering on past leadership failures, current leadership challenges, future trends, and the new context for leading (and following) in the decades to come, including a myriad of anticipated adaptive challenges. By distilling the latest thinking on leadership from scholars, experts, and practitioners, and by looking to the needs of the future, a relational and outcome driven model of global leadership has been presented. This model will enable leaders to meet these current and emerging challenges and to gain the respect and credibility required to lead with high-level purpose and unprecedented levels of integrity. Such leadership will unleash constituents' highest levels of connectedness, creativity, innovation, grit, decisiveness, and bold collective action. Finally, it is important to highlight that the GLPC model is offered as a way to prevent potentially devastating world events in 2050. The GLPC model provides the mental software and a set of practices needed to equip individuals to lead and follow in ways that will unite, enrich, and allow a collective shaping of the world, to better the human condition and to create a worthwhile legacy for future generations.

References

Amabile, T. M., Conti, R., Coon, H., Lazenby, J., & Herron, M. (1996). Assessing the work environment for creativity. *The Academy of Management Journal, 39*(5), 1154–1184.

Avolio, B. J., Sosik, J. J., Kahai, S. S., & Baker, B. (2014). E-leadership: Re-examining transformations in leadership source and transmission. *The Leadership Quarterly, 25*(1), 105–131.

Bauman, D. C. (2013). Leadership and the three faces of integrity. *The Leadership Quarterly, 24*, 414–426.

Bersin, & Deloitte. (2013). *Predictions for 2014: Building a strong talent pipeline for the global economic recovery.* Deloitte Consulting LLP. Retrieved from http://www.cdmn.ca/wp-content/uploads/2014/02/C-inetpub-wwwroot-Prod-uploadedFiles-122013PSGP.pdf. Accessed on April 17, 2014.

Bolden, R. (2011). Distributed leadership in organizations: A review of theory and research. *International Journal of Management Reviews, 13*(3), 251–269.

Bolden, R., & Gosling, J. (2006). Leadership competencies: Time to change the tune? *Leadership, 2*(2), 147–163.

Chang, H. T., Hsu, H. M., Liou, J. W., & Tsai, C. T. (2013). Psychological contracts and innovative behavior: A moderated path analysis of work engagement and job resources. *Journal of Applied Social Psychology, 43*(10), 2120–2135.

Contractor, N. S., DeChurch, L. A., Carson, J. B., Carter, D. R., & Keegan, B. (2012). The topology of collective leadership. *The Leadership Quarterly, 23*(6), 994–1011.

Conway, N., & Briner, R. B. (2005). *Understanding psychological contracts at work: A critical evaluation of theory and research.* Oxford: Oxford University Press.

Crevani, L., Lindgren, M., & Packendorff, J. (2007). Shared leadership: A post-heroic perspective on leadership as a collective construction. *International Journal of Leadership Studies, 3*(1), 40–67.

Cullen, K. L., Palus, C. J., Chrobot-Mason, D., & Appaneal, C. (2012). Getting to 'We': Collective leadership development. *Industrial & Organizational Psychology, 5*(4), 428–432.

Day, D. V., Fleenor, J. W., Atwater, L. E., Sturm, R. E., & McKee, R. A. (2014). Advances in leader and leadership development: A review of 25 years of research and theory. *The Leadership Quarterly, 25*(1), 63–82.

De Jong, J., & Den Hartog, D. (2007). How leaders influence employees' innovative behaviour. *European Journal of Innovation Management, 10*(1), 41−64.

De Jong, J., & Den Hartog, D. (2010). Measuring innovative work behaviour. *Creativity & Innovation Management, 19*(1), 23−36.

Earley, P. C., & Ang, S. (2003). *Cultural intelligence: Individual interactions across cultures*. Stanford, CA: Stanford University Press.

Guest, D. E. (1998). Is the psychological contract worth taking seriously? *Journal of Organisational Behavior, 19*(1), 649−664.

Gurdjian, P., Halbeisen, T., & Lane, K. (2014). Why leadership-development programs fail. *McKinsey Quarterly*, January. Retrieved from http://www.mckinsey.com/insights/leading_in_the_21st_century/why_leadership-development_programs_fail. Accessed on April 17, 2015

Hamilton, W. D. (1996). *Narrow roads of gene land vol. 1: Evolution of social behaviour*. Oxford: Oxford University Press.

Harman, W., & Horman, J. (1993). The breakdown of the old paradigm. In M. Ray & A. Rinzler (Eds.), *The new paradigm in business: Emerging strategies for leadership and organizational change* (pp. 16−27). New York, NY: G.P. Putnam's Sons.

Heifetz, R. A., & Linsky, M. (2002). *Leadership on the line: Staying alive through the dangers of leading*. Boston, MA: Harvard Business School Press.

Heifetz, R. A., Linsky, M., & Grashow, A. (2009). *The practice of adaptive leadership: Tools and tactics for changing your organization and the world*. Boston, MA: Harvard Business Press.

Hernez-Broome, G., & Hughes, R. L. (2004). Leadership development: Past, present, and future. *Human Resource Planning, 27*(1), 24−32.

Hoch, J. (2013). Shared leadership and innovation: The role of vertical leadership and employee integrity. *Journal of Business & Psychology, 28*(2), 159−174.

Holt, K., & Seki, K. (2012). Global leadership: A developmental shift for everyone. *Industrial and Organizational Psychology, 5*, 196−215. doi:1754-9426/12

House, R. J., Dorfman, P. W., Javidan, M., Hanges, P. J., & Sully de Luque, M. F. (2014). *Strategic leadership across cultures: GLOBE study of CEO leadership behavior and effectiveness in 24 countries*. Thousand Oaks, CA: Sage.

Hunt, J. G., & Dodge, G. E. (2000). Leadership déjà vu all over again. *Leadership Quarterly, 11*(4), 435−458.

Hunter, S. T., Cushenbery, L., Fairchild, J., & Boatman, J. (2012). Partnerships in leading for innovation: A dyadic model of collective leadership. *Industrial & Organizational Psychology, 5*(4), 424−428.

Janssen, O. (2001). Fairness perceptions as a moderator in the curvilinear relationships between job demands, and job performance and job satisfaction. *Academy of Management Journal, 44*(5), 1039−1050.

Kannan-Narasimhan, R., & Lawrence, B. (2012). Behavioral integrity: How leader referents and trust matter to workplace outcomes. *Journal of Business Ethics, 111*(2), 165−178.

Karp, T., & Helgø, T. (2008). The future of leadership: The art of leading people in a "post-managerial" environment. *Foresight, 10*(2), 30−37.

Kegan, R., & Lahey, L. L. (2009). *Immunity to change: How to overcome it and unlock the potential in yourself and your organization*. Boston, MA: Harvard Business Press.

Krause, D. E. (2004). Influence-based leadership as a determinant of the inclination to innovate and of innovation-related behaviors: An empirical investigation. *The Leadership Quarterly, 15*(1), 79−102.

Lenski, G., Lenski, J., & Nolan, P. (1991). *Human societies: An introduction to macrosociology* (7th ed.). New York, NY: McGraw-Hill Book Company.

Mayer, D. M., Aquino, K., Greenbaum, R. L., Kuenzi, M. (2012). Who displays ethical leadership, and why does it matter? An examination of antecedents and consequences of ethical leadership. *Academy of Management Journal, 55*(1), 151–171.

McDermott, A. M., Conway, E., Rousseau, D. M., & Flood, P. C. (2013). Promoting effective psychological contracts through leadership: The missing link between HR strategy and performance. *Human Resource Management, 52*(2), 289–310.

Mendenhall, M. E., Reiche, B. S., Bird, A., & Osland, J. S. (2012). Defining the 'global' in global leadership. *Journal of World Business, 47*(4), 493–503.

Modelski, G. (1987). *Long cycles in world politics*. Seattle, WA: University of Washington Press.

Mumford, M. D., Friedrich, T. L., Vessey, W. B., & Ruark, G. A. (2012). Collective leadership: Thinking about issues vis-à-vis others. *Industrial and Organizational Psychology, 5*(4), 408–411.

Naisbitt, J. (1984). *Megatrends: Ten new directions transforming our lives*. New York, NY: Warner Books.

National Intelligence Council. (2012). *Global trends 2030: Alternative worlds*. Washington, DC: US Government Printing Office. Retrieved from http://publicintelligence.net/global-trends-2030/

Ng, K. Y., Dyne, L. V., & Ang, S. (2012). Cultural intelligence: A review, reflections, and recommendations for future research. In A. M. Ryan, F. T. L. Leong, & F. L. Oswald (Eds.), *Conducting multinational research: Applying organizational psychology in the workplace* (pp. 29–58). Washington, DC: American Psychological Association.

Oc, B., & Bashshur, M. R. (2013). Followership, leadership and social influence. *The Leadership Quarterly, 24*(6), 919–934.

Osland, J., Bird, A., & Oddou, G. (2012). The context of expert global leadership. In W. H. Mobley, Y. Wang, & M. Li (Eds.), *Advances in global leadership* (Vol. 7, pp. 107–124). Oxford, MA: Elsevier.

Park, M. J. (2014). Leadership 2030: The six megatrends you need to understand to lead your company into the future. *Journal of Applied Management and Entrepreneurship, 19*(2), 137–139.

Petrie, N. (2014). *Future trends in leadership development: The Center for Creative Leadership (CCL)*. Retrieved from http://www.ccl.org/leadership/pdf/research/futuretrends.pdf. Accessed on April 17, 2015.

Rousseau, D. M. (1989). Psychological and implied contracts in organisations. *Employee Responsibilities and Rights Journal, 2*(2), 121–139.

Rousseau, D. M. (1995). *Psychological contracts in organisations: Understanding written and unwritten agreements*. Thousand Oaks, CA: Sage.

Salicru, S., & Chelliah, J. (2014). Messing with corporate heads? Psychological contracts and leadership integrity. *Journal of Business Strategy, 35*(3), 38–46.

Schaubroeck, J. M., Hannah, S. T., Avolio, B. J., Kozlowski, S. W., Lord, R. G., Treviño, L. K., ... Peng, A. C. (2012). Embedding ethical leadership within and across organizational levels. *Academy of Management Journal, 55*(5), 1053–1078.

Schaubroeck, J. M., Peng, A. C., & Hannah, S. T. (2013). Developing trust with peers and leaders: Impact on organizational identification and performance during entry. *Academy of Management Journal, 56*(4), 1148–1168.

Sergi, V., Denis, J. L., & Langley, A. (2012). Opening up perspectives on plural leadership. *Industrial & Organizational Psychology, 5*(4), 403–407. doi:10.1111/j.1754-9434.2012.01468.x

Story, J. S. P., Youssef, C. M., Luthans, F., Barbuto, J. E., & Bovaird, J. (2013). Contagion effect of global leaders' positive psychological capital on followers: Does distance and quality of relationship matter? *The International Journal of Human Resource Management, 24*(13), 2534–2553.

Tainter, J. (1988). *The collapse of complex societies*. Cambridge: Cambridge University Press.

The Economist. (2013). *The world economic forum in Davos: Leaders without followers*. January. Retrieved from http://www.economist.com/blogs/newsbook/2013/01/world-economic-forum-davos#comments. Accessed on April 17, 2015.

Uhl-Bien, M., Riggio, R. E., Lowe, K. B., Carsten, M. K. (2014). Followership theory: A review and research agenda. *The Leadership Quarterly, 25*(1), 83–104.

Vaccaro, I. G., Jansen, J. P., Van Den Bosch, F. A. J., & Volberda, H. W. (2012). Management innovation and leadership: The moderating role of organizational size. *Journal of Management Studies, 49*(1), 28–51.

Vielmetter, G., & Sell, Y. (2014). *Leadership 2030: The six megatrends you need to understand to lead your company into the future*. New York, NY: Amacom.

Volmer, J., Spurk, D., & Niessen, C. (2012). Leader-Member Exchange (LMX), job autonomy, and creative work involvement. *The Leadership Quarterly, 23*, 456–465.

Wilde, O. (2015). *Oscar wilde quotes*. Retrieved from http://www.goodreads.com/author/quotes/3565.Oscar_Wilde

World Economic Forum. (2014a). *Global risks 2014 report*. Geneva: World Economic Forum. Retrieved from http://www3.weforum.org/docs/WEF_GlobalRisks_Report_2014.pdf. Accessed on April 17, 2015

World Economic Forum. (2014b). *Outlook on the Global Agenda 2015*. Geneva: World Economic Forum. Retrieved from http://www3.weforum.org/docs/GAC14/WEF_GAC14_OutlookGlobalAgenda_Report.pdf. Accessed on April 17, 2015

Yammarino, F. J., Salas, E., Serban, A., Shirreffs, K., & Shuffler, M. L. (2012). Collectivistic leadership approaches: Putting the "we" in leadership science and practice. *Industrial and Organizational Psychology, 5*(4), 382–402.

Zenger, J., & Folkman, J. (2009). *The extraordinary leader: Turning good managers into great leaders*. New York, NY: McGraw-Hill.

Zhang, X., & Bartol, K. M. (2010). Linking empowering leadership and employee creativity: The influence of psychological empowerment, intrinsic motivation, and creative process engagement. *Academy of Management Journal, 53*(1), 107–128.

 11 Creative Leadership and Social Intelligence: The Keys to Leading in the Digital Age

Cathleen Clerkin

A ccording to 10-year forecaster Johansen, "we are now in the midst of a threshold decade: our natural, business, organizational, and social systems will reach tipping points of extreme challenge, and some of those systems are likely to break" (Johansen, 2012, p. xix). As we prepare to face these tipping points, leaders must develop new skills and capabilities in order to lead effectively in a changing and quickly accelerating world. However, assumptions about leadership and leadership development are not currently changing rapidly enough to keep up with the changing demands of work environments and cultures (Petrie, 2014). In order for leaders to be successful in 2050, we have to now start changing our approach to leadership.

Why the Digital Revolution Is Changing Leadership

One of the main forces behind the current changes in our world is the digital revolution. The digitalization of information has provided us with more quick access to knowledge than ever before. Where once leaders had to consult many different people, institutions, and publications to garner the information necessary to run a business, today, much of the information we seek is available 24/7 on the internet and via cloud computing. The positive effects of this are exponential, allowing leaders to catch errors, resolve conflict, learn, and make informed decisions. But there is a trade-off for this convenience. The digital age is also responsible for a great deal of today's complexity and volatility. The rapid increases in new technologies and emerging global markets have made businesses less stable and less predictable, while also cultivating a work climate that never clocks out.

DIGITALIZATION REQUIRES US TO RETHINK LEADERSHIP DEVELOPMENT

Traditionally, leadership programs tend to treat leaders as static systems which can be programed with the same code to produce identical desired outcomes. This mind-as-computer analogy has limited how we think of developing leaders, resulting in leadership programs that are past-focused and fractured. In other words, leadership development programs generally analyze what specific skillsets have been effective in the past, rather than what will be needed in the future, and examine thin slices of leadership skills rather than looking at leadership as a holistic and dynamic role (Ruderman, Clerkin, & Connolly, 2014). This strategy is no longer effective in the digital age.

In a recent field study, leadership scholar Petrie spent a year interviewing 30 leadership experts on the future trends of leadership development (2014). The experts believed that the work environment is changing at a fundamental level (due in part to new technologies, information overload, and new values and expectations), and that leadership development methods have not changed enough to accommodate for this transformation. In particular, they reported that content-heavy training which focuses on strategies that have been effective in the past are increasingly misaligned with the leadership challenges of the future (Petrie, 2014). This gap points to a larger systemic issue that we are facing in this threshold decade: the digital revolution requires us to rethink how we approach leadership education.

Typically, education systems reflect the needs and structure of society. Therefore, it makes sense that education during the industrial revolution resembled assembly lines that prized math and science, followed by the humanities, and then the arts (Diamandis & Kotler, 2012). However, in the digital age, this old system is no longer effective for success. Fact-based learning is not important in today's culture of digital information (Makel, 2009). Success today requires moving away from rote knowledge and moving toward developing hands-on, practical skillsets that cannot be easily programmed, Googled, or replaced.

DIGITIZATION HAS DECREASED THE VALUE OF INFORMATION

Traditionally, one of the privileges of being in charge was having access to information, and one of the ways to earn leadership status was by garnering knowledge. Our entire education system is built on the premise of transferring information to deserving minds. Universities were created as a centralized location to pass knowledge down from one generation to the next. But today, information is everywhere. Thanks to the World Wide Web, people of all ages and backgrounds can learn new skillsets and access information at any time. When the internet first went public in the early 1990s, around 1% of Americans had access to it; today, around 85% of Americans (and 40% of the entire world) are internet users (DataBank, 2014).

Because of this, the internet has been called the greatest self-improvement tool in history (Diamandis & Kotler, 2012). It also has made information cheap. As information becomes increasingly easy to access, facts and rote knowledge will become less important to leadership success. After all, why spend months taking an MBA class on how to balance a finance spreadsheet when you can just Google it? Conversely, the information era has also boosted the demand of certain skillsets and capabilities. Internet searches do little to cultivate "softer" skills such as social adeptness, open mindedness, or creativity. Thus, it is precisely these types of skills that will be among the most important for leaders as we look toward the midcentury (Diamandis & Kotler, 2012; Goleman, 2008; Johansen, 2012; Makel, 2009; Petrie, 2014).

DIGITIZATION HAS MADE PEOPLE REPLACEABLE

Another important factor when it comes to leadership is that the digitization of information has increased the ability for technology to replace humans for a variety of jobs and tasks. Up until recently, computers, robotics, and other data-based programs were limited to answering yes/no questions, solving limited problems with clear and rigid rules, and completing tasks that were routine and repetitive (Levy & Murnane, 2004). Consequently, the only "job prospects" for computers were entry level, or blue collar positions, such as the self-check-out lines in grocery stores or assisting with factory assembly lines. But today, "big data" and the wealth of digital information are beginning to change this. For instance, in 2011, Watson, a room-sized IBM supercomputer, made history by beating out two (human) trivia champions and winning *Jeopardy* (IBM, 2014). Within the last few years, computers have also successfully been used for other complex problem solving challenges such as detecting fraud quicker than human accountants, and diagnosing medical illnesses with the accuracy of a skilled doctor (Economist, 2014).

In 2013, researchers at the University of Oxford released a report on the future of employment, analyzing how susceptible over 700 different occupations would be to computerization (Frey & Osborne, 2013). The report concluded that about 47% of US employment can be considered at high risk of becoming computerized within the next 20 years (it is important to note that computerization also creates new jobs, so it is unlikely that the unemployment rates will change drastically). The researchers also identified three "engineering bottlenecks" that currently inhibit the computerization of careers: *perception and manipulation* (e.g., physical flexibility, dexterity, and balance), *creative intelligence* (e.g., artistic ability, originality, and cognitive flexibility), and *social intelligence* (e.g., persuasion and negotiation, social adeptness, and caregiving) (Frey & Osborne, 2013). These skillsets highlight the attributes that are most uniquely human, and least likely to be replaced by technology. In particular, this chapter will focus on two of these broad capabilities which stand out as imperative for leadership in the age of digital information: *our ability to create and innovate*, and *our ability to connect with others as social beings*.

Creating and Innovating in the Digital Age

According to urban studies theorist Florida (2005), technology and globalization has transformed the world from an industrial economy into a creative economy, and creative ideas and innovation have become the new international currency. Creativity can be defined as new ideas that are original and add value; while innovation is the implementation of these ideas (Amabile, 1988). As previously mentioned, human creativity is extremely hard for technology to duplicate (Frey & Osborne, 2013). This is because, while the information superhighway is effective for finding established ideas and products, the ability to create something new still largely relies on the human mind. Hence, creativity has been proclaimed one of the most important business skills for the next century, and the "ultimate resource" in a technology-and-information-based culture (Diamandis & Kotler, 2012).

Notably, not only does digitalization call for increased creativity, it also increases the potential to create and innovate. According to the *creative cognition approach*, creativity requires people to have access to diverse knowledge systems (Ward, Smith, & Finke, 1999).

This is because every knowledge system provides one way to accomplish a task, thus, access to multiple knowledge systems presents a variety of solutions and allows for the recombination of elements into something new. Consider the following example. When Dutch and English traders explored China in the 1600s, they encountered a new type of sauce made of fermented fish that would not go bad on long journeys. They brought this information back to Europe, and combined it with their knowledge of European sauces to create new versions of this "koe-chiap" ("fish pickle sauce") from ingredients such as mushroom, walnut, and oyster (Gandhi, 2013). About 200 years later, the recipe traveled to the United States, where people added tomatoes and sugar to the recipe and tomato ketchup was born (Gandhi, 2013).

The creation of modern-day ketchup demonstrates how globalization and diverse knowledge systems can lead to innovation. However, this invention took centuries, largely due to how slow information traveled. Today, globalization and instant information means that we have unprecedented and constant access to different knowledge systems and thus, we currently have the possibility for more creativity than ever before. Consider the case of Jack Andraka. At only 15 years old, Jack won Intel's International Science and Engineering fair by inventing a new method to test for pancreatic cancer using filter paper, carbon nanotubes, and protein antibodies. He said he figured out how to create the test largely based on information he found on Google, Wikipedia, and YouTube (ascp.org, 2012). Jack did not have any exclusive access to information, nor was he an expert on pancreatic cancer. What Jack possessed was creativity. This allowed him to recombine existing materials, methods, and information in a way that produced something new and useful.

CULTIVATING CREATIVE LEADERSHIP

While creativity is important to future success in general, it is crucial when it comes to leadership. Creativity has been shown to be central to leadership effectiveness, especially during times of change or uncertainty (Bennis & Biederman, 1997). Consequently, creative leadership will be needed to survive our current "threshold decade" in which change and uncertainty is expected to increase (Johansen, 2012). Case in point, IBM recently asked more than 1500 CEOs from 60 countries and 33 industries which leadership skills they believed would be most important in the future. They reported that creativity is the number one most important skill for future leaders (IBM, 2010). This is not an anomaly. Creativity and innovation are some of the most commonly mentioned skills when it comes to new trends in leadership (e.g., Criswell & Martin, 2007; Johansen,

2012). By 2050, the successful leaders are likely to be the most creative ones.

However, creativity and innovation are also areas in which many leaders and organizations currently struggle. In a recent survey, 485 leaders from around the globe were asked about innovation in their organizations (Clerkin & Cullen, 2014). Sixty-two percent of leaders agreed that innovation is "very important" to the success of their companies; however, only 14% believed that their organizations were "very effective" at innovation. Interestingly, around three-fourths of leaders said that their organizations have tried to improve innovation in the workplace, but many have been ineffective. Among organizations that struggled with innovation, respondents pointed to lack of culture that supports innovation, and lack of leadership around innovation as the two biggest setbacks.

This creativity-gap highlights the fact that most leadership development and executive training programs have not yet incorporated creativity into their curriculums (Petrie, 2014). There are likely two reasons for this. First, industrialized notions of education still perceive creativity to be an elective skillset — one that is nice but not necessary to succeed (Makel, 2009). Second, culturally, we tend to see creativity as a gift, a talent, or an innate ability. People self-categorize as the "creative type" or not, which then leads to the incorrect perception that creativity does not need to be — or cannot be — taught or learned (Plucker, Beghetto, & Dow, 2004).

These belief systems need to change if we are going to develop creative leaders in the future. Creativity needs to be a fundamental facet of education — especially when it comes to leadership development. Research shows that creativity is an ability that can be learned, developed, and enhanced; and that many people's apparent "lack" of creativity is due to the fact that they have not worked to cultivate it (Shalley & Gilson, 2004). Creativity takes practice and first-hand experience. Leaders should take the time to cultivate their own creativity, such as exploring a new hobby, or perhaps, reclaiming a long lost one. Additionally, practitioners should consider how they can bring creativity into the classroom.

Connecting with Others in the Digital Age

In addition to creativity, one other facet of leadership that is virtually irreplaceable by technology is the human connection (Frey & Osborne, 2013). This is because — as humans — we are uniquely wired to respond to other human beings (Lieberman, 2013). The latest neuroscience research has proven that during social interactions, human brains "interlock" in such a way that the patterns of neurons firing in one person's brain can actually influence the firing of neurons in the other person's brain (Goleman, 2006). This, in turn, allows us to affect other people's thoughts, emotions, and even physical and mental health. For instance, during stressful situations, our brains become calmer (i.e., threat-related neural activation decreases) when someone holds our hand, and this effect becomes stronger when our hand is held by a loving partner (Coan, Schaefer, & Davidson, 2006). Similarly, research shows that positive physical contact (such as hugging) and perceived social support can buffer against stress and illness (Cohen, Janicki-Deverts, Turner, & Doyle, 2015).

This new understanding of social interactions has important implications for the digital age. Unlike computers and artificial intelligences, which are programed around data and if/then commands, humans are uniquely designed to adapt and change in response to others. We are able to "catch" other people's emotions, read subtle facial expressions and vocal tones, and even rewire neural connections based on social interactions (Goleman, 2006). Therefore humans have the ability to influence others in ways that artificial intelligence will probably never be able to.

Yet paradoxically, the digital age has also led to a decrease in social interpersonal interactions. Where once people would talk to the person next to them in line, on the bus, or at a bar, now we stare at our smart phones or tablets and barely acknowledge the people who surround us. This is particularly notable considering that social skills and social adeptness takes time and repeated practice in order to master (Snow, 2009). Because of this, experts predict that interpersonal capabilities – or "social intelligence" – is likely to decrease in the future if we are not careful and do not make an effort to cultivate it (Goleman, 2006, 2013).

STRENGTHENING LEADERS' SOCIAL INTELLIGENCE

Social intelligence can be defined as the capability to understand other people and engage in adaptive social interactions, and is the key to making effective human connections (Thorndike, 1920). Social intelligence is of particular importance for leaders because leadership is inherently social and requires the ability to build strong interpersonal relationships with others. Socially intelligent leaders have strong conversation and listening skills, a keen understanding of social roles and rules, confidence in interacting with different types of people, and a fine-tuned ability to understand others' thoughts and feelings (Cantor & Kihlstrom, 1987; Riggio & Murphy, 2002). According to Goleman, author of *Social Intelligence: The New Science of Human Relationships*: self-mastery can lead to outstanding individual performance, but social intelligence is required for outstanding leadership (Goleman, 2008).

Consider the following: In the 1950s, a girl was born to a single teen mother in Mississippi. She grew up in poverty, was passed between care-givers, survived repeated sexual assault, and was nearly sent to a juvenile detention home. Today, she is the richest African American in the world and the first black woman to make the *Forbes* billionaire list (Academy of Achievement, 2013; Nsehe, 2012, 2014). How did Oprah Winfrey manage this transformation? Obviously, she was intelligent, capable, hardworking, and tenacious. However, by all accounts, "the foundation of her success is said to be the ability to connect on a personal level with audiences" (Vitale & Palmer-Mehta, 2010, p. 619). Unsurprisingly, Oprah is often cited as the paragon of success via social intelligence (Seligman, 2004).

Empirical evidence also shows that social intelligence is a strong predictor of both leadership experience and leadership success (Kobe, Reiter-Palmon, & Rickers, 2001). For example, a recent study by the executive recruitment firm Egon Zehnder International, examined the reasons behind hiring and firing of CEOs. They found that CEOs were most often hired based on ambition, intelligence, and business expertise, but were most commonly fired when they lacked social skills and the ability to work well with others (Goleman, 2008). This is consistent with research from the Center for Creative Leadership which shows that across decades of data, the number one predictor of leader derailment (i.e., when leaders are fired, demoted, or held on a career plateau) is "an inability to relate to people in meaningful ways" (Chappelow & Leslie, 2001, p. 7).

Importantly for leaders and leadership development, research shows that social intelligence can be learned and developed. For instance, leaders can become more socially intelligent by simply practicing attending to other people and interpreting social cues. Studies have shown that skills such as empathy, active listening, reading non-verbal information (e.g., body language, facial expressions, tone of voice), and picking up on cultural differences all improve with training (Earley & Ang, 2003; Gentry, Weber, & Sadri, 2007; Lieberman, 2013; Snow, 2009).

Leaders can also strengthen their social intelligence through practicing awareness and control over their own minds. When leaders become more aware of their own thought processes, emotions, and internal states, they are better able to control their reactions and become more mindful in their interactions with others (Ruderman et al., 2014). Renowned psychiatrist Siegel calls this *mindsight*: the ability to observe mental processes and "the capacity to perceive the mind in yourself and others" (Siegel, 2010, p. x). Siegel argues that mindsight is the basis for all social intelligence. Indeed, research has shown that various contemplative practices such as mindsight, mindfulness, and meditation have positive effects on awareness, perspective-taking, and emotional regulation – abilities that contribute to social intelligence (Holzel et al., 2011; Siegel, 2010).

Leaders would greatly benefit if executive and leadership training programs spent more time strengthening social intelligence and social connections as part of leadership development. Additionally, leadership programs that are designed with interpersonal connection in mind may also see an increase in motivation and information retention. Research shows that students who feel socially connected in the classroom perform better; and that people are more likely to remember information when their brains' social neural networks are engaged (Lieberman, 2013).

Leading Others' Creativity and Social Connections

The empirical and theoretical evidence outlined above suggests that creativity and social intelligence will become increasingly desirable skillsets for leaders as we look toward 2050. But above and beyond this, leaders will also likely become increasingly responsible for leading creativity and human connections among their teams and organizations. As teams become increasingly global and virtual, and economies become increasingly creative, contributors will turn to leaders for creative direction and social facilitation. Managers and leaders have the ability to influence the creativity of their subordinates both directly through their behaviors, practices, support, and instructions, and indirectly through their influence on the culture and context of the working environment (Carmeli, Gelbard, & Reiter-Palmon, 2013; Shalley & Gilson, 2004). Similarly, subordinates tend to follow the social cues and norms set by their leaders, which allows leaders to influence the social connectivity of their workgroups (Goleman, 2013).

However, learning to cultivate both creativity and social connection among teams may be easier said than done. There is reason to believe that creativity can sometimes be at odds with social connection. Research has shown that highly creative people tend to be intelligent, imaginative, ambitious, and open – but also individualistic, domineering, arrogant, competitive, and have low emotional stability and sociability (Martinsen, 2011; Reiter-Palmon, de Vreede, & de Vreede, 2013). Because of this, creative people may have difficulties collaborating, working with others, and taking supervision (Reiter-Palmon et al., 2013). Conversely, individuals and teams who are overly focused on harmony and collaboration may limit their creative potential, given that group creativity is aided by diverse viewpoints and challenging the status quo (e.g., Page, 2008).

This apparent paradox highlights the key role of leaders in striking a balance between creative and socially intelligent organizations. Future leadership development programs should train leaders on how to strengthen both creativity and social intelligence without damaging each other. One potential way to do this could be to train leaders in mindfulness, which has been demonstrated to facilitate both creativity and social intelligence simultaneously (Marturano, 2014; Ostafin & Kassman, 2012). Another possibility is to train leaders in participatory leadership techniques, which have been shown to be effective for facilitating collaboration among creative individuals (Reiter-Palmon et al., 2013).

Finally, future leadership development programs need to expand beyond strictly information-and-rote-knowledge based classes, and begin to develop more holistic, dynamic, and experiential-based approaches in order to effectively facilitate creativity and connection. Both leadership experts and technology experts agree that the future of education needs to be applied, decentralized, personal, and interactive (Diamandis & Kotler, 2012; Petrie, 2014). Excitingly, modern technology actually allows for more sophisticated personalization and experience-based learning and delivery than ever before (e.g., blended learning, interactive video games, apps, biofeedback, etc.). In today's complex and volatile business world, leadership development needs to be hands-on: leaders must practice being creative, attempt new innovations, learn to be mindful, and exercise their abilities to pick up social cues in order to become successful in the future.

Summary and Conclusion

The digitalization of information has made knowledge easy, fast, and cheap. By and large, this digital revolution has benefited leaders and businesses. However, it is also changing the skillsets that are most important to success as we look toward the midcentury. In particular, the digitalization of information has made rote information less valuable and routine skills replaceable. Because of this, abilities to that are not easily programmable − such as the ability to create and innovate and the ability to connect to others as social beings, will become some of the most important skills in the future of business and leadership. Notably, research shows that leaders are in a unique position to help cultivate and facilitate both creativity and social connection in their organizations. However, these skillsets are not yet typically emphasized in most leadership development programs. Thus, as we look toward 2050, leaders and practitioners need to begin rethinking traditional leadership development in order to develop the creative and socially connected leadership skills that will be needed in the near future.

References

Amabile, T. M. (1988). A model of creativity and innovation in organizations. *Research in organizational behavior*, 10(1), 123–167.

ASCP. (2012). *Jack Andraka's recipe to make a difference in the world: YouTube, Google, Wikipedia, a Laboratory*. American Society for Clinical Pathology. Retrieved from ascp.org

Bennis, W., & Biederman, P. W. (1997). *Organizing genius. The secrets of creative collaboration*. Reading, MA: Addison Wesley.

Cantor, N., & Kihlstrom, J. F. (1987). *Personality and social intelligence*. Englewood Cliffs, N.J.: Prentice-Hall.

Carmeli, A., Gelbard, R., & Reiter-Palmon, R. (2013). Leadership, creative problem solving capacity, and creative performance: The importance of knowledge sharing. *Human Resource Management*, 52, 95–122.

Chappelow, C., & Leslie, J. B. (2001). Throwing the right switches: How to keep your executive career on track. *Leadership in Action*, 20(6), 6–9.

Clerkin, C., & Cullen, K. (2014). *Innovation leadership solutions*. Unpublished raw data. Center for Creative Leadership.

Coan, J. A., Schaefer, H. S., & Davidson, R. J. (2006). Lending a hand: Social regulation of the neural response to threat. *Psychological Science*, 17(12), 1032–1039.

Cohen, S., Janicki-Deverts, D., Turner, R. B., & Doyle, W. J. (2015). Does hugging provide stress-buffering social support? A study of susceptibility to upper respiratory infection and illness. *Psychological Science*, 26(2), 135–147.

Criswell & Martin. (2007). *10 trends: A study of senior executives' views on the future*. Center for Creative Leadership White Paper.

DataBank. (2014). *The World Bank*. Retrieved from http://databank.worldbank.org/data/home.aspx. Accessed on April 17, 2015.

Diamandis, P. H., & Kotler, S. (2012). *Abundance: The future is better than you think*. New York, NY: Simon and Schuster.

Earley, P. C., & Ang, S. (2003). *Cultural intelligence: Individual interactions across cultures*. Redwood City, CA: Stanford University Press.

Economist. (2014). Coming to an office near you: The effect of today's technology on tomorrow's jobs will be immense—and no country is ready for it. *The Economist*. Retrieved from http://www.economist.com/news/leaders/21594298-effect-todays-technology-tomorrows-jobs-will-be-immenseand-no-country-ready. Accessed on April 17, 2015.

Florida, R. (2005). *The flight of the creative class: The new global competition for talent*. New York, NY: Harper Business.

Frey, C. B., & Osborne, M. A. (2013). *The future of employment: How susceptible are jobs to computerisation*. Oxford Martin School, Working Report.

Gandhi, L. (2013). Ketchup: The all-American condiment that comes from Asia. *National Public Radio*. Retrieved from http://www.npr.org/blogs/codeswitch/

2013/12/02/248195661/ketchup-the-all-american-condiment-that-comes-from-asia. Accessed on April 17, 2015.

Gentry, W. A., Weber, T. J., & Sadri, G. (2007). *Empathy in the workplace: A tool for effective leadership*. A Center for Creative Leadership White Paper.

Goleman, D. (2006). *Social Intelligence: The new science of human relationships*. New York, NY: Bantam Books.

Goleman, D. (2008). *Leadership: Social intelligence is essential*. Retrieved from http://www.danielgoleman.info/leadership-social-intelligent-is-essential/. Accessed on April 17, 2015.

Goleman, D. (2013). *Focus: The hidden driver of excellence*. New York, NY: Harper Collins.

Holzel, B. K., Carmody, J., Vangel, M., Congleton, C., Yerramsetti, S. M., Gard, T., & Lazar, S. W. (2011). Mindfulness practice leads to increases in regional brain gray matter density. *Neuroimaging, 191*(1), 36−43.

IBM. (2010). Capitalizing on complexity: Insights from the global chief executive officer study: Executive summary. Somers, NY. Retrieved from http://www-304.ibm.com/businesscenter/cpe/download0/200422/ceostudy_2010.pdf. Accessed on April 17, 2015.

IBM. (2014). *What is Watson*. Retrieved from http://www.ibm.com/smarterplanet/us/en/ibmwatson/what-is-watson.html. Accessed on April 17, 2015.

Johansen, B. (2012). *Leaders make the future: Ten new leadership skills for an uncertain world*. San Francisco, CA: Berrett-Koehler Publishers.

Kobe, L. D., Reiter-Palmon, R., & Rickers, J. D. (2001). Self-reported leadership experiences in relation to inventoried social and emotional intelligence. *Current Psychology, 20*(2), 154.

Levy, F., & Murnane, R. J. (2004). *The new division of labor: How computers are creating the next job market*. Princeton, NJ: Princeton University Press.

Lieberman, M. D. (2013). *Social: Why our brains are wired to connect*. Oxford: Oxford University Press.

Makel, M. C. (2009). Help us creativity researchers, you're our only hope. *Psychology of Aesthetics, Creativity, and the Arts, 3*(1), 38−42.

Martinsen, Ø. L. (2011). The creative personality: A synthesis and development of the creative person profile. *Creativity Research Journal, 23*(3), 185−202.

Marturano, J. (2014). *Finding the space to lead: A practical guide to mindful leadership*. New York, NY: Bloomsbury Press.

Nsehe, M. (2012). The black billionaires 2012. *Forbes*.

Nsehe, M. (2014). The black billionaires 2014. *Forbes*. Retrieved from http://www.forbes.com/sites/mfonobongnsehe/2014/03/04/the-black-billionaires-2014/. Accessed on April 17, 2015.

Oprah Winfrey Biography—Academy of Achievement. (2013). Retrieved from http://www.achievement.org/autodoc/page/win0bio-1. Accessed on April 17, 2015.

Ostafin, B. D., & Kassman, K. T. (2012). Stepping out of history: Mindfulness improves insight problem solving. *Consciousness and Cognition, 21*(2), 1031−1036.

Page, S. E. (2008). *The difference: How the power of diversity creates better groups, firms, schools, and societies*. Princeton, NJ: Princeton University Press.

Petrie, N. (2014). *Future trends in leadership development*. Center for Creative Leadership White Paper.

Plucker, J., Beghetto, R. A., & Dow, G. T. (2004). Why isn't creativity more important to educational psychologists? Potential, pitfalls, and future directions in creativity research. *Educational Psychologist, 39*, 83–96.

Reiter-Palmon, R., de Vreede, T., & de Vreede, G. J. (2013). Leading creative interdisciplinary teams: Challenges and solutions. In S. Hemlin, C. M. Allwood, B. Martin, & M. D. Mumford (Eds.), *Creativity and leadership in science, technology and innovation* (pp. 240–267). New York, NY: Routledge.

Riggio, R. E., & Murphy, S. E. (Eds.). (2002). *Multiple intelligences and leadership.* Mahwah, NJ: Lawrence Erlbaum Associates.

Ruderman, M. N., Clerkin, C., & Connolly, C. (2014). *Leadership development beyond competencies: Moving to a holistic approach.* Center for Creative Leadership White Paper.

Seligman, M. E. P. (2004). *Character strengths and virtues: A handbook and classification.* Washington, DC: American Psychological Association.

Shalley, C. E., & Gilson, L. L. (2004). What leaders need to know: A review of social and contextual factors that can foster or hinder creativity. *The Leadership Quarterly, 15*, 33–53.

Siegel, D. J. (2010). *Mindsight: The new science of personal transformation.* New York, NY: Bantam Books.

Snow, N. (2009). *Virtue as social intelligence: An empirically grounded theory.* New York, NY: Routledge.

Thorndike, E. L. (1920). Intelligence and its use. *Harper's Magazine, 140*, 227–235.

Vitale, D. R., & Palmer-Mehta, V. (2010). Oprah Winfrey. In R. Chapman (Ed.), *Culture wars: An encyclopedia of issues, viewpoints, and voices.* New York, NY: M.E. Sharpe.

Ward, T. B., Smith, S. M., & Finke, R. A. (1999). Creative cognition. In R. J. Sternberg (Ed.), *Handbook of creativity.* New York, NY: Cambridge University Press.

12

The Strategist Competency Model: The Future of Leadership Development

Susan Cannon, Michael Morrow-Fox and Maureen Metcalf

The qualities of effective leadership can be paradoxical – requiring effective leaders to be passionate and unbiased, detailed and strategic, hard driving and sustainable, fact-focused and intuitive, self-confident and selfless – all often at the same time. Such complexity is rarely found in leaders even under optimal conditions. As we move toward 2050, new contexts and conditions are poised to emerge that will create challenges beyond the abilities of most leaders or any single nation to manage. This powerful contextual shift – a time of great stress and constraint – has the potential to drive a new and more complex stage of human culture and consciousness to meet these challenges.

Historically, as new stages of human culture and consciousness have emerged, the requirements for effective leadership have shifted accordingly. Such a shift is already underway in small pockets; in the next few decades, we expect its significance to increase. This shift will call for and catalyze what researchers and scholar-practitioners of adult developmental maturity (developmentalists) call "Strategist" leadership skills (B. Brown, 2011; Cook-Greuter, 2000,

2004, 2013; Cook-Greuter & Soulen, 2007; O'Fallon, 2013;[1] Rooke, 2001; Rooke & Torbert, 2005). Strategist[2] leaders have a world-centric, truly inclusive capacity to see, make meaning, and respond in a way that facilitates consistent, flexible, holistic, meta-systemic, broadly collaborative, and transformative problem-solving that endures even during times of times of stress and constraint. In this chapter, the authors describe research-based probable futures that will require more Strategist leaders, and outline a Strategist Competency Model that will help to cultivate and support Strategist leaders' development.

Future Trends

A review of current literature in futures/foresight studies, research-based scenarios, and think tank and government research on global trends, is sobering. Prominent trends include transnational change drivers such as abrupt climate change, sudden global economic disruption, unsustainable production and consumption that rapidly and dangerously degrades the biosphere, runaway pandemics, spreading armed conflict, including failing states and terrorism, (potentially with weapons of mass destruction), and catastrophic water shortages over large parts of the earth (L. Brown, 2011; Franklin & Andrews, 2012; Gore, 2013; Moore & Rees, 2013; Moran, 2011; National Intelligence Council [NIC], 2012; Organisation for Economic Co-operation and Development [OECD], 2011; Orr, 2013; Randers, 2012; The Arlington Institute [TAI], 2014; United Nations [UN], 2013; World Resource Institute [WRI], 2014; Watson & Freeman, 2012).

These are but a few of the probabilities, any of which could drive myriad secondary trends, such as mass refugee migrations, and the potential collapse of urban population centers due to food and resource supply chain disruption. Despite the challenges, positive indicators also exist. Critical advances are being made in global health (Gore, 2013; Franklin & Andrews, 2012; UN, 2013), women's empowerment (McKinsey & Company, 2013), literacy (UNESCO, 2010), and more freely available, lower-cost, renewable sources of energy (Franklin & Andrews, 2012; OECD, 2012;

---

[1] In O'Fallon's StAGES model, the Strategist is not named directly in the paper but correlates to Stage 4.5, Late Fourth Person Perspective (p. 20). In public presentations of the StAGES model, O'Fallon does use the term Strategist.

[2] Developmentalists have used different terms interchangeably for the Strategist stage, for example, Autonomous or Integral. In this chapter we will use Strategist only.

Randers, 2012; Watson & Freeman, 2012.). In the developing world, extreme poverty is decreasing as middle class segments grow (Franklin & Andrews, 2012; Kupchan, 2012; UN, 2013). Biological advancements have emerged out of the convergence of the Digital Revolution, and the Life Sciences Revolution is on the way to expanding not only our lifespan but also our "healthspan" (Gore, 2013, loc. 4841). Movements such as Transition Towns and permaculture seek to build collective resilience and proliferate sustainable practices in towns and cities. The emergence of "green" or sustainable MBA programs, and the growing acceptance of triple bottom-line approaches in business are signals of a shift in values toward sustainability and sensitivity in the business and economic sector.

The literature varies significantly on projected visions of the future — for example, from technology and a more conscientious capitalism aligning to solve our biosphere and material problems, to a future of self-interested exploitation and breakdown. One point of agreement does exist: unprecedented and disruptive change is upon us for decades to come. Kurzweil (2001), renowned technology forecaster[3] and director of engineering at Google predicts that at the comparative rate for technological change in 2001, the twenty-first century will experience 20,000 times more than did the twentieth century, accelerating techno-economic evolution beyond the ability to reliably forecast. In his recent synthesis of the drivers of global future change, former U.S. Vice President Al Gore noted that there is a clear consensus that "the future now emerging will be extremely different from anything we have ever known ..." (2013, loc. 62). "These emergent revolutionary changes are threatening to overtake us at a moment in history when there is a dangerous vacuum of global leadership" (2013, loc. 74).

Leadership Needed for the Future

This perfect storm of increasing complexity, accelerating change, and near constant uncertainty is creating conditions that exceed the mental and emotional capacities of most leaders (Brown, 2013). According to Rawlings, Smith, and Bencini (in Mayes, 2014), while technology is advancing exponentially, our laws, culture, and social contracts are moving in a linear fashion. The same is true for conventional approaches to leadership development. Four recent global studies on the future needs and gaps of organizational leadership concluded that current leadership lacks the higher ordered skills and capacities to meet the complexity of even today's challenges

---

[3]See Kurzweil (2010) for technology prediction accuracy data.

(Development Dimensions International & The Conference Board [DDI], 2014; Gitsham, 2009; IBM Corporation, 2010; Leslie, 2009). For example, current leaders lack the ability to function in environments that have a high degree of ambiguity and uncertainty, to build cross-cultural strategic relationships, to facilitate collaboration between diverse groups, or to sense the crucial and unspoken undercurrents and relational dynamics in a meeting. The systematic cultivation of such higher ordered capacities in leaders requires more than training — it means they must psychologically evolve to a more complex way of being.

THE DEVELOPMENTAL PERSPECTIVE

The leadership development approach proposed in this chapter is grounded in constructive-developmental psychology. (B. Brown, 2011). In this field, individuals evolve through times of change or stability to stages of greater complexity and capacity. The interpretations, and the frameworks or "constructs" they use to make sense of what is happening, become more complex. Growth occurs in a predictable sequence of stages from birth through adulthood, often likened to an ever-widening spiral (Cook-Greuter & Soulen, 2007). Each later stage is "more differentiated, integrated, flexible and capable of optionally functioning in a rapidly changing and complexifying world," and most importantly, can be "encouraged and facilitated by appropriate support and challenge" (2007, p.184).

In other words, adult psychological capacity or "ego maturity" is developed in a stage progression — if the appropriate conditions are created. Scholar-practitioners in the field of leadership development have defined ego maturity stages of combined cognitive-affective-behavioral growth using accurately measurable, statistically verified instruments (Cook-Greuter, 2000, 2004, 2013; Rooke, 2001; Rooke & Torbert, 1998, 1999, 2005).

RELATIONSHIP BETWEEN LEADERSHIP AND CULTURAL STAGES OF DEVELOPMENT

The stages of a leader's growth have a direct correlation, and thereby a natural fit, with stages of cultural evolution. To understand the leader best suited to the emerging future, we need to look at a brief summary of how leadership and culture have evolved together over time.

Historically, whenever the pressures of "life conditions," or times of stress and constraint, consistently exceed the ability of humans to meet existential challenges, a new and more complex stage of culture and a corresponding advanced stage of adult maturity have emerged. As shown in Table 1, a corresponding new

Table 1: Relationship between Cultural Stage and Leadership.

Cultural Stage[a]	Techno-Economic Era	Social Organization	Adult Maturity Stage[b]	Leader Type Example[c]
Archaic	Hunting and foraging	Clans	Symbiotic	Clan Wo/Man
Tribal	Horticultural	Tribes/Villages	Impulsive	Chieftain
Warrior	Early agricultural	City-state empires	Opportunist/ Egocentric	Emperor/ Dictator
Traditional	Late agricultural	Kingdoms	Conformist	Monarch
Modern	Industrial-scientific	Nation-states	Expert and achiever[d]	Executive
Postmodern	Informational	Virtual-transnational networks	Individualist/ Pluralist	Co-leader
Integral (emerging)	(Post-informational – emerging)	(Global emerging)	Strategist	Meta-system transformer

[a]See McIntosh (2007).
[b]See Cook-Greuter (2013) and Rooke and Torbert (2005); the leading edge stage of adult maturity for that stage of culture; one of a variety of interchangeable terms used by developmentalists to designate that stage.
[c]These leader examples are representative of the leadership paradigm that emerged at the corresponding cultural stage, not the only kind of leader at that stage. No clear leader type existed at the Clan stage, though informal leadership would be taken by a particular Man or Woman given the existing conditions.
[d]The Expert and the Achiever are actually two distinct stages of adult maturity that emerged during the Modern cultural stage, and comprise the majority of organizational managers today (Rooke & Torbert, 2005).

techno-economic era encompassing a wider span of social organization and a new leadership paradigm has resulted (Cannon, 2014). Developmentalists generally agree that approximately five or six such cultural stages have emerged and are still in existence in various parts of the world (Beck & Cowan, 1996; Gebser, 1985; McIntosh, 2007; Wilber, 1996).[4]

Each techno-economic era offered an innovation, a vertical leap typically in modes of technology, communication, and energy, catalyzing out-of-the-box solutions to the thorny problems of human existence that the previous stage was unable to solve. For example, as the nomadic hunting and foraging bands of Archaic culture grew in population, the increasing distance and effort required to gather

---

[4]Although there is general agreement on the nature and number of these cultural stages, the naming conventions can differ between authors. We have chosen the names used by integral philosopher Steve McIntosh (2007).

and hunt sufficient food catalyzed the innovations of horticulture, animal domestication, and permanent settlement.

The new leader that emerged with each cultural stage had the requisite capacities and developmental maturity to reach beyond what came before. For example, someone seeking to become a term-limited Chief Executive of a Modern era nation-state democracy must have the more complex, nuanced, and emotionally intelligent capacity to gather support and communicate with the electorate and representatives in a way that a Traditional era bloodline monarch, ruling by fiat, would not need or understand.

LEADERSHIP FOR 2050: STRATEGIST LEADERS

According to a lineage of past and current developmentalists such as Gebser (1985), Graves (1974), Beck and Cowan (1996), McIntosh (2007), and Wilber (1996, 2001, 2012, 2013), an emerging stage of "Integral Culture" is next on our horizon, with a more flexible, inte-grative, and complex worldview. In December 2013, in his welcome speech to participants of the Integral movement in Russia, Wilber (para. 3) wrote:

> In particular, we are facing, for the first time in human his-tory, the emergence of a truly holistic or integral conscious-ness – meaning a consciousness that is all-inclusive, embracing, caring, pervading, outreaching, enveloping. Never before in humankind's history has this significant a transformation occurred. All previous transformations – each important, to be sure – were nonetheless partial, frag-mented, and excluding – whether magic, mythic, rational, or pluralistic. And yet, starting just a few decades ago, developmentalists began observing the emergence, in rare individuals, of an entirely new type of awareness or new type of consciousness – one that fully appreciated and embraced all earlier stages of development, and did not exclude, marginalize, or attempt to suppress them, but transcended and included them all. Maslow called this self-actualizing; Gebser called it integral-aperspectival; for Loevinger, it was autonomous and integrated; Graves called it systemic. But by whatever name, this consciousness was radically new and altogether revolutionary.

This emerging cultural stage of development structurally corre-lates to the Strategist leader. It is considered the first "Integral" stage, holistically capable of embracing and embodying the tenets of a global worldview. Having internalized systems thinking, "They not only see the interconnected aspects of the external world, but also that of their own meaning making. With the expanded time frame and wider social networks, [these] persons can perceive systemic patterns or long-term trends and are often valued for that 'strategic' capacity and vision" (Cook-Greuter, 2013, p. 63). According to Wilber, "Integral Leadership is very important because, for the first time in history our problems are global, which means that our solutions must be global. When it comes to problemsolving, leadership – and its capacity to influence people and guide them toward these new integral solutions – is crucial" (2012, p. 2).

Strategist leaders are uniquely prepared to navigate the complexities of the future both behaviorally and developmentally. Behaviorally, researchers have identified "Four I's" of effective leadership executed by transformational leaders such as Strategists (Avolio, Waldman, & Yammarino, 1991). These "Four I's" are Individualized consideration, Intellectual stimulation, Inspirational motivation, and Idealized influence, and they are particularly effective at building teams, managing change, increasing individual effectiveness, and strategic planning.

Strategist leaders have been linked to attaining the highest level of business results. In a study of CEOs by Rooke and Torbert (2005), Strategists were found to have the greatest ability to create transformational results for their companies. These transformations included profitability, market share, and reputation over a four-year period. The researchers concluded that "Strategists typically have socially conscious business ideas that are carried out in a highly collaborative manner. They seek to weave together idealist visions with pragmatic, timely initiatives and principled actions" (2005, p. 72).

Equally important as the behaviors and the results, the key to the effectiveness of the Strategist leader is that these behaviors are not born of external prompting or skill mimicking. They are intuitive, innate actions arising from developmental maturity. Strategist leaders don't have to examine innovation because they are innovational, they don't need to ponder transformation because they are transformational, and they don't need to study collaboration because they have become collaborative. This "being" rather than "acting" facilitates a clarity and consistency that endures during times of stress and constraint.

It is not a simple matter to hire a Strategist to fill a leadership position. Rooke and Torbert (2005) claim that only 5 percent of leaders are Strategists. Wilber (2014 cited in Putoshkin, 2014) claims that only about two percent of the world population has reached the Strategist level, though developmentalists predict it could potentially reach 10 percent of world population within another decade. However, this is not a foregone conclusion. In order to fill the need for Strategist leaders able meet the challenges of 2050, much will depend upon the conditions and environments fostered by influential institutions such as business, government, nonprofit, and education to develop them.

Approaches for Leadership Development

Our current leadership development programs are not effective at supporting or developing the Strategist level leaders able to navigate the future. Leadership development has traditionally followed two tracts: horizontal development and vertical development (B. Brown, 2011; Cook-Greuter, & Soulen, 2007). Horizontal development deepens a leader's abilities and skills at a given level of maturity – it adds tools to an existing toolset. The leader acquires new skills and information, but perceives the world in the same limited way. Horizontal programs that teach skills such as crucial communication, situational delegation, and SWOT analysis certainly enhance the abilities of a leader; however, they do very little to transform them. Vertical development advances the ego maturity of the leader, which widens her or his perspective. A vertical development experience, such as Nelson Mandela's years of incarceration and reflection, challenges a leader's view of the world, changes her or his views, and leaves them with more cognitive, affective, and behavioral capability than before. With an increase in the complexity of their consciousness, they perceive the world and respond to it in more skillful, wise, nuanced, and sensitive ways that were not possible before.

Typical leadership development programs are almost exclusively horizontal and do not expose the leaders to experiences that will promote vertical growth (B. Brown, 2011; Cook-Greuter, & Soulen, 2007; Fisher, Merron, & Torbert, 1987). Conditions for vertical development in a leadership program must be created – it does not happen by just sitting in a classroom. Vertical development is a fundamental reorganizing to a higher order of entrenched cognitive-affective-behavioral patterns. The leader literally grows new neural networks.

According to the rapidly advancing field of neuroscience, an individual's feelings, thoughts, and physical movements generate precisely timed electrical signals that travel through a chain of neurons, or nerve fibers. Think of an electrical current moving through a wire. Myelin, a fatty insulation that wraps around these wires (nerve fibers), makes this possible. In *The Talent Code*, Coyle argues that the targeted growth of myelin – not inborn talent – is the key to building new skills and capacities that result in high performance. "The more we fire a particular circuit," says Coyle, "the more myelin optimizes that circuit, and the stronger, faster and more fluent our movements and thoughts become" (2009, p. 32).

Coyle's research with talent hotbeds revealed that myelin grows best through struggle and persistent practice. The metaphoric hero's journey is the neophyte encountering unexpected challenge, failing at first, reorienting and trying again, and finally mastering the new capacities to succeed. Leaders must be willing to go outside their comfort zone, and take on particular challenges that are uniquely theirs.

Practice design is critical. Vertical development requires the ability to reflect on one's experience – for example, thoughts, feelings, bodily sensations, interpretations – to gain insight for change. Reflective practices working with the leaders' actual life experiences and challenges are almost always a constituent. This can include noticing and challenging the unskillful and limiting habits in one's accustomed way of being, and committing to the initial discomfort of trying out unfamiliar behaviors. In *Integral Life Practice*, Wilber, Patten, Leonard, and Morelli (2008) propose that an accelerating synergy is generated by cross-training with specific practices targeting physical, mental, emotional, and spiritual growth as well as the removal of unconscious psychological barriers through "shadow work." A coach, trainer, or consultant skilled in vertical development can help an individual or group design practice sets in the appropriate sequence and specifically tuned to the clients' needs, objectives, and current ways of being.

One caveat is that vertical development does not substitute for having basic organizational and functional competencies, and knowledge intrinsic to success in one's field. Hiring someone based solely on the fact that they are at the Strategist level does not mean that they have the basic skills or knowledge to fill that particular position. Nevertheless, competent leaders growing to the Strategist level tend to intuitively master many horizontal skills without specialized coaching or training. Rooke and Torbert (2005, p.75) explain, "They [Strategist leaders] will already have mastered many of those skills. Rather, they are exploring the disciplines and commitments entailed in creating projects, teams, networks, strategic alliances, and whole organizations on the basis of collaborative inquiry."

Given the turbulent times ahead, we propose that leadership development be approached with more urgency, and that methods to facilitate vertical development be used with capable prospective leaders with the specific aim of increasing the percentage of Strategists in organizations and institutions. To that end we offer a rethinking of the traditional leadership competency model: The Strategist Competency Model.

Leadership Competency Models

Businesses and other institutions have used leadership competency models for decades. Serving as a roadmap for the acquisition, development, and promotion of leaders, they also set the tone for an organizational or institutional culture. Integrated into most major corporations and leadership development organizations, leadership competency models are foundational to leadership development. The models facilitate feedback mechanisms such as performance reviews and 360 assessments, training programs, coaching practices, and succession programs. Human performance experts base these models upon leadership KSABs (Knowledge, Skills, Attitudes, and Behaviors). The leadership KSABs employed most widely today have been developed to increase and measure horizontal growth. These horizontal KSABs are aimed at deepening specific leadership skills, but do nothing to address the developmental maturity of the leader.

THE STRATEGIST COMPETENCY MODEL

Strategists consistently exhibit traits that both differentiate their developmental maturity and contribute to their transformative effectiveness. In reviewing the literature, we have identified seven specific traits that turn up in both outcome research and developmental descriptions (Cook-Greuter, 2000, 2002; Fisher et al., 1987; Fisher, Rooke, & Torbert, 2003; Kuhnert, & Lewis, 1987; Merron, Fisher, & Torbert, 1987; Metcalf, 2008; Metcalf & Brenza, 2014; Metcalf & Palmer, 2011; Metcalf, Stoller, Pfeil, & Morrow-Fox, 2014; Rooke, 2001; Rooke & Torbert, 2005; Young, 2002). The seven traits are humility, commitment to right action, strategic perspective, versatility, authenticity, ability to inspire followership, and innate collaboration.

Operating from evolved ego strength, the Strategist has developed a temperament and developmental maturity that gives rise to these traits. Cook-Greuter (2002, pp. 24–25) writes

> Strategists have access to a logical system that can integrate psycho-logically paradox elements, therefore less energy needs to be spent on "defending." This in turn, allows them to be *more tolerant* and *spontaneous* than adults at conventional stages. Self and others are accepted as complex human beings with good and bad traits. Exchange with others makes it possible to get in touch with things one would otherwise tend to overlook.

The traits of strategic perspective and intellectual versatility may arise from the Strategist's expanded worldview and decreased need for artificial boundaries. Strategists have also been well recognized as having the ability to be highly committed to right action and mission. This high commitment allows them to find new ways to solve complex problems rather than abandoning goals under conditions of duress.

Table 2:   Strategist Competencies.

Competency	Explanation
Professionally humble	*Cares about getting it right ahead of being right*
	Committed to personal and organizational mission as "north star" and focal point for where to invest energy in service of leaving a legacy
	Cares more about the organization and the result than her/his image
	Freely, happily, and instinctively gives credit to others
	Puts principles ahead of personal gain
Unwavering commitment to right action	*Is unstoppable and unflappable when on a mission*
	Has the ability to be fully committed, hard driving, fully focused, and yet not experienced as either myopic or stubborn
	Has the ability to "stay the course" when under pressure
A 360 degree thinker	*Has the "Balcony View"*
	Innately understands the systems, constraints, perceptions, near-term, long-term, and secondary impacts of strategy and decisions – and how to transform them to complete amazing results
	Balances competing commitments of multiple constituents on a regular basis
	Thinks in terms of systems, dialogues, and transformations when focusing on constraints and perceptions – consider the organizational context when making recommendations
	Strong commitment to continual personal learning and building learning systems
	Understands cross organizational impact – striving to understand the interconnection across multiple complex systems and make highly informed decisions considering implications across broader contexts
Intellectually versatile	*Has developed interests, expertise, and curiosity beyond the job and organization*
	Despite a devout commitment to the job and the organization, they are always interested and involved with areas beyond their comfort zones
	Takes a special interest in political, national, and international developments
	Use external interest to enhance legacy and provide balance in life
Highly authentic and reflective	*Is not constrained by personal appearance but is highly focused on personal behavior*
	Highly committed to personal growth and development and growing and developing others
	Is so undefended and open to feedback it may be surprising

Table 2: (*Continued*)

Competency	Explanation
	Seeks out discussions and feedback even in uncomfortable situations
	Able to manage emotions in the most difficult situations — understand the impact and contagious nature of emotions so they develop skills to recognize them, manage/metabolize them, and relate to others productively
	Able to maintain perspective in times of stress, taking a long-term view and remaining vision focused, they are less challenged by difficult situations than others
	Demonstrates emotional courage — willing to confront challenging situations
	Continually looking for ways to enable the organization to improve its ability to meet its mission more efficiently and effectively
Able to inspire followership	*Has the special ability to connect with people at all levels of the organization to create a shared vision*
	Intuitively understands change, the steps to managing change, and how to help the organization overcome its resistance to change
	Has an innate ability to diffuse conflict without avoiding or sidestepping the source of the conflict
	Has a great ability to use humor effectively to put people at ease
	Able to relate to a broad range of people and understand their motivators and stressors
	Innately connect projects to the individual goals while working to overcome barriers
	Able to provide valuable feedback to others in a manner that is supportive of growth and development of the recipient
Innately collaborative	*Welcomes collaboration in a quest for novel solutions that serve the highest outcome for all involved*
	Seeks input from multiple perspectives — valuing diverse points of view
	Creates solutions to complex problems by creating new approaches that did not exist, pulling together constituents in novel ways, creating broader and more creative alliances
	Understands that in a time of extreme change, input from multiple stakeholders with diverse points of view are required

Taking these seven research-attributed traits, we developed a Strategist Competency Model that will allow businesses, institutions, and leadership development groups to support and develop Strategist leaders (Metcalf, Stoller, Pfeil, & Morrow-Fox, 2014). Like other competency models, this model is useful in recruiting, assessing, and developing leaders, as well as facilitating leadership succession. The Strategist Competency Model also serves as a touchstone for organizational and institutional cultural change. It is explained in Table 2.

The Strategist competencies promote vertical leadership development; competencies such as professional humility and high authenticity are intrinsically different from fostering innovation and customer orientation. Fostering innovation is what I do (horizontal); demonstrating professional humility is how I am (vertical). In order to foster innovation, a leader may learn a set of techniques or support a business focus. In order to become humble, a leader may need to fundamentally transform their perspective on who they are and how they engage with the world.

There are several statistically validated assessment instruments that measure developmental maturity and provide a means to assess Strategist competencies. Susanne Cook-Greuter's Maturity Assessment for Professionals (MAP) and Terri O'Fallon's StAGES assessment instrument have undergone rigorous academic review for their reliability, validity, and utility. Rooke and Torbert's Leadership Development Profile (LDP) is a derivative of MAP. In addition, 360 review assessments using Strategist competencies add a further measurable component. These assessments are extremely useful for both the measurement and design of a leadership development process.

Conclusion

In the years preceding 2050, the leaders of our time will enter a perfect storm of disorienting dilemmas, and face an unprecedented wave of change that could swallow or advance them at any moment. Future trends indicate this change may include global economic shocks, catastrophic climate events, demographic shifts, or unexpected disruptions and innovations in business and technology cycles. This chapter argues that we need Strategist level capacities in leadership roles in order to meet these upcoming and ongoing challenges. Research shows that if a leader − with the appropriate experience and functional skills and knowledge for his or her position − views and engages the world with a Strategist perspective, the important business and political metrics are likely to follow.

In the face of historic change, it is fortunate that the means and practices are available to support vertical development toward

Strategist level leadership. Currently, Strategist leaders are few in number, in part because the organizational cultures and leadership development practices of most organizations do not support vertical growth. The Strategist Competency Model as a mainstay of a vertically-oriented leadership development program will go a long way toward increasing this number. A future that is fully staffed with Strategist leaders is a possibility, but certainly not a foregone conclusion. It will require commitment to a leadership development path that is less familiar and more personally provocative than most leaders and organizations are currently accustomed. Some may ask: Can this be done? Our response is that we can't afford not to try.

Acknowledgments

We would like to acknowledge Dr. Michael Marien, Director of Global Foresight Books, for his valuable and timely consolidation, organization, and reviews of futures-relevant books, reports, and articles. We have benefitted from his prolific service to the field of professional futures research since the 1990s when he was editor of the monthly publication *Futures Survey* for the World Future Society. To create the Strategist Competency Model, we drew extensively from the work of several renowned developmentalists and integral theorists including: Barrett Brown, Susanne Cook-Greuter, Terri O'Fallon, Steve McIntosh, David Rooke, Bill Torbert, and Ken Wilber. Their work in integrating developmental psychology and leadership development serves as the foundation for our model of future leaders.

References

Avolio, B. J., Waldman, D. A., & Yammarino, F. (1991). Leading in the 1990s: The four I's of transformational leadership. *Journal of European Industrial Training*, 15(4), 9−16.

Beck, D., & Cowan, C. (1996). *Spiral dynamics*. Malden, MA: Blackwell Business.

Brown, B. (2011). *Conscious leadership for sustainability: How leaders with a late-stage action logic design and engage in sustainability initiatives*. Doctoral dissertation. Retrieved from Dissertations and Theses database (UMI No. 3498378).

Brown, B. (2013). *The future of leadership for conscious capitalism*. Retrieved from https://associates.metaintegral.org/sites/default/files/MetaIntegral_Brown_The futureofleadershipforconsciouscapitalism_20140402.pdf. Accessed on April 17, 2015.

Brown, L. (2012). *Full planet, empty plates: The new geopolitics of food security* [Kindle Cloud Reader]. Retrieved from Amazon.com. Accessed on September 10, 2012.

Cannon, S. (2014). *Developing extraordinary leaders: The masculine, the feminine, and the future* [PowerPoint]. Presented at the HR Vision conference, Osney Media, June 4−5, 2014, Amsterdam. Available upon request.

Cook-Greuter, S. (2000). Mature ego development: A gateway to ego transcendence? *Journal of Adult Development, 7*(4), 227–240.

Cook-Greuter, S. (2002). *A detailed description of the development of nine action logics adapted from ego development theory for the leadership development framework.* Wayland, MA: Cook-Greuter & Associates. Retrieved from http://nextstepintegral.org/wp-content/uploads/2011/04/The-development-of-action-logics-Cook-Greuter. pdf. Accessed on April 17, 2015.

Cook-Greuter, S. (2004). Making the case for a developmental perspective. *Industrial and Commercial Training, 36*(7), 275–281.

Cook-Greuter, S. (2013). *Nine levels of increasing embrace in ego development: A full-spectrum theory of vertical growth and meaning making.* Wayland, MA: Cook-Greuter & Associates. Retrieved from http://www.cook-greuter.com/ Cook-Greuter9levelspapernew1.1%271497p%5B1%5D.pdf. Accessed on April 17, 2015.

Cook-Greuter, S., & Soulen, J. (2007). The developmental perspective in integral counseling. *Counseling and Values, 51*(3), 180–192.

Coyle, D. (2009). *The talent code: Greatness isn't born. It's grown. Here's how.* New York, NY: Bantam Dell.

Development Dimensions International & The Conference Board. (2014). *Ready-now leaders: Meeting tomorrow's business challenges. Global leadership forecast 2014| 2015.* Retrieved from http://www.ddiworld.com/DDI/media/trend-research/global-leadership-forecast-2014-2015_tr_ddi.pdf?ext=.pdf

Fisher, D., Merron, K., & Torbert, W. (1987). Human development and managerial effectiveness. *Group & Organizational Studies, 12*(3), 257–273.

Fisher, D., Rooke, D., & Torbert, W. (2003). *Personal and organizational transformations: Through action inquiry.* Boston, MA: Edge/Work.

Franklin, D., & Andrews, J. (Eds.). (2012). *Mega change: The world in 2050.* Hoboken, NJ: Wiley.

Gebser, J. (1985). *The ever-present origin.* Athens, OH: Ohio University Press. (Original work published as Part 1, 1949, and Part 2, 1953).

Gitsham, M. (2009). *Developing the global leader of tomorrow.* Ashridge and EABIS report. Retrieved from http://www.ashridge.com/Website/IC.nsf/ wFARPUB/Developing+the+Global+Leader+of+Tomorrow+Report+-+2009?open document

Gore, A. (2013). *The future: Six drivers of global change* [Kindle Cloud Reader]. Retrieved from Amazon.com. Accessed on September 13, 2014.

Graves, C. W. (1974). Human nature prepares for a momentous leap. *The Futurist, 8*(2), 72–85. Retrieved from http://www.global-change-seminar.org/raps/Graves1974 Article.pdf

IBM Corporation. (2010). *Working beyond borders: Insights from the global chief human resource officer study.* Retrieved from http://www-935.ibm.com/services/c-suite/chro/study/

Kuhnert, K. W., & Lewis, P. (1987). Transactional and transformational leadership: A constructive/developmental analysis. *Academy of Management Review, 12*(4), 648–657.

Kupchan, C. (2012). *No one's world: The west, the rising rest, and the coming global turn.* Oxford: Oxford University Press.

Kurzweil, R. (2001). *The law of accelerating returns.* Retrieved from http://www.kurzweilai.net/the-law-of-accelerating-returns. Accessed on September 14, 2014.

Kurzweil, R. (2010). How my predictions are faring. Retrieved from http://www.kurz-weilai.net/predictions/download.php

Leslie, B. (2009). *The leadership gap: What you need and don't have when it comes to leadership talent.* Center For Creative Leadership. Retrieved from http://www.ccl.org/leadership/pdf/research/leadershipGap.pdf

Mayes, R. (August 10, 2014). Review of the book in C. Rawlings, J. R. Smith, & R. Bencini, Pardon the disruption: The future you never saw coming. *The Futurist*, 48 (5). Retrieved from http://www.wfs.org/blogs/randall-mayes/book-review-pardon-disruption-future-you-never-saw-coming-wasteland-press-2013-r

McIntosh, S. (2007). *Integral consciousness and the future of evolution.* St. Paul, MN: Paragon.

McKinsey & Company. (2013). *Gender diversity in top management: Moving corporate culture, moving boundaries.* Women Matter. Paris: McKinsey & Company. Retrieved from http://www.mckinsey.com/features/women_matter. Accessed on April 17, 2015.

Merron, K., Fisher, D., & Torbert, W. (1987). Meaning making and management action. *Group & Organizational Studies*, 12(3), 274–286.

Metcalf, M. (2008). Level 5 leadership: Leadership that transforms organizations and creates sustainable results. *Integral Leadership Review*, 1–14. Retrieved from http://www.metcalf-associates.com/wp-content/uploads/2010/10/Maureen-Metcalf-Level-5-Leadership-Article-for-Integral-Leadership-Review.pdf

Metcalf, M., & Brenza, J. (2014). *Innovative leadership workbook to implementing analytics programs.* Tucson, AZ: Integral Publishers.

Metcalf, M., & Palmer, M. (2011). *Innovative leadership fieldbook.* Tucson, AZ: Integral Publishers.

Metcalf, M., Stoller, J., Pfeil, S., & Morrow-Fox, M. (2014). *Innovative leadership workbook for physician leaders.* Tucson, AZ: Integral Publishers.

Moore, J., & Rees, W. (2013). Getting to one-planet living. In E. Assadourian & T. Prugh (Eds.), *State of the world 2013* (pp. 39–50). Washington, DC: Island Press. September 12, 2014. Retrieved from http://blogs.worldwatch.org/sustainabilitypossible/wp-content/uploads/2013/05/SOW2013-04-Moore-and-Rees-.pdf. Accessed on April 17, 2015.

Moran, D. (Ed.). (2011). *Climate change and national security: A country-level analysis.* Washington, DC: Georgetown University Press.

National Intelligence Council. (2012). *Global trends 2030: Alternative worlds.* Retrieved from http://www.dni.gov/files/documents/GlobalTrends_2030.pdf

OECD. (2011). *Future global shocks: Improving risk governance.* OECD International Futures Programme. Paris: Organisation for Economic Co-operation and Development.

OECD. (2012). Energy and climate policy: Bending the technological trajectory. OECD Studies on Environmental Innovation, OECD Publishing. Retrieved from http://dx.doi.org/10.1787/9789264174573-en. Accessed on September 13, 2014.

O'Fallon, T. (2013, July). The senses: Demystifying awakening. Presented at the 2013 Integral Theory Conference, San Francisco, CA. Retrieved from https://metaintegral.org/sites/default/files/O'Fallon_ITC2013.pdf. Accessed on April 17, 2015.

Orr, D. (2013). Governance in the long emergency. In E. Assadourian & T. Prugh (Eds.), *State of the world 2013* (pp. 279–291). Washington, DC: Island Press. Retrieved from http://blogs.worldwatch.org/sustainabilitypossible/wp-content/uploads/2013/11/SOW2013-26-Orr-.pdf

Putoshkin, E. (2014). The integral movement in Russia: Bigelow, Fuhs and Wilber. *The Integral Leadership Review*, (April–June). Retrieved from http://integralleadershipreview.com/8062-the-integral-movement-in-russia-bigelow-fuhs-and-wilber/. Accessed on May 8, 2014.

Randers, J. (2012). *2052: A global forecast for the next forty years*. White River Junction, VT: Chelsea Green Publishing.

Rooke, D. (2001). Organizational transformation requires the presence of leaders who are strategists and magicians. *Organizations and People, 4*(3), 16–23.

Rooke, D., & Torbert, W. (1998). Organizational transformation as a function of CEO's developmental stage. *Organization Development Journal, 16*(1), 11–28.

Rooke, D., & Torbert, W. (1999). The CEO's role in organizational transformation. *Systems Thinker, 10*(7), 1–5.

Rooke, D., & Torbert, W. (2005, April). Seven transformations of leadership. *Harvard Business Review, 83*(4), 67–76. Retrieved from https://hbr.org/2005/04/seven-transformations-of-leadership. Accessed on April 17, 2015.

The Arlington Institute. (2014). *The world's biggest problems*. Retrieved from http://www.arlingtoninstitute.org/wbp. Accessed on September 12.

UNESCO Institute for Statistics. (2010). September 20, 2014. Retrieved from http://www.uis.unesco.org/literacy/Pages/adult-youth-literacy-data-viz.aspx. Accessed on April 17, 2015.

United Nations. (2013). *A new global partnership: Eradicate poverty and transform economies through sustainable development*. Report of the High-Level Panel of Eminent Persons on the Post-2015 Development Agenda. United Nations Publications, NY. Retrieved from http://www.un.org/sg/management/pdf/HLP_P2015_Report.pdf. Accessed on April 17, 2015.

Watson, R., & Freeman, O. (2012). *Futurevision: Scenarios for the world in 2040*. Brunswick: Scribe Publications.

Wilber, K. (1996). *A brief history of everything*. Boston, MA: Shambhala Publications.

Wilber, K. (2001). *A theory of everything: An integral vision for business, politics, science, and spirituality*. Boston, MA: Shambhala publications.

Wilber, K. (2012). The international integral leadership collaborative. Ken Wilber Keynote Presentation Notes – ILC. May 08, 2014. Retrieved from http://www.integralleadershipcollaborative.com/fe/16462-the-time-has-come-for-integral-leadership-ken-wilber. Accessed on April 17, 2015.

Wilber, K. (2013). The integral movement in Russia: Bigelow, Fuhs and Wilber. *The Integral Leadership Review, April–June 2014*. Retrieved from http://integralleadershipreview.com/8062-the-integral-movement-in-russia-bigelow-fuhs-and-wilber/. Accessed on April 17, 2015.

Wilber, K., Patten, T., Leonard, A., & Morelli, M. (2008). *Integral life practice: A 21st-century blueprint for physical health, emotional balance, mental clarity, and spiritual awakening*. Boston, MA: Integral Books.

World Resource Institute. (2014). *Climate: Advancing transformative solutions for climate change mitigation and adaptation*. Retrieved from http://www.wri.org/our-work/topics/climate. Accessed on September 11.

Young, J. E. (2002). A spectrum of consciousness for CEOs: A business application of Ken Wilber's spectrum of consciousness. *The International Journal of Organizational Analysis, 10*(1), 30–54.

13 Quantum Leadership: Collapsing the Wave Function

Michael A. Piel and Karen K. Johnson

Quantum Leadership: A Wave of Probability

When considering the complex phenomenon of leadership, one becomes aware of the marvelous richness and diversity of leadership behaviors, dimensions, and perspectives. Not only has leadership been a core focus of mankind for millennia, the intricacy of the various behaviors have allowed for an amazing and vibrant diversity of best practices, definitions, theories, and models.

Prevailing scientific paradigms have often influenced how we theorize and model leadership behavior. Toward the end of the 20th century, chaos theory and the science of complexity captivated the imagination of leadership scholars and practitioners. Margaret Wheatley's *Leadership and the New Science* (Wheatley, 2006), Kathleen Allen and Cynthia Cherrey's *Systemic Leadership* (Allen & Cherrey, 2000), and Mary Uhl-Bien and Russ Marion's volumes on *Complexity Leadership* (Marion & Uhl-Bien, 2001, Uhl-Bien & Marion, 2007; Uhl-Bien, Marion, & Noe, 2009) are but a few of the examples of this trend. Complexity theory helped elucidate and gave us a way to talk about distributed leadership and the ability of small shifts to effect large change, but as the world moves into a future that is built on volatility, uncertainty, and ambiguity, the paradigm of quantum physics has much more to offer.

Quantum theory emerged as a paradigm shift decades ago and has increasingly influenced how scientists view the world around us

(Chopra & Kafatos, 2014). While quantum theory suggests views that radically differ from our normal perceptions (Bohm, 1951), questions regarding the validity of applying these principles to the macroscopic world remain open (Rakovic et al., 2014). Although divergent views are held by physicists on the complex intricacies of quantum mechanics (Gargiulo, 2013), a growing group of scientists, academics, philosophers, and authors have begun to apply quantum theory concepts to many wide-ranging fields, including leadership. Such cross-pollinations of ideas often yield rich and novel insights. As researchers and innovators continue to expand quantum concepts' influence across their various diverse disciplines, soon no future academic field will be left untouched.

Reframing leadership as "the collapsing of the wave function" introduces the leadership community to an evolving understanding and perspective of leadership grounded in quantum principles. To assist readers in deciding whether to accept, reject, or suspend judgment of the quantum theory and model of leadership, we explore quantum leadership in context of the quantum principles of duality, superposition, entanglement, and observation.

The leadership challenges of the future will require adopting innovative thinking capable of effectively addressing emerging unknowns. Applying the kernel insights from quantum physics to leadership behavior opens the possibility for seeing leadership in fresh, inventive, and novel ways and enables leaders and managers to take advantage of this rapidly evolving, science-based, enriching, and inspirational thought. A quantum leadership theory and model are presented in this chapter, accompanied by an exploration of the dynamics of leadership behavior emerging from this perspective.

The Quantum World Untangled: Duality, Superposition, Entanglement, and Observation

Quantum particles possess some strange and interesting properties (Bohm, 1951; Zhao & Schöllkopf, 2012). While the academic literature on quantum physics is rich and complex, four key quantum principles serve as the groundwork for entering into our leadership discussion: duality, superposition, entanglement, and observation. These serve as the fundamental principles of quantum leadership. By establishing a baseline understanding of these principles, one can more effectively evaluate the merits of accepting and applying these remarkable principles to the quantum leadership perspective.

QUANTUM DUALITY

From the quantum theory's perspective, light, which is a photon, exists as both a particle and wave (Arbab, Widatallah, & Khalafalla, 2012; Lehnert, 2006). While the dynamics of wave-particle duality has been researched for many decades, understanding the meaning and implications remains remarkably obscure and elusive (Greulich, 2010; Lehnert, 2006). With varying interpretations of the duality of a photon's wave-like and particle-like properties, verifying these property relationships in context of various theories remains challenging (Greulich, 2010).

Scientific deliberation seems ongoing regarding light, light properties, and their relationships to other quantum principles like uncertainty (Unruh & Georgiev, 2007). While most scientists agree that light is a particle, deciphering the exact meaning of the word *particle* is problematic (Greulich, 2010). Light has a dual nature of a particle and wave but these properties are not visible concurrently (Arbab et al., 2012). A photon has no mass or charge (Hansson, 2014). Since light is neither a pure wave nor a pure particle, Arbab et al. (2012) suggested a distinction between a field wave and a particle wave.

Whether additional distinctions bring further clarity or add increasing confusion, the dual nature of light remains a theoretical challenge to physicists (Rinaldi, 2011). Attempting to further our understanding of the duality of light is sure to inspire theoreticians and researchers for decades to come. For now, besides the headache, whether light presents itself to us as a particle or wave simply remains the determination of our own observation.

QUANTUM LEADERSHIP DUALITY

Without others no one leads; leadership is empty without followership (Bass, 1990). Both leaders and followers are potentially both leaders and followers; observation determines whether an individual becomes a follower or leader in the present moment. Quantum leaders perceive themselves as potential followers and see others as potential leaders. Reminiscent of quantum particles in a *Heisenberg Uncertainty Principle* inspired dance, where one can know only one property at a time, either position or momentum, quantum leadership mirrors that dance. Leaders are presented with a changing world that is anything but certain. Understanding the certainty-uncertainty dynamic as ubiquitous, quantum leaders giving equal weight to what is known and not known seek out multiple differing perspectives.

Observation determines whether light becomes a particle or wave; similarly, leadership determinations unfold from observations that create what is perceived. Observation is dependent on thinking which is a process, a continuum, always progressing forward in an irreversible flow. Reflecting on thinking reveals how one understands the dynamic. No matter which philosophical heuristic or definition one applies, understanding thinking primarily occurs in context of results and utility. Since thinking creates one's present and future (Kirby & Goodpaster, 2002), quantum leaders stalwartly value reflection.

QUANTUM SUPERPOSITION

Known as superposition, quantum particles simultaneously exist in all of their possible states. Quantum theory posits that reality is neither this nor that but rather a wave of probability (Heisenberg, 1958/1999). *Schrödinger's Cat* paradox is a well-known thought experiment on this concept designed by Erwin Schrödinger in 1935 (Stepuk, 2014). In the thought experiment, a cat is placed inside a closed box accompanied by radioactive material, a radiation-detecting Geiger counter, and a vial of hydrocyanic acid (Meland, 2014; Stepuk, 2014). If the radioactive material decays, the vial will be shattered. Since the cat cannot be observed in the box, one cannot determine whether the cat is dead or alive until the box is opened.

Schrödinger's Cat illustrates the superposition concept in quantum systems; the cat being neither dead nor alive, being both dead and alive until observed (Aharonov, 2013). The cat is in a superposed state which is in all possible states simultaneously until viewed. Numerous experiments have demonstrated this exceptionally unique principle of quantum superposition (Walther, Jian-Wei, Aspelmeyer, & Ursin, 2004).

Brumfiel (2012) suggested that quantum particles exist simultaneously in numerous "mutually exclusive" states. For quantum systems, reality is concurrently both potentially this and potentially that. In such a background, the concept of uncertainty moves beyond the absence of outcome knowledge into the domain of possible different outcomes knowledge (Ross & Ladyman, 2013).

QUANTUM LEADERSHIP SUPERPOSITION

Approximating quantum particles existing simultaneously in all possible states, the world leaders encounter potentially exists as this or as that dependent on observation. Being able to see other possibilities is one result of creative intelligence merging with intuition. Intuition-inspired innovation and creativity empowers leaders to deal with the unexpected and uncertain (Bass, 1990). Intuition opens the doors to seeing in new ways, to seeing beyond what current thinking sees (Bass). Intuition sparks intellectual stimulation. Intellectually stimulating and innovative quantum leaders see outside the box seeing all the possibilities. In creating innovative images, quantum leaders fundamentally create the possibility itself.

Everyone in the work world has an idea, mostly all differing, of what leadership is to them. The differences among these varying ideas make leadership extremely challenging to understand and even more difficult to improve. No matter what idea one has of leadership, the kind of leader one is and becomes is rooted in what one thinks leadership is. Quantum leaders understand that the concept of leadership simultaneously exists in all possible states. Leadership is not this or not that until leadership is observed, observed by oneself and others. Quantum leaders appreciate the value and importance of authentically listening to the perceptions of others.

QUANTUM ENTANGLEMENT

Quantum entanglement describes the phenomenon where objects become linked regardless of proximity even if extremely distant (Brumfiel, 2012; Ormerod, 2013; Weidemüller, 2013; Zhao & Schöllkopf, 2012). Quantum energy influences other quantum energy non-locally. Quantum entanglement is often referred to simply as what Einstein called *spooky-action-at-a-distance* (Aharonov, 2013; Weidemüller, 2013; Zhao & Schöllkopf, 2012).

The strange, unusual, and *spooky* phenomenon of entanglement challenges our normal perspectives and common senses (Matthews & Thompson, 2012; Ormerod, 2013). No matter how far apart components of an entangled system are, measuring one of the components determines immediately the state of the other (Weidemüller, 2013). When one particle selects its spin, the entangled particle instantaneously chooses the opposite spin (Sachdev, 2013, as cited by Gargiulo, 2013). The measurements of the components of an entangled system are correlated no matter how long the distance is (Merali, 2012).

Although quantum properties are difficult to observe because the mere act of observation causes interference, experimental techniques developed by Wineland and Haroche provide scientists visibility to the phenomenon (Brumfiel, 2012). Quantum entanglement has been demonstrated in various experiments at various laboratories around the world (Matthews & Thompson, 2012; Weidemüller, 2013).

Both entanglement and non-locality are key quantum mechanics principles (Massar, 2012). The beautiful magic in quantum entanglement is that quantum particles appear to communicate non-locally with each other (Bohm, 1980). Regardless of distance, the entangled interaction is instantaneous. Sachdev (2013) frames this phenomenon as the entangled particle *knowing* the quantum state of the other (as cited by Gargiulo, 2013). This non-locality feature of the quantum world strongly suggests a significant degree of connectedness and level of consciousness present in all of a wave-collapsed reality.

QUANTUM LEADERSHIP ENTANGLEMENT

From a quantum perspective, when change occurs to one part of a composite component, other related parts of the unit change accordingly regardless of distance (Aerts, Broekaert, Gabora, & Sozzo, 2013). More than simply non-locality, quantum entangled change indicates connectedness and a knowing presence. Quantum leaders leverage this dual dynamic by encouraging collaborative thinking. Facilitating collaborative thinking and maintaining an authentic thinking space are key to establishing knowledge communities (Katz, 2003). As the world continues to face changing challenges, the sharing of multiple perceptions and perspectives yields the most effective solutions (Aghababaei, Hoveida, & Rajaiepour, 2013).

Buber (1937/1970) suggested that our world mirrors our twofold attitudes, seeing the world as objects and as encounters. While management focuses on objects, leadership focuses on people. Quantum leaders grasp that leading is encounter relations which are interconnected and interdependent; we are mirrors to each other. One encounter creates a ripple forward touching all encounters.

An individual has visibility only to parts as parts, not to the whole as a whole. For quantum leaders, continuous learning ensures doors of possibility remain open to seeing and creating more of the whole. Continuous learning and the counterpart continuous unlearning are like listening. The role of the hearer and sound are dynamically interrelated. What the hearer hears is as much a contributor to what is heard as the sound itself. Authentic listening hears beyond mere sounds to hearing the underlying delightful wonder (Kroodsma, as cited by Arnold, 2005). Quantum leaders hear and help others hear the underlying wonder.

QUANTUM OBSERVATION

Observation, in collapsing the wave function of probability, reifies quantum particles into existence (Gargiulo, 2013; Lee & Wexler, 1999). The observer determines what actual outcome occurs. Only when *Schrödinger's Cat* is observed does the cat become dead or alive. The observer collapses the wave function of probability shifting potential reality to actual reality (Gargiulo, 2010).

While explaining the macro world in context of quantum theory remains challenging, some researchers suggest the phenomenon of decoherence (Gargiulo, 2013; Seife, 2006). Decoherence states that everything in the finite universe is in a continuous and increasing entanglement with everything else in the universe (Epperson, 2012; Seife, 2006). Since everything in the nature is interacting, interdependent, and interconnected (Hawking & Mlodinow, 2005), the collapsing of the wave function is ubiquitous and ongoing (Gargiulo, 2013).

Gargiulo (2010) acknowledged that quantum principles have helped our understanding of the macroscopic world. There is still an ongoing debate among physicists regarding the extent of quantum connectedness and non-locality at macro levels (Rakovic et al., 2014), suggesting that an observer not only collapses the wave function but is initially virtually connected to all possible probability waves is a position both logically valid and worth considering.

Without the paramount role of the observer, the quantum world remains a world of mere possibility (Lee & Wexler, 1999). Chopra and Kafatos (2014) suggested that consciousness is fundamental to observation with the observer, observed, and observation process being linked. Our experiences of reality are grounded in our consciousness Gargiulo (2013). From the quantum theory perspective, consciousness being composed of awareness and wakefulness is contingent on self-observation (Vithoulkas & Muresanu, 2014). In consciousness, the observer and observed become one.

QUANTUM LEADERSHIP OBSERVATION

Considering the mind as a quantum wave phenomenon (Lee & Wexler, 1999), consciousness through observation grounds reality (Chopra & Kafatos, 2014; Gargiulo, 2013). At the quantum and leadership levels, observation is the nucleus which links duality, superposition, and entanglement. Awareness is a core component of consciousness (Vithoulkas & Muresanu, 2014). Awareness is a product of the merging together of self-awareness and reflection. Self-awareness is a pivotal component of quantum leadership providing the instrument for collapsing wave functions.

The collapsing of the wave function does not occur in isolation of others. Collapsing the wave function is an integrated, interconnected, and interdependent endeavor. Quantum leaders appreciate the importance of other's self-awareness and act to ensure others gain an enhanced appreciation of the wave of possibilities.

Harrison (1999) highlighted how one's world view is contingent on the lenses one learns to use. Weick and Sutcliffe (2007) framed categories as tools which assist in our activities of controlling, planning, and predicting. Some human experiences either defy categorization or the categorization itself seems inadequate and meaningless.

Multifaceted phenomena like leadership lend themselves to phenomenological bracketing. Placing these types of phenomena in a category equally illuminates as well as de-illuminates them.

From a quantum leadership perspective, we are mirrors of each other; we create each other and create our shared reality. When considering self, understanding how another perceives self may be one of the greatest collapsing challenges for quantum leaders. Quantum leaders are authentic helping-hands, connecting with people and creating collaborative possibilities.

Collapsing Future Wave Functions

While as yet unwritten, the future to 2050 continues megatrending from the past. Numerous factors continue forming the landscape upon which future quantum leaders will stand. Globalization, environmental contexts, individualization, digitalization, demographic shifting, and technological convergence are dominant signposts directing world focus (Vielmetter & Sell, 2014). As interconnectedness and interdependencies rise, the potential for troublesome risks follows (Olu-Daniels & Nwibere, 2014). One fact unquestionably remains invariable – leadership will be indispensable to future survival.

The leadership approaches exercised by today's leaders will determine how future wave functions collapse. In the rest of this chapter, we look at the act of determining an organization's design, a capstone activity of organizational leaders (Mueller, 2014), through the lens of quantum leadership (see Figure 1). By exploring key areas of organizational design in context of quantum leadership's interaction with evolving megatrends and assessing the tangible value of adopting this paradigm, the potential worth to leaders becomes evident.

THE VISION WAVE FUNCTION

Organizational vision no longer exists as a shared common single meaning. Rather, the meaning of the organizational vision is fractal, interconnected, interdependent, and multidimensional. What each team member of the organization understands the vision to be, that is what the vision is for the organization. Organizational vision is not an accumulation of the individual team members understanding of a single vision but rather each member's vision *is* the vision. The organizational vision collapses from every individual's vision, being identical yet different at the self-same time. The quantum leader, being aware of this dual nature of vision, collaboratively collapses the vision wave function.

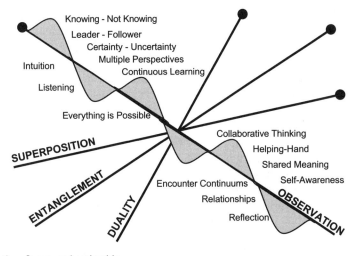

Figure 1.   Quantum Leadership.

As individual empowerment (NIC, 2012) and individualistic attitudes continue to increase in significance in the coming years (Vielmetter & Sell, 2014), these megatrends require leaders to adopt a differing perspective from the past. Megatrends do not exist as discrete entities but as interconnected and interdependent trends (Valencia, 2013). While these trends have the potential to establish inner and outer boundaries of human possibility, quantum leaders understanding that thought creates reality empower individuals to collaboratively visualize preferred states. Individual empowerment becomes a mechanism for advancing organizational objectives and increasing overall agility in addressing interconnected emerging challenges.

THE STRUCTURE WAVE FUNCTION

Concerning organizational structure, quantum leaders minimize the significance of formal structure and highlight the importance of the informal. Leaders perceive structure in the parts as reflective at larger scales. Both the structure, and more significantly, the meaning of the structure appear fractal.

Meaning and interpretation defines the reality of the organizational structure. The meaning of the formal structure emerges from the meaning given by each of the individuals in the informal structure. The informal structure, which itself is fractal — a concept from complexity science —, influences meaning in quantum fashion through entanglement. How organizational meaning changes is not reducible to a cause-effect relationship. Meaning itself occurs within the realm of the *in-between* of encountering continuums. Quantum leaders create the possibility for authentic encounters to arise within the organizational structure.

Referred to as the diffusion of power, this megatrend covers the migration of power away from being hegemonic (NIC, 2012). Power is shifting from organizations to individuals (Vielmetter & Sell, 2014) while at the same time trending toward a multi-polar world (NIC, 2012). Increases in instability and uncertainty are extremely possible in these landscapes. How organizations respond to these megatrends is delimited by structures selected. Quantum leaders engage others to collaboratively craft structures that increase the potentialities and decrease the limitations of the organization.

THE CULTURE WAVE FUNCTION

A twofold characteristic of culture is the meaning provided to life and the corresponding knowledge transfers (Nejad, 2013). Culture is both fractal and quantum. Organizational culture is a fractal of what the culture is for any team member. The culture of a team member is a fractal of organizational culture. The relationships between the cultural fractals are quantum; each influences the other in a non-localized fashion. How cultural shifts occur cannot be isolated to a single cultural fractal, for all fractals are interrelated.

Culture is not experienced but encountered. Individuals create the organizational culture through encountering others and their cultures in the continuum of the in-between. With approximately 3000 cultures in the world (Slaus, 2014), every culture has a distinctive richness (Hammou, Galib, Steiger, & Mellou, 2014). Organizational cultures are constantly changing in response to the changing world. To change an organizational culture means simply to see the encountering continuum, to see the *in-between*, in a new way.

As demographic patterns change due to ageing (NIC, 2012), interrelated phenomena equally vibrate. Workforces will become increasingly intergenerational (Vielmetter & Sell, 2014). Population migrations will increase toward urban areas (NIC, 2012; Valencia, 2013) while mounting pressures will intensify for increasingly limited resources (NIC, 2012). These forces transform culture and perceptions of international relations.

Views of international relationships and problems are colored by the ontology and epistemology one adopts (Nejad, 2013). Quantum leaders make possible seeing cultures and international relationships as interrelated and interconnected. Injecting considering what is possible into cultural perspectives opens a passageway to new solutions.

THE ENVIRONMENT WAVE FUNCTION

An organization's relationship to the environment, no matter which environmental aspect is being considered, is one of an encountering continuum. The global environment is perceived as encounters where the reality of any individual encounter exists in the in-between of the continuum. Individuals make possible the environment that becomes reality.

All organizational environmental relationships are fractal and quantum. What is seen in the singular is a reflection of what is seen in the plural. What is seen in the plural is a reflection of what is seen in the singular. Non-local causality is in effect within the realm of the in-between. Changes in one environment virtually instantly cause changes in all other environments. To influence or impact one environment is to influence and impact all.

Environmental concerns are increasing as life-enabling resources persist toward scarcity (Vielmetter & Sell, 2014). Slaus (2014) framed this increasingly unsustainable progression as requiring a duplicate earth. While the solutions are within grasp of mankind, a lack of effective world-wide leadership endures (Glenn, 2014). Effective world leadership starts with seeing the possibility; quantum leaders help others see the potential.

Having the aptitude, agility, and management savvy to effectively respond to change is imperative (Shirokova, Berezinets, & Shatalov, 2014). Learning is a solution to problems budding from relentless change (Chow, 2014; Shirokova et al., 2014). Continued learning is valued by quantum leaders who create the possibility for the same in others.

THE TECHNOLOGY WAVE FUNCTION

Technology is viewed as an encountering continuum. Beyond specific technologies, one's perspective toward technology is a significant component to an organization's perspective and use of technology. The views of technology held by individuals are both fractal and quantum, influencing all aspects of an organization. Similar to the view of technology, what an organization does with technology, which is also fractal and quantum, is equally central. Using technology in one manner impacts how that technology is used throughout the organization. Quantum leaders, sensitive to the technological force as both fractal and quantum, in collaboration with others, help others see what technological and non-technological opportunities are possible.

The movement from scientific knowledge to implemented technology is impressively efficient (Komazec & Delic, 2014). Technology is a force which is driving the world forward (Vielmetter & Sell, 2014). The dimensions of nano-technology and bio-technology are increasingly changing lives with this megatrend expected to increasingly influence society (Bhukuvhani et al., 2013; Vielmetter & Sell, 2014). A fresh way of thinking, sensitive to technology, and the knowledge world, is required to tackle these challenges (Komazec & Delic, 2014). While addressing such complexity is beyond the capabilities of one individual, quantum leaders understanding the sum of collaborative thinking is greater than the sum of the parts, open doors of possibility for others.

THE PEOPLE WAVE FUNCTION

The disciplines of management and leadership encompass different activities (Bass, 1990; Gilstrap, 2013). Leadership is a multifaceted phenomenon involving an influential relationship between leaders and followers (Osula & Ng, 2014) often leading to a transcendence of expectations (Hirtz, Murray, & Riordan, 2007; Kark & van Dijk, 2007). Relationships define the inner and outer boundaries of leadership possibilities.

Without the other, no one leads. From the quantum leadership perspective, relationships are encounter continuums. The social realm, whether from a formal or informal perspective, is both fractal and quantum. The organization and the activity of organizing become reified in the dialogue that occurs between intra-organizational members. Quantum leaders advance individual's awareness of relationship connectedness and interdependence.

The world is a world of relationships (Wheatley, 1992). The reality of an organization does not reside in individuals, structures, or environments but rather in the in-between of encounter continuums. People's perceptions themselves are fractal and quantum, changing instantaneously and reflecting both the parts and the total. Organization perceptions mirror an identical relationship as people; both perceptions are similarly fractal and quantum.

The digital age and encompassing personal and societal perceptions of empowerment are altering organizational dynamics. The past international order is animatedly shifting (Valencia, 2013). These megatrends tend to amplify in scope and significance over time (Vielmetter & Sell, 2014). New information and communication technologies (ICT) are empowering individuals (NIC, 2012). Global enterprises freed by ICT advances have embarked on innovative activities through international coordination (Komazec & Delic, 2014). The arising needs from these megatrend relationship dynamics will require quantum leadership which helps others visualize and create international relationships and possibilities.

Quantum Leaders Creating Shared Future Reality

Many philosophers throughout the ages have suggested that there exists a natural oneness and connectedness throughout and within all reality. From a quantum leadership perspective, a leader is connected to all probability waves, being connected to all the follower probability waves as well. Quantum leadership transmutes the idea that the person an individual becomes emerges from what one thinks (Singh, 2013) into the collaborative and shared idea of "as we think, so we become."

Often obscured by convincing illusions and foggy deceits and tricks, true experience is not always what one perceives. One needs only the experience of the Ebbinghaus, Ponzo, or Müller-Lyer illusions to gain an understanding that differentiating between reality and non-reality is not always as straight-forward as one normally thinks. Sometimes, one may give more weight to things that only seem to be real over those things that are real.

Understanding the significance of any given experience is equally a challenging endeavor subject to numerous potential errors. Böll (1963/1975) in his work of fiction framed his clown character as a perceiver of a world flashing-by who struggles to understand his experience, to make sense of the world he finds himself in, and give the world meaning. Whatever experiences we might have, we attempt to understand those events and create a meaning.

While this same quandary applies to leadership, the meaning being searched is not from inside isolation but from within collaboration. The power of thought, that ability to control the collapse of the wave function, empowers leaders to create shared reality. For quantum leaders, all is connected. Leaders collapse the wave function in conjunction with and in connection with all their followers.

Opening the doors to new possibilities frequently requires moving outside comfort zones (Baltar & de Coulon, 2014; Osula & Ng, 2014). Seeing in new collaborative ways, turning left when everyone else is turning right are often cited as hallmarks of entrepreneurial, innovative, agile, and thought-provoking leaders and managers. Quantum leadership provides the essential ontological, phenomenological, and epistemological shifts necessary to take advantage of the power of quantum dynamics at the macro-level within organizations. While Einstein's dreams of catching a wave unfolded the wonders of our universe (Sweeney, 2014), quantum leaders with analogous intuition and passion, together with others, collapse the wave functions creating our shared future reality.

Whether or not one accepts the quantum principles energizing and being applied to the quantum leadership perspective, no one can doubt that today's leaders are influencing our future world which in turn creates our future leaders. With so much at stake at so many different levels in so many places in our sometimes imperfect, fractured, and increasingly struggling Anthropocene world, incorporating the quantum leadership perspective into the leadership toolset seems categorically indispensable. Able to liberate and coalesce the positive energies from within all interconnections, quantum leadership is essentially about becoming more human. As a consequence, our global world becomes more humane making the quantum leadership perspective significantly imperative for our shared future.

References

Aerts, D., Broekaert, J., Gabora, L., & Sozzo, S. (2013). Quantum structure and human thought. *Behavioral and Brain Sciences*, *36*(3), 274–276. doi:10.1017/S0140525X12002841

Aghababaei, R., Hoveida, R., & Rajaiepour, S. (2013). The analysis of relationship between self-leadership strategies and components of quantum organization at universities. *International Journal of Academic Research in Economics and Management Sciences*, *2*(5), 192–203.

Aharonov, D. (2013). Trusted entanglement. *Nature*, *496*(7446), 436–437.

Allen, K. E., & Cherrey, C. (2000). *Systemic leadership: Enriching the meaning of our work* (1st ed.). Washington, DC: University Press of America.

Arbab, A. I., Widatallah, H. M., & Khalafalla, M. A. H. (2012). Toward a complete wave-particle duality: Do matter waves have inertia? *Advances in Natural Science*, *5*(3), 32–34.

Arnold, E. (2005, June). *Searching out 'the singing life of birds'*. NPR radio expeditions. Retrieved from http://www.npr.org/templates/story/story.php?storyId=4699207. Accessed on June 15, 2014.

Baltar, F., & de Coulon, S. (2014). Dynamics of the entrepreneurial process: The innovative entrepreneur and the strategic decisions. *Review of Business & Finance Studies*, *5*(1), 69–81.

Bass, B. M. (1990). *Handbook of leadership: Theory, research, & managerial applications* (3rd ed.). New York, NY: The Free Press.

Bhukuvhani, C., Tigere, A., Sana, A., Mhishi, M., Sunzuma, G., & Mupa, P. (2013). Science and technology education curriculum reforms for the nanoscience and nanotechnology (NST) revolution. *Journal of Education*, *3*(1), 44–47.

Bohm, D. (1951). *Quantum theory*. New York, NY: Dover.

Bohm, D. (1980). *Wholeness and the implicate order*. New York, NY: Routledge.

Böll, H. (1975). The clown (L. *Viennewitz, Trans.*). New York, NY: Bard. (Original work published in 1963).

Brumfiel, G. (2012). Physics nobel for quantum optics. *Nature*, *490*(7419), 152.

Buber, M. (1970). I and thou (W. *Kaufmann, Trans.*). New York, NY: Charles Scribner's Sons. (Original work published 1937).

Chopra, D., & Kafatos, M. C. (2014). From quanta to qualia: How a paradigm shift turns into science. *Philosophy Study*, 4(4), 287–301.

Chow, A. (2014). Leading change and the challenges of managing a learning organisation in Hong Kong. *Journal of Management Research*, 6(2), 22–38.

Epperson, M. (2012). *Quantum mechanics and the philosophy of Alfred North Whitehead*. New York, NY: Fordham University Pres.

Gargiulo, G. J. (2010). Mind, meaning, and quantum physics: Models for understanding the dynamic unconscious. *Psychoanalytic Review*, 97(1), 91–106.

Gargiulo, G. J. (2013). Some thoughts about consciousness: From a quantum mechanics perspective*Psychoanalytic Review*, 100(4), 543–558. doi:10.1521prev 20131004543

Gilstrap, D. L. (2013). Leadership and decision-making in team-based organizations: A model of bounded chaotic cycling in emerging system states. *Emergence: Complexity and Organization*, 15(3), 24–54.

Glenn, J. C. (2014). Our global situation and prospects for the future. *The Futurist*, 48(5), 15–20.

Greulich, K. O. (2010). Single molecule experiments challenge the strict wave-particle dualism of light. *International Journal of Molecular Sciences*, 11(1), 304–311. doi:10.3390/ijms11010304

Hammou, K. A., Galib, M. H., Steiger, J., & Mellou, J. (2014). The effect of national culture on strategic behavior and financial performance: Evidence from the cement industry in Morocco and the United States of America. *Journal of Management Research*, 6(1), 70–90.

Hansson, J. (2014). On the origin of elementary particle masses. *Progress in Physics*, 10(2), 71–73.

Harrison, B. (1999). The nature of leadership: Historical perspectives & the future. *Journal of California Law Enforcement*, 33(1), 24–30.

Hawking, S., & Mlodinow, L. (2005). *A briefer history of time*. New York, NY: Bantam Dell.

Heisenberg, W. (1999). *Physics and philosophy: The revolution in modern science*. Amherst, NY: Promedieus Books. (Original work published 1958).

Hirtz, P. D., Murray, S. L., & Riordan, C. A. (2007). The effects of leadership on quality. *Engineering Management Journal*, 19(1), 22–27.

Kark, R., & van Dijk, D. (2007). Motivation to lead, motivation to follow: The role of the self-regulatory focus in leadership processes. *Academy of Management Review*, 32(2), 500–528.

Katz, R. (2003). *The human side of managing technological innovation* (2nd ed.). New York, NY: Oxford University Press.

Kirby, G. R., & Goodpaster, J. R. (2002). *Thinking* (3rd ed.) Upper Saddle River, NJ: Prentice Hall.

Komazec, G., & Delic, M. V. (2014). New technologies generate need for a new organizational practice. *Acta Technica Corviniensis – Bulletin of Engineering*, 7(1), 59–67.

Lee, B. X., & Wexler, B. E. (1999). Physics and the quandaries of contemporary psychiatry: Review and research. *Psychiatry*, 62(3), 222–234.

Lehnert, B. (2006). Photon physics of revised electromagnetics. *Progress in Physics*, 2, 78–85.

Marion, R., & Uhl-Bien, M. (2001). Leadership in complex organizations. *The Leadership Quarterly*, 12(4), 389–418. doi:10.1016/S1048-9843(01)00092-3

Massar, S. (2012). Quantum information: Bad randomness comes good. *Nature Physics*, *8*(6), 447–448. doi:10.1038/nphys2310

Matthews, J. C. F., & Thompson, Mark G. (2012). An entangled walk of photons. *Nature*, *484*(7392), 47–48.

Meland, C. (2014). Talking tribalography: LeAnne Howe models emerging worldliness in "the story of America" and Miko Kings. *Studies in American Indian Literatures*, *26*(2), 26–39. 113.

Merali, Z. (2012). The quantum space race. *Nature*, *492*(7427), 22–25.

Mueller, J. R. (2014). Alternative organizational design and its impact on the future of work. *Journal of Strategic Innovation and Sustainability*, *9*(1), 48–58.

Nejad, M. S. (2013). A review study about quality of democracy from the view of international law and the definitions related to democracy. *International Journal of Academic Research in Business and Social Sciences*, *3*(10), 269–279.

Olu-Daniels, S., & Nwibere, B. M. (2014). Trust and organizational resilience in the Nigerian oil and gas industry. *International Journal of Business and Management*, *9*(2), 291–312.

Ormerod, N. (2013). Bernard Lonergan and the recovery of a metaphysical frame. *Theological Studies*, *74*(4), 960–982.

Osula, B., & Ng, E. C. W. (2014). Toward a collaborative, transformative model of non-profit leadership: Some conceptual building blocks. *Administrative Sciences*, *4*(2), 87–104. doi:10.3390/admsci4020087

Rakovic, D., Dugic, M., Jeknic-Dugic, J., Plavsic, M., Jacimovski, S., & Setrajcic, J. (2014). On macroscopic quantum phenomena in biomolecules and cells: From Levinthal to Hopfield. *BioMed Research International*. doi:10.1155/2014/580491

Rinaldi, A. (2011). When life gets physical: Quantum effects in selected biological systems have been confirmed experimentally, but how widespread is their role remains unclear. *EMBO Reports*, *13*(1), 24–27. doi:10.1038/embor.2011.236

Ross, D., & Ladyman, J. (2013). Quantum probability, choice in large worlds, and the statistical structure of reality. *Behavioral and Brain Sciences*, *36*(3), 305–306. doi:10.1017/S0140525X1200310X

Sachdev, S. (2013, January). Strange and stringy. *Scientific American*, *308*(1), 44–51.

Seife, C. (2006). *Decoding the Universe: How the new science of information is explaining everything in the cosmos, from our brains to black holes*. New York, NY: Penguin Books.

Shirokova, G., Berezinets, I., & Shatalov, A. (2014). Organisational change and firm growth in emerging economies. *Journal for East European Management Studies*, *19*(2), 185–212.

Singh, T. (2013, May 25). *As you think, so you become*. Retrieved from http://www.gurbani.org/articles/webart180.htm. Accessed on November 7, 2014.

Slaus, I. (2014). Transition to a new society. *Cadum*, *2*(2), 1–8.

Stepuk, A. (2014). Offshore investments investments-cui prodis? Schrodinger's cats in offshore financing: Both alive and dead. Paper presented at the Fifth International Science Conference, Belgrade, Megatrend University. Abstract retrieved from http://www.esd-conference.com/book_of_proceedings_Belgrade_2014.pdf

Sweeney, J. H. (2014). Einstein's dreams. *The Review of Metaphysics*, *67*(4), 811–834.

Uhl-Bien, M., & Marion, R. (Eds.). (2007). *Complexity leadership: Part 1: Conceptual foundations*. Charlotte, NC: Information Age Publishing.

Uhl-Bien, M., Marion, R., & Noe, R. A. (Eds.). (2009). Leadership and complexity. In *Empirical evidence and practical applications* (Vol. 2). Charlotte, NC: Information Age Publishing.

Unruh, W. G., & Georgiev, D. D. (2007). Comment on "single photon experiments and quantum complementarity" by D. Georgiev. *Progress in Physics*, *3*, 27−33.

U.S. National Intelligence Council (NIC). (2012). *Global Trends 2030: Alternative Worlds*, Washington, DC.

Valencia, C. R. (2013). *The future of the chemical industry by 2050*. Weinheim: Wiley-VCH.

Vielmetter, G., & Sell, Y. (2014). *Leadership 2030: The six megatrends you need to understand to lead your company into the future.* New York, NY: American Management Association (AMACOM).

Vithoulkas, G., & Muresanu, D. F. (2014). Conscience and consciousness: A definition. *Journal of Medicine and Life*, *7*(1), 104−108.

Walther, P., Jian-Wei, P., Aspelmeyer, M., Ursin, R., et al. (2004). De Broglie wavelength of a non-local four-photon state. *Nature*, *429*(6988), 158−161.

Weick, K. E., & Sutcliffe, K. M. (2007). *Managing the unexpected: Resilient performance in an age of uncertainty* (2nd ed.). San Francisco, CA: Jossey-Bass.

Weidemüller, M. (2013). Spooky action gets collective. *Nature*, *498*(7455), 438−439.

Wheatley, M. J. (1992). *Leadership and the new science: Learning about organizations from an orderly universe.* San Franscisco, CA: Berrett-Koehler.

Wheatley, M. J. (2006). *Leadership and the new science: Discovering order in a chaotic world* (3rd ed.). San Francisco, CA: Berrett-Koehler.

Zhao, B. S., & Schöllkopf, W. (2012). Fundamental physics: Molecules star in quantum movie. *Nature Nanotechnology*, *7*(5), 277−278. doi:10.1038/nnano.2012.44

14

Social Artistry: A Whole System Approach to Sustainable Analysis and Leadership Practice

Skye Burn and Jean Houston

We are living in a time of whole system transition involving the breakdown of the membrane between peoples, cultures, and nations; the re-patterning of human nature and re-genesis of society; a radical deconstruction and reconstruction of social structures; and uprisings from the depths of the emerging new world order. To lead us successfully through this transition, leaders need the capacities and skills of social artists (Houston, 2003, 2004).

Social Artistry brings to leadership the experience and acumen of the master artist. The challenges we face in the world today – climate change, economic instability, resource depletion, population pressure, food and water insecurity, violence – cannot be resolved by technological and material solutions that ignore the intangible realms of emotion and spirit. The power of art comes from giving tangible form to something intangible, in a way that resonates (Burn, 2013). To create a world that embodies the spirit of unity and evokes the sense of peace, leaders need the capacity to integrate the internal and external dimensions of life.

Re-Patterning of Human Nature

The re-patterning of human nature is changing how we collectively think and process information, changing our behavior, and changing how we relate to other cultures and the environment. In every field of human endeavor, the re-patterning is profound.

In *The Future*, Al Gore observes that the "the emergence of a planet-wide electronic communications grid, connecting the thoughts and feelings of billions of people and linking them to rapidly expanding volumes of data" is coalescing the global mind (2013, p. xiv). Computer technology allows people to access and process vast amounts of information very rapidly, while the internet is giving us the capacity to transmit and receive information instantaneously, a kind of digital telepathy bringing spontaneity, innovation, and open sourcing to the workings of the global mind. Old paradigms and belief patterns are decomposing as new connections are made and synapses are activated.

Today, no part of the world is isolated from the workings of the whole or exempt from the changes. In *The Zero Marginal Cost Society*, Jeremy Rifkin speaks of an emerging collaborative commons, a new economic paradigm replacing capitalism, and the Internet of Things (IoT), which "will connect every thing with everyone in an integrated global network. People, machines, natural resources, production lines, logistics networks, consumption habits, recycling flows, and virtually every other aspect of economic and social life will be linked via sensors and software to the IoT platform, continually feeding Big Data to every node—businesses, homes, vehicles—moment to moment, in real time" (2014, p. 11). The Internet of Things is not only a means to integrate the magnificently diverse and seemingly disparate parts of humanity into a highly coordinated network; its emergence is tangible evidence that the integration is occurring. As we become more connected, the growing interdependence is wakening us to the reality of global citizenship. We are gradually, and with considerable resistance, accepting that as global citizens we are individually and collectively responsible for the health and well-being of the whole, as well as the well-being of our local communities.

As we come into different relationships, with each other and with the environment, we are experiencing the need to adjust the systems we use to structure and support our collective activities (economic system, judicial system, healthcare system, etc.). Historically, our lives have been patterned for a different time. In the past, for example, the education system was geared to the needs of the industrial era. Students were taught to sublimate their passions and do work they did not love. Today, the emphasis is shifting. In *Leading from the Emerging Future*, Otto Scharmer and Katrin Kaufer explain: "In order to meet the challenges of our time, we need to shift our thinking as individuals and as a society." We must "relink work—the profession we choose to pursue—with Work—what we really love doing" (2013, p. 77). Others also recognize that it is time to focus on doing work we are genuinely called to do (Stigler & Saionji, 2014; Wheatley, 2012). In effect, changing the education system to support students in discovering their callings and doing work they love is the trim tab to tremendous change, which exemplifies the re-patterning that humanity is experiencing globally.

To navigate this tumultuous sea change and lead us safely into the emerging future, to change the systems without incurring a collapse of the systems, leaders need the capacities of social artists: the ability to connect with "Source" and sense where "it" wants to go (Jaworski, 2012; Scharmer, 2007; Scharmer & Kaufer, 2013), the artistic capacity to sense what wants to emerge, and give it tangible form in the world.

Re-Genesis of Society

The re-genesis of society occurs as social movements rise from the depths, gathering force and momentum, transforming the dynamic of culture, and redefining what it means to be human. Through such uprisings – the civil rights movement, women's movement, environmental movement, Tea Party, Arab Spring, gay marriage – we discover "new styles of interpersonal connection and new ways of being in community, within a global society" (Houston, 2003).

Grassroots movements that take hold and develop a life of their own are beyond any leader's power to control, except through often heartless, inhumane, and harsh modes of repression. While leaders and artists prize the moment when a work comes alive, the moment when a project takes on a life of its own and becomes self-organizing, the re-genesis of society expands the concept to a massive scale. Social movements leverage power to jack existing social structures, institutions, and governments off their foundations in order to replace the foundations with a different set of values and mores. Because our lives are invested in the systems and we depend on the systems to support our collective activity, whole system change is vastly disturbing. Lives and livelihoods are threatened by the re-genesis of society, with its toppling infrastructures.

These challenges call for a new style of leadership. The re-genesis of society elicits resistance and opposition, as some members of society work to change the system, while others resist the changes and work to conserve the values and organizational structures of the old world order. Whatever their affiliation, be it progressive or conservative, old-style leaders eschew the collaborative commons. Old-style leaders seek to further their self-interests and the interests of their organizations at the expense of the whole and, as a consequence, society remains mired in competition and conflict. In contrast, new-style leaders rise above the conflict. They make the health and well-being of the whole their priority, even while pursuing their own interests and the interests of their organizations. New-style leaders understand the creative value of conflict and resistance and they purposefully work with tension to facilitate change in their communities, organizations, institutions, and society.

Social Artistry fosters the new style of leadership, by providing a whole systems approach to situational analysis and leadership practice and by affirming the rightness and beauty of this moment in history. In *Artful Leadership*, Michael Jones notes that "pure expressions of beauty often have a sense of inner inevitability about them" (2006, p. 98). Today, change is inevitable. The life-threatening situations that we face in the world demand systemic change. It is not possible to sustain an economic system based on the unbridled consumption of natural resources, or a transportation system and industrial activities that discharge asphyxiating pollution into the atmosphere, or a polarizing political system that stymies collaboration and erodes trust. We must change the systems if we want to survive in 2050 and beyond. The beauty of the situation is that we are collectively being forced to find within ourselves and bring forth the capacity to create a world that really does justice to what it means to be human.

Four Levels of Social Artistry

The Social Artistry model provides skills to create the enabling environment for participatory democracy and coherent decision-making. The Social Artistry model, initiated by Houston (2004, 2003, 2000, 1996), and practices Houston and Sanders (2004), have been used in leadership development and education worldwide, through the United Nations Development Program, non-governmental organizations, and individual consulting. The Social Artistry model offers a four-level framework for developing leadership capacities, as well as a framework for analyzing situations and developing strategies. The four levels are the sensory-physical, psychological-historical, mythic-symbolic, and integral-unitive.

SENSORY-PHYSICAL LEVEL

On the sensory-physical level, leaders take note of information available through the physical senses. Through training, they become acutely aware of the space, or environment, in which they operate and the density of connectedness on the sensory-physical level. They develop the capacity for somatic knowing, the ability to sense, and interpret undercurrents in the group. They listen to their bodies and discern what their bodies are telling them. This sensory acuity enhances the imagination and the capacity to produce leadership strategies that awaken the sense of unity, sense of peace, and sense of connection in the world body.

In analyzing situations on the sensory-physical level, leaders ask: What are the features of the physical environment? What does the space feel like, look like, smell like, sound like? How does the condition of the environment affect people? What is the status of the economy? How are financial resources allocated? What do people eat? Do they have enough food and water? Are they healthy? Do they have access to education and healthcare? How are people gathered and in what configurations? Who are the stakeholders and are they evenly represented in the decision-making of the whole? This cultural intelligence profile informs leadership decisions and strategies on the sensory-physical level.

Developments in leadership research and practice affirm the importance of somatic knowing and sensory acuity. In the introduction to *Leading with Spirit, Presence, & Authenticity*, the 2014 volume of the International Leadership Association *Building Leadership Bridges* series, Kathryn Goldman Schuyler observes that we humans "have not yet learned how to fully use all of our equipment: we haven't yet mastered the fine art of living with the rich and complex body/mind/sensing apparatus (or self) that we are" and she suggests that "simply paying attention might trigger a different way of approaching life and action" (Goldman Schuyler, Baugher, Jironet, & Lid-Falkmann, 2014, p. xxii). Goldman Schuyler explains that "Embodiment offers a potential for sensing our interconnectivity with one another and with the air, water and earth with which we are in constant interaction" (p. xix). Lois Ruskai Melina, lead editor of *The Embodiment of Leadership*, the 2013 volume in the ILA series, emphasizes that "leadership practice originates in and is informed by bodily experiences" (Melina, Burgess, Lid-Falkmann, & Marturano, 2013, p. xiii) and embodiment is part of "an integrated mind-body approach to the theory, practice, and development of leadership" (p. xv).

Developing leadership capacities on the sensory-physical level is important for the future because we need to pay attention to what our bodies and the world body are telling us in order to discern what feels right. Globally, the world is in transition and there is massive disruption. Statistical analysis and the intellect can measure the level of disruption and incidents of violence and can tell us when progress is being made in their reduction. However, the sense that something is missing or wrong, which goads so much social action, comes from within and leaders need to be cognizant of what is driving people. Leaders are instruments of collective agency and our ability to resolve the life-threatening situations that we face in the world depends, in part, on the breadth and acuity of the sensory awareness that informs our collective agency.

PSYCHOLOGICAL-HISTORIC LEVEL

Leadership education on the psychological-historical level involves personal self-development, psychological literacy, and learning to free oneself and others from messy internal narratives that perpetuate endless hamster wheels of misery, self-criticism, and resentment toward others. Psychological adeptness means not just crossing the great divide of otherness; it means being radically empathetic to otherness in a non-defensive, friendly, and playful manner.

Leaders learn to recognize and address psychological factors that affect agency. Agency is defined as the capacity to make choices and execute our choices in the world. Leadership is an instrument of collective agency, in that leaders help groups make and execute their choices. Such factors include the self-schema (the story we tell ourselves about what we are doing and why we are doing it); self-image (how we see ourselves); how the past influences the present; identity, entelechy, and calling; naming the parts of the self; silencing the self (Jack & Ali, 2010); and complexes. Leaders discover how to liberate themselves from unconscious, habitual ways of reacting to life and instead embrace ways of being that allow them to move through life with exuberance and an appetite for celebration and gratitude.

In analyzing situations on the psychological-historic level, leaders ask: What factors impact the group's ability to make choices and execute their choices in the world? Are cultural complexes active in the situation (Singer & Kimbles, 2004)? How do peoples' past experiences influence their present relationships? How do the people see themselves? Are they self-critical? Are any stakeholders silenced, marginalized, or repressed in the decision-making of the whole? Are people struggling to make themselves heard?

Again, developments in leadership research and practice affirm the need to understand and take into account the psychology of the situation. In *Leadership Is An Art*, Max Depree explains, "Without forgiveness [for what happened in the past], there can be no real freedom to act within a group" (1987, p. 132). Having an open heart, the ability to love and be loved, is the core of psychological adeptness. In *Leadership on the Line*, Martin Linsky and Ronald Heifetz, the originator of Adaptive Leadership, explain the capacity to love and be loved is "the compass heading that orients people most directly," and developing a "sacred heart" lets one

"encompass the entire range of human experience without harden-
ing or closing yourself" (Heifetz & Linsky, 2002, p. 211). Like
Social Artistry, Adaptive Leadership teaches people to remain connected to other people and to the sources of our "most profound
purposes" (p. 230). Both approaches teach us to step back, onto the
balcony, and avoid taking things personally and reacting
defensively.

Developing leadership capacities on the psychological-historical
level is necessary for the future because unresolved psychological
issues stand in the way of world peace and creating a world that
works. Residues of past experiences, the lingering effects of trauma,
and the lack of integration in the collective psyche keep the diverse
parts of humanity from working together with a sense of common
purpose (Burn, 2013). Instead of working together, we are fighting
and working against each other. The situations that we face in the
world are complex, systemic, and globally interconnected. To
resolve these situations we collectively need to work together with a
sense of common purpose. We need to focus attention, energy, and
resources on resolving the issues that hold us apart, instead of letting
fear, insecurity, and defensiveness undermine our capacity to work
together effectively.

MYTHIC-SYMBOLIC LEVEL

Mythically, we are in the midst of an immense weaving of a new
story (Elgin, 2009; Houston, 1996; Korten, 2006). Along with the
global mind, humanity is experiencing the emergence of a global
identity. This emerging identity requires a new story, or self-schema,
which provides thematic continuity from ancient times and explains
what we are doing and why we are doing it in a way that resonates
across cultures, without obfuscating or weakening our unique sepa-
rate identities, for our creative resilience relies on diversity (Burn &
Moreva, 2006). As we move toward a world civilization with high
individuation of culture and high individuation of its participants,
we are discovering that our old stories may no longer serve and new
stories are needed to release and actuate the enormous creativity
that is now permitted us. On the mythic-symbolic level, social artists
consistently seek aspects of the new story, or new understanding of
old stories, that will encourage greater freedom, equality, health,
and flexibility for humanity as a whole.

In analyzing situations on the mythic-symbolic level, leaders
ask: What are the prominent symbols of the culture or organization
(flags, statues, memorials, landmarks, logos)? What are the stories
behind the symbols? What is the dominant cultural narrative, and
what are its origins? Are any stakeholders disenfranchised by the

story? If so, how do their stories differ? Does the cultural narrative support a culture of collaboration? Does the contextual framing of the narrative allow all members of the organization or society to be in alignment and work together with a sense of common purpose toward a common goal? How are people's roles defined by the story?

Again, developments in leadership research and practice affirm the importance of understanding the mythic-symbolic elements of the situation. In *Leadership Can Be Taught*, Sharon Daloz Parks explains:

> Myth cannot be dismissed as mere fiction. Myths are epic, powerful stories that arise from, pervade, and shape the cultures we breathe. They are formed from our collective capacity to understand, interpret, and shape our world. The potency of myths is that they provide ways for us to make sense of our experience, to make meaning we can count on and share with others. Myths give us anchoring images and stories, and they seed the assumptions by which we understand who we are, what is true and untrue, right and wrong. Myths interpret the past, locate us in the present, and shape our expectations of the future. Myths define reality … [and] … The transformation of myth is always an adaptive challenge.
>
> Parks (2005, p. 202)

In *A Passion for the Possible*, Houston elaborates, "Myth is like a force field charging the incidents of our personal history with meaning and significance. It sustains and shapes our emotional attitudes, provides us with life purposes, and energizes our everyday acts. It gives life meaning and momentum" (1997, p. 129).

Developing leadership capacities on the mythic-symbolic level is vital for the future because leaders articulate and interpret the cultural narrative in ways that inspire people to act, which directly impacts organizational and community dynamics, on both the local and global levels. If, for example, leaders promote the story that we are "fighting to make the world a better place," the characters who represent what we are striving to eradicate become the enemy and we end up fighting one another, to the detriment of our communal well-being. Other stories promote a victim mentality. By changing the story, we can change the dynamic and the cultural mentality. Leaders need to understand the mythic structures of the stories we bring to life and they need to know how to use narrative constructively to induce healthy, positive, life-affirming dynamics in their organizations and communities.

INTEGRAL-UNITIVE LEVEL

The integral-unitive level represents a threshold concept in leadership education. Erik Meyer and Ray Land explain that threshold concepts are "akin to passing through a portal" or "conceptual gateway" that opens up "previously inaccessible way[s] of thinking about something" (2008, p. 261). On the integral-unitive level, the consciousness of separation gives way to the holistic awareness of being part of all that is. The personal self seems to disappear, and one enters mind at large — a unitive condition in which one discovers oneself to be the knower, the knowledge, and the known.

Leadership bridges with artistic mastery on the integral-unitive level. Timeless works of art capture something universal, which touches and speaks to the soul, and leaders who operate on this level tap into the substrate of universal consciousness and timeless wisdom. Artists understand that a work of art has a life of its own and intelligence of its own (McNiff, 1998). Leaders who operate on this level understand the dynamic of culture — our collective world making activity — is self-organizing. Like artists, leaders speak of connecting with Source (the nexus of self-organization), surrendering, and going where it leads (Jaworski, 1998, 2012; Scharmer, 2007; Scharmer & Kaufer, 2013). In surrendering, the ego-centric mode of operations gives way to the world-centric mode, ego-system awareness yields to eco-system awareness (Scharmer & Kaufer, 2013), and we attain the flow state (Burn, 2011, 2013). Leaders acknowledge that "if we are to participate in the unfolding process of the universe, we must let life *flow* through us, rather than attempt to *control* life" (Jaworski, 1998, p. 44).

In analyzing situations on the integral-unitive level, leaders ask: Are people thinking globally and acting locally? Is the health and well-being of the whole their priority? To what extent and how consciously do they participate in the collaborative commons? How is the local situation a fractal of the global situation? Have synchronicities affirmed the alignment with the self-organization of the whole? Do people feel time pressure? Are all stakeholders respected and honored for their contributions to the life of the whole? Are the people able to respond to conflict without defensive or violent reactions?

Again, developments in research and practice indicate that leadership is evolving toward integral-unitive level awareness. In the 1970s, the publication of *Servant Leadership* by Greenleaf (1977) intrinsically signaled a shift from the egoic command and control mode of operations to serving what wants to emerge. Connective Leadership, originated by Jean Lipman-Blumen, emphasizes that "As the leadership paradigm shifts from independence to *interdependence*, from control to *connection*, from competition to *collaboration*, from individual to *group*, and from tightly linked geopolitical alliances to loosely coupled global *networks*, we need to encourage a new breed of leaders who can respond effectively to such conditions" (1996, p. 226). Complexity Leadership (Uhl-Bien & Marion, 2007) is based on understanding the dynamic of culture as a self-organizing system. Parks observes, "The new commons in which we now find ourselves is both global in scope and relentlessly local in impact" (2005, p. 3) and Jaworski explains that in connecting with Source and surrendering, one yields "to the design of the universe," which speaks "through the design of my own person" (2012, p. 74).

Objectively, as we move toward holistic politics, "We become less concerned with keeping the peace and more concerned with utilizing diversity and conflict well, to generate insight, energy and power" (Atlee, 2003, p. 90). Michael Ray advises: "The world is in crisis—filled with danger and opportunity. The danger is the end of our existence. The opportunity is for a new kind of creativity, a co-creation based on a new level of consciousness. We have to get into the flow of the process of the world as it is transformed. The charge for us individually, in groups and in the larger systems of the world is to find out how we can relate to each other in this way—and out of that begin to participate in creating a sustainable system" (1999, p. 296).

Developing leadership capacities on the integral-unitive level is essential for the future because our success or failure as a global society, our collective longevity or demise, depends on our ability to sustain and nourish a deep sense of connectedness and shared meaning. In this time of global transformation and unrest, leaders in every sector elicit the sense of connection through tapping into and cultivating integral-unitive awareness in their organizations and communities.

Social Artistry in Action

The categories of social artistry in action include leadership education, community of practice, and leadership development. Three examples.

In 2014, the University of Aruba began offering a nine-month Professional Development Certificate Program in Educational Leadership for Collaboration based on the social artistry model, as part of a strategy for systemic change. Leaders in the Aruban education system (department of education policy administrators, school board administrators, community college deans, school principals, and school management team members) comprise the cohorts. The program coordinator is Juliet Chieuw, Coordinator of the Center for Quality Assurance at the University of Aruba. Janet Sanders, of People Energy and the Jean Houston Foundation, designed the course and is the lead instructor. Douglas Banner, of The Flow

Project, and Robertson Work, of Innovative Leadership Services, and additional faculty broaden the scope of the training. The program blends four local seminars with monthly cohort meetings and international coaching sessions. The seminars progress through the four levels, starting with the sensory-physical and culminating with the integral-unitive. In addition to reading and writing assignments, each student is required to complete a Personal Learning Agenda, including objectives and outcomes; a Cultural Intelligence Profile, analyzing the Aruban culture on the four levels; and an Action Research Project in their institution, targeting an issue on one of the levels and applying principles and practices of leadership for collaboration in its resolution. Participants also learn practices from Technology of Participation (Institute of Cultural Affairs International, 2015) in building collaboration in the schools. The final report from the first cohort concluded that the participants fully infused the new thinking and new skills into their leadership practice and created positive outcomes in their schools.

Social Artistry training programs develop a growing global community of practice. Practitioners share their projects and receive peer support at annual Social Artistry Summits, generally held in Ashland, Oregon, the United States. One such project is Swamp Gravy, a community performance theater in Colquitt, Georgia, the United States, since replicated in other locations. Colquitt is the county seat of Miller County, economically the poorest county in Georgia. Swamp Gravy, co-founded by Joy Jinks and Richard Geer in 1991, addresses the four levels. On the sensory-physical level, the theater project has become a source of revenue, attracting audiences from around the world. A cotton warehouse was converted into a theater, rundown buildings have been renovated, and an inn was created. Landscaping and parks have been made more appealing. On the psychological-historical and mythic-symbolic levels, Miller County, like other areas in the southern United States, has a history of slavery, Civil War ravages, segregation, and racism. Swamp Gravy addresses underlying tensions by going into the local community and recording stories, which are then woven into plays by a professional playwright. The interracial casts consist of community members, up to 100 for each production, who act out the stories on Cotton Hall stage, with a professional director. Among many positive outcomes, Swamp Gravy influenced the Fire Chief to integrate the previously all-white Miller County fire department. The project has also inspired the creation of award-winning murals on landmark buildings, which illustrate the stories of community. On the integral-unitive level, Swamp Gravy participants learn to hold their own as characters on the stage, as they simultaneously act together in bringing the stories to life. Most importantly, they have serious fun working together.

Social Artistry training has been used by the United Nations Development Program (UNDP) as part of a strategy for localizing the Millennium Development Goals (MDGs). In 2003, five days of social artistry training occurred in Albania. Participation was mandatory for UNDP staff and regional project members. The instructors included Robertson Work, UNDP senior policy advisor on decentralized governance; Jean Houston, senior consultant to the UN and the founder of social artistry; Janet Sanders, whose work with UNDP has included special projects in Nepal and Africa; Margaret Rubin, a theater artist; and Elisabeth Rothenberger. The participants, including several representatives from organizations associated with the work of UNDP, were mostly young adults in their late twenties and early thirties. Mornings focused on skills development, using theater, brain exercises, and psycho-physical exercises to awaken the kinesthetic body and demonstrate its use and enhance sensory perception and inner sensing. Afternoons focused on the role of culture and use of culture to fulfill the MDGs. On the psychological-historical level, the main challenge was to counteract the sense of hopelessness and anger. Albania has a history of constant invasion or fear of invasion. From 1945 until the 1990s, Enver Hoxha, the Communist dictator, kept the country prisoner. Hoxha had 900,000 bunkers built, and many still stand like poisonous gray mushrooms in the landscape. After the fall of Communism, attempts to allow democratic possibilities resulted in outrageous money schemes by the government, which collapsed into chaos and hopelessness. Tito of Yugoslavia claimed Kosovo as part of his country and began killing Albanian Moslems. The Serbs carried out "ethnic cleansing" against Kosovar Albanians, until halted by NATO bombing in 1999. On the mythic-symbolic level, the Albanian folktale "The Seven Skillful Brothers" provided a text for teaching teamwork and collaboration. On the integral-unitive level, the participants looked beyond the Albanian narrative to realize they are part of a world story, which is demanding radical change. They realized that patterns changed locally contribute to global change, and the sense of being part of something larger engendered a sense of empowerment and possibility. After the Social Artistry training, the Albania UNDP staff developed adaptations of the curriculum for the local and regional levels. In the following years, additional trainings were given in Kenya, Philippines, and Barbados.

Conclusion

There are certain points where we wake up in our understanding of the suchness of we — where we discover new aspects of what it means to be human and we outgrow the social structures that suited our previous understanding. The notion of the collaborative commons is arising as part of our waking to the phenomenal opportunity of the present situation. The level of crisis, especially the ecological crisis, is so vast, that it can only be resolved through such enormous collective uprisings, which birth new ways of being and doing.

In the coming decades, as the systems we use to structure and support our collective activities become fundamentally unworkable in their present configuration, the four-level Social Artistry model gives leaders and leadership educators a way of assessing and addressing the full complexity of the situation and a framework for developing leadership capacities to meet the needs and challenges of systemic change on the four levels.

The relevance of an artistic approach to leadership is primarily a matter of need, timing, and readiness (Burn, 2005). In *Crossing the Unknown Sea*, David Whyte explains, "There is a good practical reason for encouraging our artistic powers within organizations that up to now might have been unwelcoming or afraid of those qualities …. A good artist, it is often said, is fifty to a hundred years ahead of their time, they describe what lies over the horizon in our future world" (2001, p. 241). As social artists, leaders help us see what is coming and, as Parks concludes, "When the practice of leadership and teaching are recognized as art and artistry, we are honoring the capacity of every human being to respond to the cries and wonder of the world *as an artist* and to co-create with others; that is, to cultivate a collective creativity—a shared excellence in the art of life—a practice rigorous in its own terms" (2005, p. 230).

References

Atlee, T. (2003). *The tao of democracy: Using co-intelligence to create a world that works for all.* Cranston, RI: The Writer's Collective.

Burn, S. (2011). What art offers leadership: Looking beneath the surface. In J. Barbour & G. Hickman (Eds.), *Leadership for Transformation* (pp. 106–123). Building Leadership Bridges. San Francisco, CA: Jossey-Bass.

Burn, S. (2013). Seeking alignment in the world body: The art of embodiment. In L. Melina, G. Burgess, L. Lid-Falkman, & A. Marturano (Eds.), *The embodiment of leadership* (pp. 65–83). Building Leadership Bridges. San Francisco, CA: Jossey-Bass.

Burn, S., & Moreva, L. (2006). Preface. Unity and diversity in religion and culture: Exploring the psychological and philosophical issues underlying global conflict. In L. Moreva (Ed.), International readings on theory, history and philosophy of culture (Vol. 22). St. Petersburg, Russia: St. Petersburg Branch of the Russian Institute for Cultural Research and the Philosophical and Cultural Research Centre "Eidos", under UNESCO auspices.

DePree, M. (1987). *Leadership is an art.* East Lansing, MI: Michigan State University Press.

Elgin, D. (2009). *The living universe: Where are we? Who are we? Where are we going?* San Francsco, CA: Berrett-Koehler.

Goldman Schuyler, K., Baugher, J. E., Jironet, K., & Lid-Falkman, L. (Eds.). (2014). *Leading with spirit, presence, and authenticity.* Building Leadership Bridges. San Francisco, CA: Jossey-Bass.

Gore, A. (2013). *The future: Six drivers of global change.* New York, NY: Random House.

Greenleaf, R. (1977). *Servant leadership: A journey into the nature of legitimate power and greatness.* New York, NY: Paulist Press.

Heifetz, R., & Linsky, M. (2002). *Leadership on the line: Staying alive through the dangers of leading.* Boston, MA: Harvard Business School Press.

Houston, J. (1996). *A mythic life: Learning to live our greater story.* New York, NY: HarperCollins.

Houston, J. (1997). *A passion for the possible: A guide to realizing your true potential.* San Francisco, CA: HarperSanFrancisco.

Houston, J. (2000). *Jump time: Shaping your future in a world of radical change.* New York, NY: Jeremy P. Tarcher/Putnam.

Houston, J. (2003). *Applying social artistry to decentralized governance for human development, delivered during the United Nations 5th Global Forum on Reinventing Government, Innovation, and Quality in Government of the 21st century.* Mexico City. 3–7 November 2003. Retrieved from http://jeanhoustonfoundation.org/resources/applying-social-artistry-to-decentralized-governance-for-human-development/ Accessed on April 17, 2015.

Houston, J. (2004). *Social artistry.* Baltimore, MD: Johns Hopkins School of Education. Retrieved from http://education.jhu.edu/PD/newhorizons/future/articles/social-artistry/index.html. Accessed on April 17, 2015.

Houston, J., & Sanders, J. (2004). *The social artist's fieldbook: Book one: Developing your inner capacities.* New York, NY: United Nations Development Program. Available from the Jean Houston Foundation website.

Institute of Cultural Affairs International. (2015). *Technology of participation.* Retrieved from http://ica-international.org/top/top-intro.htm. Accessed on April 17, 2015.

Jack, D., & Ali, A. (Eds.). (2010). *Silencing the self across cultures: Depression and gender in the social world.* Oxford: Oxford University Press.

Jaworski, J. (1998). *Synchronicity: The inner path of leadership.* San Francisco, CA: Berrett-Koehler.

Jaworski, J. (2012). *Source: The inner path of knowledge creation.* San Francisco, CA: Berrett-Koehler.

Jones, M. (2006). *Artful leadership: Awakening the commons of imagination.* Victoria: Trafford Publishing.

Korten, D. (2006). *The great turning: From empire to earth community.* San Francisco, CA: Berrett-Koehler.

Land, R., & Meyer, J. G. (2008). Cited by Cousin, G., In *Threshold concepts: Old wine in new bottles or new forms of transactional inquiry.* In Land, R., Meyer, J. & Smith, J. (Eds.), *Threshold concepts within the disciplines* (pp. 261–272). Rotterdam: Sense Publishers. Retrieved from http://www.ee.ucl.ac.uk/~mflanaga/thresholds.html. Accessed on April 17, 2015.

Lipman-Blumen, J. (1996). *Connective leadership: Managing in a changing world.* New York, NY: Oxford University Press.

McNiff, S. (1998). *Trust the process: An artist's guide to letting go.* Boston, MA: Shambhala.

Melina, L. R., Burgess, G. J., Lid-Falkman, L., & Marturano, A. (2013). *The embodiment of leadership. Building leadership bridges.* San Francisco, CA: Jossey-Bass.

Parks, S. D. (2005). *Leadership can be taught: A bold approach for a complex world.* Boston, MA: Harvard Business School Press.

Ray, M. (1999). Social creativity as an heroic path in world crisis. In A. Montuori & R. Purser (Eds.), *Social creativity* (Vol. 1). Cresskill, NJ: Hampton Press.

Rifkin, J. (2014). *The zero marginal cost society: The internet of things, the collaborative commons, and the eclipse of capitalism.* New York, NY: Macmillan.

Scharmer, O. (2007). *Theory U: Leading from the future as it emerges.* Cambridge, MA: The Society for Organizational Learning.

Scharmer, O., & Kaufer, K. (2013). *Leading from the emerging future: From ego-system to eco-system economies.* San Francisco, CA: Berrett-Koehler.

Singer, T., & Kimbles, S. (2004). *The cultural complex: Contemporary Jungian perspectives on psyche and society.* New York, NY: Brunner-Routledge.

Stigler, B., & Saionji, Y. (2014). Enspirited leadership in Japan. In K. Goldman Schuyler, J. Baugher, K. Joironet, & L. Lid-Falkman (Eds.), *Leading with spirit, presence, & authenticity* (pp. 59−75). Building Leadership Bridges. San Francisco, CA: Jossey-Bass.

Uhl-Bien, M., & Marion, R. (Eds.). (2007). *Complexity leadership: Part 1: Conceptual foundations.* Charlotte, NC: Information Age Publishing.

Wheatley, M. (2012). *So far from home: Lost and found in our brave new world.* San Francisco, CA: Berrett-Koehler Publishers, Inc.

Whyte, D. (2001). *Crossing the unknown sea: Work as a pilgrimage of identity.* New York, NY: Riverhead Books.

15 Attentional Leadership Theory: A Framework for the 2050 Leader

Bruce H. Jackson

Introduction

There is no country, state, or community where leadership is not exercised. But defining leadership—even teaching people how to become a leader—remains in debate. Numerous principles, theories, and tools abound – many grounded in theoretical and empirical research – however, most convey a limited angle of vision, provide an incomplete combination of elements, and lack the dynamic understanding of this complex and evolving discipline. At the same time, studies continue to show that developing leadership skills makes a difference in academic (Komives, Lucas, & McMahon, 2009), professional (McCartney & Campbell, 2006), military, and other domains (Zenger & Folkman, 2009).

With so many moving and interconnected variables, leadership might be likened to a swarm of butterflies, each one a variable in relation to the others, with structures and patterns unclear – yet beautiful. We know leadership when we see it, but often struggle to define or frame it holistically and temporally. Leadership scholars aim to re-organize the butterflies into meaningful frameworks but often do so with a limited perspective. While progress continues, more work is needed to unify, or at least better understand how to relate these leadership variables. As we move toward 2050, scholars and practitioners alike should work together to clarify the science *and* practice of leadership – making it more understandable and more useful for a broader audience.

Some consider leadership and inside-out process, leading self first, then others to expand one's circle of influence (Covey, 2004). Others look at leadership through an outside-in or top-down perspective (balcony vs. dance floor) where problem solving and adaptive processes can be exercised within groups, organizations, and whole societies (Heifetz, 1998; Linsky & Heifetz, 2002; Williams, 2005). In a complex world, more relevant is to lead from the inside-out, outside-in, top-down, bottom-up, and multiple other angles — including time and place — as circumstances require. If there is one thing that futurists seem to agree upon it's that the world is becoming increasingly complex, whether through interconnected global economies, technologies that transcend communication, cultural boundaries, and traditional organizational practices, or the speed at which problems need to be solved individually or collectively, the 2050 leader must be able to work effectively and draw upon a multitude of leadership skill-sets on demand.

Seeing complex systems requires a distinct solution based on the intersection of multiple variables. This suggests that the exercise of leadership takes place moment by moment where attention is required using available resources and informed practices to address the complex challenges at hand. Why then is this model relevant to the future leader? Because it provides a broad framework that drills down and parcels out the complexity into 125 discrete boxes that more clearly identifies various intersecting competencies clusters — making it easier for a leader to identify knowledge and skill gaps that may be required as they address leadership challenges moment by moment. This is a new paradigm (Kuhn, 2012) for the research, understanding, and utilization of leadership theories and practices.

This chapter seeks to frame leadership theories and practices based on the allocation of attention, resources, and the time needed to influence human systems and processes in multiple dimensions to achieve valued objectives. This new paradigm, which I've termed Attentional Leadership Theory (ALT), does not suggest a single universal theory, but a *binding* or *bounding* framework that draws connections within and between intersecting dimensions, which contain a multitude of interconnected systems and processes relevant to effective leadership. Given the brevity of this chapter only a brief introduction is possible. Future efforts and publications will seek to draw further connections and applications.

The Foundation of Attentional Leadership Theory

While there are many definitions of leadership, in ALT, I define leadership as, "The capacity to influence oneself and others in the pursuit of individual, interpersonal, team, organization, or civic/ community objectives; within any Meaningful Life Arena." At this definition's core, leadership *is* influence. Leadership is more than the direct exercise of command. It is a process of using oneself to influence others at multiple levels using various theories and *informed practices* to achieve valued objectives.

ALT leadership theory draws a distinction between technical knowledge (Tk) and leadership knowledge (Lk). Technical knowledge represents the specific knowledge or skills needed within a particular profession or domain (e.g., law, aviation, athletics, engineering, medicine). By contrast leadership knowledge is often transferrable to other disciplines or Meaningful Life Arenas (MLA's). In ALT, those who develop both Tk and Lk develop an "X Factor" (Plimpton, 1995), which translates into higher levels of performance or influence − inside and out − whether performing individually, in dyads, teams, organizations, or even communities (Figure 1).

Attentional Leadership Theory emphasizes the importance of scientific inquiry − where rigorous research leads to five levels of knowledge and informed practice. Scientific inquiry begins with questions inside a conceptual domain (Level 1) − where new Principles, Laws, and/or emerging Knowledge (PLKs) are discovered and found valid and reliable (if only temporarily given the null hypothesis; Level 2). New PLKs lead to emergent paradigms that often require translation (using models, schemas, illustrations, etc.) to make them comprehensible and applicable (Level 3). New PLKs and paradigms (Kuhn, 2012), whether in the hard sciences (e.g., astronomy, biology, or chemistry) or the soft sciences (e.g., political, organizational, interpersonal, or personal), increase our understanding of underlying systems and/or processes in action. Examples of natural systems include planetary rotation, photosynthesis in plants, or chemical bonding, while examples of human systems include thought/emotion processes within the brain, uses of power, organizational communications, or legislative process. This

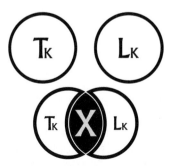

Figure 1.   Technical Knowledge Linked to Leadership Knowledge. The "X" Factor.

is otherwise referred to as Level 4 (Bertalanffy, 1969; Blanchard, 2008; Meadows, 2008). Understanding human systems and processes (and the PLKs and paradigms that govern them) give rise to informed practice to influence self and lead others – using the interconnected dimensions hereafter discussed (Level 5).

Attentional Leadership Theory draws upon the theory of flow (Csikszentmihalyi, 1998, 2008). Central to flow theory are the following characteristics (Csikszentmihalyi, 2008):

1. An activity has clear goals and objectives;
2. An activity provides unambiguous feedback creating a coherent demand for action;
3. There is a sense of control where awareness and actions merge together;
4. There are limited distractions and high concentration power;
5. Performance seems effortless;
6. There is an altered sense of time;
7. There is a loss of ego-awareness and complete absorption in the effort;
8. The activity is intrinsically motivating; and
9. The activity provides a context where perceived challenges and perceived skills meet (see Jackson, 2003, p. 3).

The underlying theme of ALT is that leadership – at its core – is about influencing people within context. This is not dissimilar to flow and requires that attention and resources be placed *when*, *where*, and at the *time* needed, to influence human systems and processes at any level, be it individual, interpersonal, team, organization, or community. Other peak performance (Garfield, 1987; Jackson, 2011; Orlick, 2007), and positive psychology literatures (Fredrickson, 2009; Seligman, 2003, 2006) offer additional PLKs relevant to ALT.

The Framework of Attentional Leadership Theory

Attentional Leadership Theory suggests that leading self and others is more than fixed traits or mastery of competencies, behaviors, or situations. 2050 Leadership, will require a more dynamic, interconnected, and fluid process, where, moment by moment, attention is summoned to influence human systems inside the self and others, within various domains, time perspectives, or dimensions, using well researched practices, and to achieve valued objectives. This will require a more holistic and systemic mindset, with nimble focus, ready to address any challenges a leader may face – moment by moment.

ALT posits that 15 *big box* dimensions (and their intersections) contain many of the literatures often used to understand and exercise leadership. The first five dimensions (intrapersonal focus) include the physical, emotional, psychological, philosophical, and spiritual dimensions of self. The second five (external focus) include the individual, interpersonal, team, organization, and community (regional, national, or international). Third are the five dimensions of time (long future, short future, focus in the present, short past, and long past). These 15 broad dimensions, in any combination, serve the purpose of providing a meaningful structure for the many literatures and sub-literatures of leadership relevant within any technical or life arena.

THE FIVE INTRAPERSONAL DIMENSIONS

The five intrapersonal dimensions are where individuals lead themselves to achieve their best (Waitley, 1984), find personal flow (Jackson, 2011), or demonstrate excellence (Orlick, 2007). This may be called self or personal leadership (Neck & Manz, 2012) – where leaders focus attention on various internal systems and processes in order to develop their own potential (or that of others) toward full engagement (Loehr & Schwartz, 2004).

Physical Dimension

Personal leadership and the leadership of others requires the appropriate placement of attention on the body's physical systems and sub-systems that support or deny energy, general health, and well-being (Gurt, Schwennen, & Elke, 2011). Internal considerations that support physical infrastructure and optimal functioning include nutritional requirements, physical fitness (aerobic, anaerobic, strength, flexibility), sleep, rest and recovery, stress management (e.g., breathing and meditation). All are practices that influence physical systems toward optimal functioning. External physical resources (e.g., energy inputs, tools) – even physical context (Zimbardo, 2007) play a significant role in influencing human behavior. Physical assets or deficits influence the other intrapersonal dimensions (e.g., sleep deprivation on mood, nutrition on thinking) which affects human performance in work (Ford, Cerasoli, Higgins, & Decesare, 2011) and other environments.

Emotional Dimension

The study of Emotional Intelligence (Bradberry & Greaves, 2009; Goleman, 2006; Stein & Book, 2006) and resilience (Siebert, 2005) has become increasingly relevant within the field of leadership.

Developing one's capacity to identify, label, and manage emotions is at the core of personal resiliency, self-control, even grit (Cornum, Matthews, & Seligman, 2011). This gives individuals choice using cognitive and behavioral strategies to buffer emotional/affective triggers (Reynolds, 2004) within self and in relationships (Higgs & Aitken, 2003) at multiple levels.

Research continues to suggest that individuals with greater emotional awareness and strategies to regulate emotions have a greater capacity to manage stress and perform at higher levels by managing emotions which often get in the way of intentional focus (Wong & Law, 2002). Effective leaders influence not just with the head, but the heart, recognizing the importance in growing their emotional capacities, not only within self, but also within larger contexts of human relationships.

Psychological Dimension

There is a vast array of mental/cognitive capacities/skills that permeate the psychological dimension. Technical knowledge (represented earlier by Tk) in combination with other psychological skills, such as strategic and critical thinking, planning and problem solving, verbal self-guidance, visioning, mental rehearsal, perspective taking, sustained attention, self-reflection, and others are equally relevant in self as well as leading others (Lee, 1999). This includes an extensive number of psychological disciplines – with many seeking to remove "deficit-based" (i.e., psychological liabilities) while others focus on "strength-based" (Brewerton, 2011), such as positive psychology (e.g., psychological assets; Seligman, 2012) or strengths (Clifton, 2002). Meta-cognition, or *thinking about thinking* (Kruglanski & Higgins, 2007), is also applicable for the reflective leader.

Philosophical Dimension

The philosophical dimension is primarily focused on values and experiences acquired through self and others. While the spiritual dimension (see below) focuses primarily on conceptions of higher than self ideals or prescribed doctrine, the philosophical dimension taps into acquired shared values, ethics, and morals, gained through "lived experiences" (Allison & Gediman, 2007) and wisdom (Sternberg, 2001). This "values-based leadership" focuses on defining a shared set of core principles and values between leaders and followers (Frost, 2014), in teams (Shoenfelt, 2011), in organizations (Ledford Jr., Wendenhof, & Strahley, 1995), and in communities. Connecting values and ethics back to flow (at the heart of ALT) was central to the Good Work Project (Gardner, Csikszentmihalyi, & Damon, 2008), where leaders not only facilitated excellence and focus, but within an ethical and moral frame.

Spiritual Dimension

The spiritual dimension is comprised of larger-than-self factors such as principles, truths, beliefs, moral values, meaning, and purpose (Gini, 1997). One's spiritual dimension transcends the self (as compared to the philosophical dimension, which is derived from personal and collective experiences). This is a compelling dimension for leaders as it taps deeply held inner and seeded historical values derived from established faith traditions. As Daft (2007) pointed out "All leadership practices can be used for good or evil, and thus have a moral dimension" (p. 170). As such, the spiritual dimension is central to the study and practice of leadership, often taking the form of integrity, humility, respect, appreciation, fair treatment, and personal reflection (Reave, 2005) – through calling and membership (Fry, 2003) – helping people find deeper meaning through their work.

Together these five internal dimensions (physical, emotional, psychological, philosophical, and spiritual) comprise large conceptual blocks with numerous sub-literatures. Of significant value is the cross-influential nature of these dimensions and their collective influence on the individual (see Figure 2).

FIVE EXTERNAL DIMENSIONS

When engaging any change effort, "the leader must take into consideration individuals', a group's, or an organization's, as well as his or her own, contributions to the effort." (Bass, 1990, p. 33). This suggests that influence and leadership take place within oneself as well

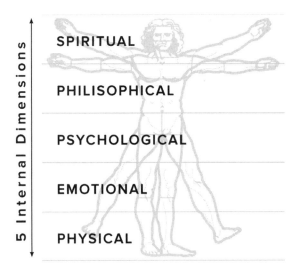

Figure 2.   The Five Internal Dimensions.

as in relationships with others, including teams, organizations – even communities.

Personal Dimension

Using the five intrapersonal dimensions already discussed, an individual may exercise personal leadership by becoming physically robust, emotionally resilient, psychologically skilled, philosophically grounded, and spiritually connected. This notion of "full engagement" (Loehr & Schwartz, 2004) suggests that we need to look at ourselves with a more comprehensive, holistic mindset – to place attention in each of the five intrapersonal dimensions to function optimally (Greene, 2012; Tracy, 2002; Waitley, 1984) – recognizing that each of the five internal and five external dimensions is interconnected (e.g., thoughts on moods, sleep on health, food on energy, beliefs on thoughts) (Wisneski & Anderson, 2004). As optimally functioning individuals, leaders may use themselves more effectively as agents of influence and change.

Interpersonal Dimension

This level represents the dyadic or interpersonal dimension. Our ability to achieve goals almost always requires others to assist in various roles and capacities. Interpersonal principles, theories, and practices are vast and complex, and are necessary to coordinate and leverage one another in the pursuit of common goals. Interpersonal leadership principles include numerable practices such as effective verbal and non-verbal communication, active listening, giving and receiving feedback, praise, understanding personality and cultural differences, interpersonal conflict, use of empathy and understanding, building rapport, motivating and rewarding, appreciating and valuing, managing, coaching, networking, negotiating, and other practices designed to support higher levels of relational influence (Canary, 2008) to achieve common goals – nested within larger relational clusters as summarized below.

Team Dimension

This level represents human relationships beyond the dyad – usually groups larger than 3 but less than 10 (Rouse & Boff, 2005). In this external dimension leaders influence and are influenced by the group or team, each influencing the other by focusing attention and energies on the needs of each to accomplish shared goals or purpose (Larson & LaFasto, 1989). There are principles and practices that inform successful teams (Katzenbach & Smith, 2006), the process of team development (Miller, 2003), types and purpose of teams, optimal team functioning (e.g., clarifying roles and responsibilities, team accountabilities, team norms, identifying strengths and weaknesses), dysfunctions of teams (Lencioni, 2002), and why teams succeed and fail (Robbins & Finley, 2000).

Relevant here are the five internal dimensions applied at the team level such as physical assets and/or liabilities of teams (e.g., general physical health of team members, adequate physical resources), emotional assets and/or liabilities of team members (e.g., emotional understanding, empathy), psychological assets and/or liabilities (e.g., shared mental models, ideas, working knowledge), philosophical assets and/or liabilities (e.g., guiding principles, norms or ethics) – even spiritual assets and/or liabilities (e.g., a connection to a valued purpose beyond self in service of the team).

Organizational Dimension

Organizations contain distinct levels, functions, and cross-functions (i.e., operations, finance, accounting, information technology, human resources, marketing, sales, etc.) that work together to produce products, services, knowledge, or other valued outputs. With consideration to many permutations and combinations of individuals, relationships, intersecting groups or teams, divisions or business lines, etc., we take into consideration these functional units and their coordination through the broader organizational system (Senge, 2010). Other organizational considerations include its mission, vision, core values, governance, strategies, structures, functional systems, and process alignment – all contributing to a collective corporate culture (Deal, Kennedy, Kennedy, & Deal, 2000; Kotter & Heskett, 2011). Connections to the five internal dimensions may be made at the physical (plant, property, equipment), emotional (organization climate/employee engagement), psychological (institutional knowledge, shared models, mindsets or "theories in use"), philosophical (corporate values, beliefs, norms and standards), and spiritual (higher than organization purposes, faith, social responsibility).

Community Dimension (Regional, National, International)

Larger environments increase the level of human complexity and number of variables based on all previous external dimensions discussed – recognizing that communities are composed of governments, organizations, groups, interpersonal dyads, and individuals.

Using this largest level, we might look at communities physically (e.g., physical infrastructure, public health/well-being, and safety), emotionally (e.g., the general climate/attitude), psychologically (e.g., shared mindset, mental models, knowledge), philosophically (e.g., core values, beliefs, culture and standards (Crowther & Gomez, 2012; Michalos & Poff, 2012)) – and spiritually (e.g., collective spiritual beliefs and practices (Marques, Dhiman, & King, 2009)) (see Figure 3). Taken together these 10 dimensions may be

Figure 3.   The Five External Dimensions.

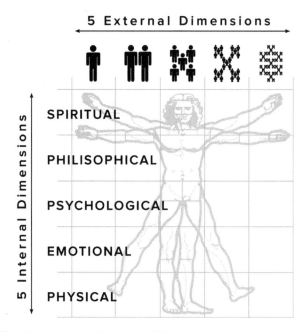

Figure 4.   The 10 Intersecting Dimensions (Static).

illustrated using the following schematic representing the intersection between the five internal and five external dimensions (see Figure 4).

This model suggests that influence and leadership, through the placement of attention and resources, can be exercised by influencing systems and processes at any of the 10 dimensions. Together they provide an initial static matrix from which to frame leadership theories and practice with 25 intersecting content areas (Table 1).

FIVE DIMENSIONS OF TIME

Exercising influence using any process is exercised moment by moment (thoughts, decisions, transactions) in time (Thoms & Greenberger, 1995). If moments were counted in hours, 8760 of these are given to each of us annually from which to exercise influence. While there is no perfect model for constructing time, five distinct blocks are used here: Long future (LF), short future (SF), focus (F), short past (SP), and long past (LP). As the third category of five dimensions, time is central to understanding and exercising leadership.

Long Future (LF)

Leadership is never static, but constantly moving toward the future from the past, through the present – moment by moment – then into the past. In the broadest sense, at every level, we plan for the LF using the SF as a bridge. In the LF dimension resides abstract forethought such as a desired future state. This may be defined as strategic leadership (Ireland & Hitt, 1999). In this dimension we explore mission, vision, and legacy building strategies, which sets standard of excellence and integrity at every level of human engagement (see Daft, 2007, p. 397).

Short Future (SF)

In this dimension, LF abstractions are broken down into concrete goals. Goals setting, strategic and contingency planning, risk management, time maximization, and preparation strategies reside within this SF dimension used by leaders at every level to ensure that progress is being made toward the LF objectives.

Focus

At the center is present moment focus (F) or attention in the moment. Various concepts such as "flow" (Csikszentmihalyi, 2008), "execution" (Bossidy, Charan, & Burck, 2002), "strategic implementation" (Bourgeois & Brodwin, 1984) "mindfulness" (Langer, 1990), and the many types of focus (Goleman, 2013) all discuss attention in the moment for different purposes.

Attentional Leadership Theory's premise is that leaders must continually monitor and focus their attention, time, and resources where they are needed now – the "work at the center" – (Heifetz, Linsky, & Grashow, 2009), to remove interferences and use

Table 1: Summary of Inter-Relationships of the 10 Dimensions (Static).

	Personal	Interpersonal	Team	Organization	Community
Spiritual	Higher than self, often religious principles, values, and beliefs applied to self.	Higher than relationship, often religious principles, values, and beliefs applied to relationships.	Higher than self, often religious principles, values, and beliefs applied to team.	Higher than self, often religious principles, values, and beliefs applied to organization (i.e., spirit in the workplace).	Higher than self, often religious principles, values, and beliefs applied to community.
Philosophical	Self-constructed values including personal beliefs, principles ethics, norms etc	Interpersonally constructed values including shared beliefs, principles ethics, norms etc	Team constructed values including shared beliefs, ethics, norms, team culture etc	Organization constructed values including shared beliefs, ethics, norms organization culture etc	Community constructed values including shared beliefs, ethics, norms and culture etc
Psychological	Mental models concepts Perceptions Thoughts Attitudes Perspective Knowledge etc	Shared mental models concepts Perceptions Thoughts Attitudes Perspective Knowledge etc	Shared mental models concepts Perceptions Thoughts Attitudes Perspective Knowledge etc	Shared mental models concepts Perceptions Thoughts Attitudes Perspective Knowledge etc	Shared mental models concepts Perceptions Thoughts Attitudes Perspective Knowledge etc
Emotional	Understanding and managing personal affect/emotions.	Understanding and managing others affect emotions (e.g., empathy, conflict, understanding).	Understanding and managing team emotions (e.g., empathy, conflict, understanding).	Understanding and managing emotional climate of the organization. (e.g., empathy, conflict, understanding).	Understanding and managing emotional climate of the community. (e.g., empathy, conflict, understanding).
Physical	Internal physical well-being. Required internal and external physical resources and context (e.g., nutrition, fitness, rest).	Interpersonal physical well-being. Required internal and external physical resources and context.	Team physical well-being. Required internal and external physical resources and context.	Organization physical well-being. Required internal and external physical resources and context (e.g., infrastructure, corporate wellness).	Community physical well-being. Required internal and external physical resources and context (e.g., infrastructure, public health).

informed leadership practices. While focus may be centered purely in the moment purely for its own sake (e.g., mindfulness), it is also the centerpiece of ALT as focus and attention go to where they are needed within the ALT model discussed throughout this chapter.

Short Past (SP)

The SP represents the receptacle of every Moment of Performance (MOP). It is from the SP where information is gathered through

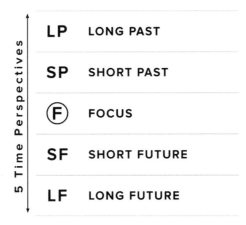

Figure 5. The Five Dimensions of Time.

Table 2:   Summary of the Five Dimensions of Time.

Long Past	Short Past	Focus	Short Future	Long Future
The collective history of an individual, a relationship, team, organization, or community. It is here that the leader learns of the relevant data that informs future practice at any intersecting space referenced above.	Exiting moments of performance or execution at the individual, interpersonal, team, organization, or community level. The primary space where leaders gather feedback and identify course corrections at any intersecting space referenced above.	In the moment focus and/or execution at the individual, interpersonal, team, organization, or community level. Where attention is being placed in the here and now at any intersecting space referenced above.	Where all relevant preparatory strategies and goals are set prior to entering moments of performance at the individual, interpersonal team, organization, or community level at any intersecting space referenced above.	The abstract and broad future constructed at the individual, interpersonal, team, organization, or community level at any intersecting space referenced above.

experience as feedback loops for future reference (Coonradt, 2012). Studies suggest that "candid, insightful feedback" is one of the more important aspects of growth and development yet most supervisors fail to provide it (Michaels, Handfield-Jones, & Axelrod, 2001). Short past work can be represented through such practices as "After Action Reports" in the military (Department of the Army, 1993), quality or statistic process control mechanisms (Wheeler, 2000, 2010), Balanced Scorecards (Kaplan & Norton, 1996), giving or receiving feedback generally (Folkman, 2006), or the simple practice of self-reflection (Branson, 2007). Short past work is primarily feedback driven and takes place in any dynamic system (Gleick, 1987).

Long Past (LP)

Long past (LP) represents a collective history or story (Loehr, 2008). Through the development of personal, interpersonal, team, organization, community histories, and stories we retrieve core lessons (Allison & Gediman, 2007; Urban, 2002), develop an evolving self or collective image, store real or imaged beliefs, and build self-efficacy (Bandura, 1997). Within the LP space is where beliefs, values, norms, cultural memes – even the challenging or building of an individual (Maltz, 1984), team (Hertel & Solansky, 2011), organization, or collective self-image (Gonzalez & Chakraborty, 2012) (see Figure 5, Table 2).

The Interconnectivity of Leadership Theories and Practice

The 15 dimensions of ALT suggest that within any arena, leadership is exercised through influence within the greater system. As discussed within the five levels of knowledge, influence, requires informed practice, within a system, governed by principles, within a given arena/context. Attentional Leadership Theory recognizes the inherent value of all relevant leadership principles, theories, and practices recognizing that there is a time, place, and duration for which to use them. These 15 "big blocks" identify 125 intersecting "mini blocks" where theoretical intersections may be explored.

By adding new variables, these "mini blocks" can be broken down further as more specific inquiries take place. In the case above, attention may be given to the physical aspects of a community within an historical time frame to better understand how it has evolved and may need to be influence or led given this historical knowledge (see Figure 6).

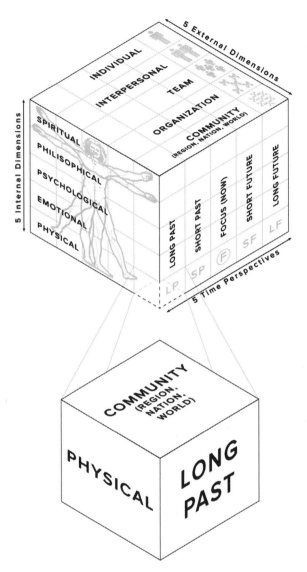

Figure 6. The 15 "Big Blocks" and the 125 "Mini-Blocks."

Practical Applications of ALT and Diagnostic Questions

At its core ALT may be a diagnostic framework from which to dive deeper into leadership theory, practice, and theoretical intersections. Addressing any current circumstance, a leader may inquire where, when, and for what duration his/her attention needs to be directed to address a problem/opportunity to influence a system or process to achieve a desired end. Five general questions may be used in exploration of this model:

1. Given current reality, situation, or challenge, where should attention and resources be placed now? Does the problem concern primarily technical or leadership challenges? If the challenge concerns a leadership challenge then consider these questions:
2. Concerning the leadership challenge, is attention needed in the long future (mission, vision, legacy), short future (goals, planing, preparation), in the moment focus/execution, short past (feedback, measurement, learning), or long past (acquired knowledge, history, wisdom)?
3. Within the time perspective, what external dimension needs attention: personal, interpersonal, team, organization, or community (regional, national, international)?
4. Within these external dimensions, what internal dimension(s)is/are most relevant: physical (i.e., well-being, resources, and infrastructure), emotional (understanding/managing affect), psychological (knowledge, concepts, perspectives), philosophical (ethics, values, standards) spiritual (purpose, beliefs, principles), or any combination of them?
5. At relevant conceptual intersections (where attention is being placed), what are the best, most reliable "informed practices" for leaders to influence most effectively to achieve desired results?

Five Development Dimensions to Consider

Taking ALT further, how might these intersecting dimensions be useful at various developmental stages and arenas? Outside of traditional corporate, organizational, civic arenas, programs within colleges/universities (Komives et al., 2009), and pre- and postsecondary schools are not far behind (Covey, 2009). Programs such as "Life Re-imagined" (Leider, 2013) offer similar leadership theories, tools, and practices for more mature populations. These roughly drawn life stages (presecondary, postsecondary, college/university, professional, and mature) add other dimensions from which to consider new research and practice. Intersecting these with the multitude of cultural and demographic differences increases the complexity exponentially but with more narrow bands of focus from which to explore new questions to inform leadership theories and practice.

The Future Implications for Developing Leaders

Attentional Leadership Theory suggests that continuous and rigorous research will ask deeper and more refined questions, providing new insights, methods, and tools that leaders can use to exercise influence where, when, and how it is needed. In contrast to books and programs that offer "off the shelf" models, the ALT framework suggests that (a) there are innumerable principles, theories, and tools (known and yet to be discovered) that may be used in the right place, at the right time, and for the right duration, to exercise influence and leadership most effectively, (b) we must consider a diagnostic approach and identify the current strengths and weaknesses of leaders to better understand what they need to learn and use now for the challenges they face today (Zenger & Folkman, 2009), and (c) that leaders may benefit from a personalized competency based approach – at every developmental stage, with consideration to various cultural, demographic, and contextual variables. Such a mindset is the clear difference between transactional leaders and transformational leaders who use multiple "informed practices" to move a systems forward (see Daft, 2007, p. 356).

Such is the 2050 leader: one who recognizes the importance of one's own physical robustness, emotional resilience, psychological complexity, flexibility and focus, philosophical grounding – even spiritual connection; to build and cultivate interpersonal relationships and high performing teams; to understand the interconnected parts of organizations – even communities (at every level). And to see each of these inter-connections in relationship to the long future, achieved through the short future, generating thoughts, making decisions, and taking actions through moment-by-moment focus and engagement, learning from every iteration in the short past, yet tapping into individual and collective histories as a significant resource for managing challenges now. Attentional Leadership Theory suggests that this is the toolkit of the future. Doing this within any distinct technical environment or domain will render leadership education and training an essential part of our education system, from Kindergarten all the way to the C-suite – recognizing that no one is genetically predestined for leadership, but instead capable of significant growth (Dweck, 2007) in the pursuit of leadership knowledge, skills, and abilities to serve in any life area. In 2050 Tk and Lk will be two equal parts of the human development equation and be the competitive advantage necessary to compete within an increasingly complex and changing world.

References

Allison, J., & Gediman, D. (Eds.). (2007). *This I believe: The personal philosophies of remarkable men and women* (1st ed.). New York, NY: Holt Paperbacks.

Bandura, A. (1997). *Self-efficacy: The exercise of control* (1st ed.). New York, NY: Worth Publishers.

Bass, B. M. (1990). *Bass & Stogdill's handbook of leadership: Theory, research & managerial applications* (3rd Sub ed.). New York, NY: Free Press.

Bertalanffy, L. V. (1969). *General system theory: Foundations, development, applications* (Rev.). New York, NY: George Braziller Inc.

Blanchard, B. S. (2008). *System engineering management* (4th ed.). Hoboken, NJ: Wiley.

Bossidy, L., Charan, R., & Burck, C. (2002). *Execution: The discipline of getting things done* (1st ed.). New York, NY: Crown Business.

Bourgeois, L. J., & Brodwin, D. R. (1984). Strategic implementation: Five approaches to an elusive phenomenon. *Strategic Management Journal, 5*(3), 241–264. doi:10.1002/smj.4250050305

Bradberry, T., & Greaves, J. (2009). *Emotional Intelligence 2.0* (Har/Dol En.). TalentSmart.

Branson, C. (2007). Effects of structured self-reflection on the development of authentic leadership practices among Queensland primary school principals. *Educational Management Administration & Leadership, 35*(2), 225–246. doi:10.1177/1741143207075390

Brewerton, P. (2011). Using strengths to drive career success. *Strategic HR Review, 10*(6), 5–10. doi:10.1108/14754391111172760

Canary, D. J. (2008). *Interpersonal communication: A goals based approach* (4th ed.). Boston, MA: Bedford/St. Martin's.

Clifton, D. O. (2002). StrengthsQuest: Discover and develop your strengths in academics, career, and beyond. Gallup Pr.

Coonradt, C. (2012). *The game of work: How to enjoy work as much as play.* Kaysville, UT: Gibbs Smith.

Cornum, R., Matthews, M. D., & Seligman, M. E. P. (2011). Comprehensive soldier fitness: Building resilience in a challenging institutional context. *American Psychologist, 66*(1), 4–9. doi:10.1037/a0021420

Covey, S. R. (2004). *The 7 habits of highly effective people: Powerful lessons in personal change* (Rev.). New York, NY: Free Press.

Covey, S. R. (2009). *The leader in me: How schools and parents around the world are inspiring greatness, one child at a time.* New York, NY: Simon and Schuster.

Crowther, D., & Gomez, A. M. D. (2012). In A. M. D. Gomez & D. Crowther (Eds.), *Ethics, psyche and social responsibility.* Aldershot: Gower.

Csikszentmihalyi, M. (1998). *Finding flow: The psychology of engagement with everyday life.* New York, NY: Basic Books.

Csikszentmihalyi, M. (2008). *Flow: The psychology of optimal experience* (1st ed.). New York, NY: Harper Perennial Modern Classics.

Daft, R. (2007). *The leadership experience.* Boston, MA: Cengage Learning.

Deal, T., Kennedy, A., Kennedy, A. A., & Deal, T. E. (2000). *Corporate cultures: The rites and rituals of corporate life* (1st ed.). New York, NY: Basic Books.

Department of the Army. (1993). *A leader's guide to after-action reviews: Training circular 25–20.* US: CreateSpace Independent Publishing Platform.

Dweck, C. (2007). *Mindset: The new psychology of success* (Reprint). New York, NY: Ballantine Books.

Folkman, J. R. (2006). *The power of feedback: 35 Principles for turning feedback from others into personal and professional change.* Hoboken, NJ: Wiley.

Ford, M. T., Cerasoli, C. P., Higgins, J. A., & Decesare, A. L. (2011). Relationships between psychological, physical, and behavioural health and work performance: A review and meta-analysis. *Work & Stress, 25*(3), 185–204. doi:10.1080/02678373.2011.609035

Fredrickson, B. (2009). *Positivity: Top-notch research reveals the 3 to 1 ratio that will change your life* (1st ed.). New York, NY: Three Rivers Press.

Frost, J. (2014). Values based leadership. *Industrial and Commercial Training, 46*(3), 124–129. doi:10.1108/ICT-10-2013-0073

Fry, L. W. (2003). Toward a theory of spiritual leadership. *The Leadership Quarterly, 14*(6), 693–727. doi:10.1016/j.leaqua.2003.09.001

Gardner, H. E., Csikszentmihalyi, M., & Damon, W. (2008). *Good work.* New York, NY: Basic Books.

Garfield, C. (1987). *Peak performers* (1st ed., 2nd Printing). New York, NY: William Morrow Paperbacks.

Gini, A. (1997). Moral leadership and business ethics. *Journal of Leadership & Organizational Studies, 4*(4), 64–81. doi:10.1177/107179199700400406

Gleick, J. (1987). *Chaos: The making of a new science* (1st ed.). New York, NY: Viking Adult.

Goleman, D. (2006). *Emotional intelligence: 10th anniversary edition; Why it can matter more than IQ* (10 Anv.). New York, NY: Bantam.

Goleman, D. (2013). *Focus: The hidden driver of excellence.* New York, NY: Harper Collins.

Gonzalez, J. A., & Chakraborty, S. (2012). Image and similarity: An identity orientation perspective to organizational identification. *Leadership & Organization Development Journal, 33*(1), 51–65. doi:10.1108/01437731211193115

Greene, R. (2012). *Mastery.* New York, NY: Viking Adult.

Gurt, J., Schwennen, C., & Elke, G. (2011). Health-specific leadership: Is there an association between leader consideration for the health of employees and their strain and well-being? *Work & Stress, 25*(2), 108–127. doi:10.1080/02678373.2011.595947

Heifetz, R. (1998). *Leadership without easy answers* (1st ed.). Boston, MA: Harvard University Press.

Heifetz, R. A., Linsky, M., & Grashow, A. (2009). *The practice of adaptive leadership: Tools and tactics for changing your organization and the world* (1st ed.). Boston, MA: Harvard Business Press.

Hertel, G., & Solansky, S. T. (2011). Team identification: A determining factor of performance. *Journal of Managerial Psychology, 26*(3), 247–258. doi:10.1108/02683941111112677

Higgs, M., & Aitken, P. (2003). An exploration of the relationship between emotional intelligence and leadership potential. *Journal of Managerial Psychology, 18*(8), 814–823. doi:10.1108/02683940310511890

Ireland, R. D., & Hitt, M. A. (1999). Achieving and maintaining strategic competitiveness in the 21st century: The role of strategic leadership. *The Academy of Management Executive, 13*(1), 43–57. doi:10.5465/AME.1999.1567311

Jackson, B. H. (2003). *In search of peak experiences through life*. Understanding the strategies for replicating the flow experience: A developmental perspective. Doctoral dissertation, The Fielding Graduate Institute, Santa Barbara, CA.

Jackson, B. H. (2011). *Finding your flow − How to identify your flow assets and liabilities − The keys to peak performance every day*. College Station, TX: Virtualbookworm.com Publishing.

Kaplan, R. S., & Norton, D. P. (1996). *The balanced scorecard: Translating strategy into action* (1st ed.). Boston, MA: Harvard Business Review Press.

Katzenbach, J. R., & Smith, D. K. (2006). *The wisdom of teams: Creating the high-performance organization*. New York, NY: Harper Business (Reprint).

Komives, S. R., Lucas, N., & McMahon, T. R. (2009). *Exploring leadership: For college students who want to make a difference*. Hoboken, NJ: Wiley.

Kotter, J. P., & Heskett, J. L. (2011). *Corporate culture and performance*. New York, NY: Free Press (Reprint).

Kruglanski, A. W., & Higgins, E. T. (2007). *Social psychology: Handbook of basic principles*. New York, NY: Guilford Press.

Kuhn, T. S. (2012). *The structure of scientific revolutions: 50th anniversary edition*. Chicago, IL: University of Chicago Press.

Langer, E. J. (1990). *Mindfulness*. Boston, MA: Da Capo Press (Reprint).

Larson, C. E., & LaFasto, F. M. J. (1989). *Teamwork: What must go right/what can go wrong*. Thousand Oaks, CA: Sage.

Ledford, G. E., Jr., Wendenhof, J. R., & Strahley, J. T. (1995). Realizing a corporate philosophy. *Organizational Dynamics, 23*(3), 5–19. doi:10.1016/0090-2616(95)90022-5

Lee, K. E. (1999). A change in the outlook for psychology in management − From skill-building to personal development. *Journal of Managerial Psychology, 14*(7/8), 586–601. doi:10.1108/02683949910292187

Leider, R. J. (2013). *Life reimagined: discovering your new life possibilities* (1st ed.). San Francisco, CA: Berrett-Koehler Publishers.

Lencioni, P. (2002). *The five dysfunctions of a team: A leadership fable* (1st ed.). San Francisco, CA: Jossey-Bass.

Linsky, M., & Heifetz, R. A. (2002). *Leadership on the line: Staying alive through the dangers of leading* (1st ed.). Boston, MA: Harvard Business Review Press.

Loehr, J. (2008). *The power of story: Change your story, change your destiny in business and in life*. New York, NY: Free Press (Reprint).

Loehr, J., & Schwartz, T. (2004). *The power of full engagement: Managing energy, not time, is the key to high performance and personal renewal*. New York, NY: Free Press (Reprint).

Maltz, M. (1984). *The magic power of self-image psychology*. New York, NY: Pocket Books.

Marques, J., Dhiman, S., & King, R. (Eds.). (2009). *The workplace and spirituality: New perspectives on research and practice*. Woodstock, VT: Skylight Paths Publishing.

McCartney, W. W., & Campbell, C. R. (2006). Leadership, management, and derailment. *Leadership & Organization Development Journal*, 27(3), 190–202. doi:10.1108/01437730610657712

Meadows, D. H. (2008). *Thinking in systems: A primer*. White River Junction, VT: Chelsea Green Publishing.

Michaels, E., Handfield-Jones, H., & Axelrod, B. (2001). *The war for talent*. Boston, MA: Harvard Business Review Press.

Michalos, A. C., & Poff, D. C. (Eds.). (2012). *Citation classics from the journal of business ethics: Celebrating the first thirty years of publication: 2* (2013th ed.). New York, NY: Springer.

Miller, D. L. (2003). The stages of group development: A retrospective study of dynamic team processes. Canadian Journal of Administrative Sciences [Revue Canadienne Des Sciences De l'Administration], 20(2), 121–134. doi:10.1111/j.1936-4490.2003.tb00698.x

Neck, C. C., & Manz, C. P. (2012). *Mastering self leadership: Empowering yourself for personal excellence* (6th ed.). Upper Saddle River, NJ: Prentice Hall.

Orlick, T. (2007). *In pursuit of excellence – 4th edition* (4th ed.). Champaign, IL: Human Kinetics.

Plimpton, G. (1995). *The X Factor: A quest for excellence*. New York, NY: W. W. Norton & Co Inc.

Reave, L. (2005). Spiritual values and practices related to leadership effectiveness. *The Leadership Quarterly*, 16(5), 655–687. doi:10.1016/j.leaqua.2005.07.003

Reynolds, M. (2004). *Outsmart Your Brain! How to Make Success Feel Easy*. Covisioning.

Robbins, H., & Finley, M. (2000). *The new why teams don't work: What goes wrong and how to make it right* (2nd ed.). San Francisco, CA: Berrett-Koehler Publishers.

Rouse, W. B., & Boff, K. R. (2005). *Organizational simulation*. Hoboken, NJ: Wiley.

Seligman, M. E. P. (2003). *Authentic happiness: Using the new positive psychology to realize your potential for lasting fulfillment*. New York, NY: Atria Books.

Seligman, M. E. P. (2006). *Learned optimism: How to change your mind and your life*. New York, NY: Vintage (Reprint).

Seligman, M. E. P. (2012). *Flourish: A visionary new understanding of happiness and well-being* (Reprint ed.). New York, NY: Atria Books.

Senge, P. M. (2010). *The fifth discipline: The art & practice of the learning organization*. New York, NY: Crown Publishing Group.

Shoenfelt, E. L. (2011). "Values Added" teambuilding: A process to ensure understanding, acceptance, and commitment to team values. *Journal of Sport Psychology in Action*, 1(3), 150–160. doi:10.1080/21520704.2010.550989

Siebert, A. (2005). *The resiliency advantage: Master change, thrive under pressure, and bounce back from setbacks* (1st ed.). San Francisco, CA: Berrett-Koehler Publishers.

Stein, S. J., & Book, H. (2006). *The EQ edge: Emotional intelligence and your success* (2nd ed.). San Francisco, CA: Jossey-Bass.

Sternberg, R. J. (2001). Why schools should teach for wisdom: The balance theory of wisdom in educational settings. *Educational Psychologist*, 36(4), 227–245. doi:10.1207/S15326985EP3604_2

Thoms, P., & Greenberger, D. B. (1995). The relationship between leadership and time orientation. *Journal of Management Inquiry*, 4(3), 272–292. doi:10.1177/105649269543009

Tracy, B. (2002). *The psychology of achievement* (Abridged). New York, NY: Simon & Schuster Audio/Nightingale-Conant.

Urban, H. (2002). *Life's greatest lessons: 20 things that matter* (Original). New York, NY: Touchstone.

Waitley, D. (1984). *The psychology of winning*. New York, NY: Berkley.

Wheeler, D. J. (2000). *Understanding variation: The key to managing chaos* (2nd Rev.). Knoxville, TN: SPC PRESS (Statistical Process Control).

Wheeler, D. J. (2010). *Understanding statistical process control* (3rd ed.). Knoxville, TN: SPC PRESS (Statistical Process Control).

Williams, D. (2005). *Real leadership: Helping people and organizations face their toughest challenges* (Annotated). San Francisco, CA: Berrett-Koehler Publishers.

Wisneski, L. A., & Anderson, L. (2004). *The scientific basis of integrative medicine*. Boca Raton, FL: CRC Press.

Wong, C.-S., & Law, K. S. (2002). The effects of leader and follower emotional intelligence on performance and attitude: An exploratory study. *The Leadership Quarterly, 13*(3), 243–274. doi:10.1016/S1048-9843(02)00099-1

Zenger, J., & Folkman, J. (2009). *The extraordinary leader: Turning good managers into great leaders* (2nd ed.). New York, NY: McGraw-Hill.

Zimbardo, P. (2007). *The lucifer effect: Understanding how good people turn evil* (1st ed.). New York, NY: Random House.

About the Authors

Stan Amaladas is currently a Research Associate with the Arthur Mauro Centre for Peace and Justice, St. Paul's College, University of Manitoba. Stan has consciously embraced the spirit of being a scholar-practitioner in his various capacities as Associate Professor, Leadership Studies, Leadership Learning, and Change Specialist, Leadership Coach, and Leadership Learning Program Developer, He is particularly committed to leading leadership learning and change "sanctuaries" through the performance of story-telling. "Chase your passion, not your pension" defines his life choices.

Anthony C. Andenoro, Ph.D., is an Assistant Professor of Leadership Education within the Department of Agricultural Education, the Challenge 2050 Project Director, and the Coordinator of the campus-wide Leadership Minor at the University of Florida. His research interests include the development of emotionally engaged thinking and resilient and sustainable communities capable of addressing complex adaptive global challenges. He also served as the Project Lead for the National Leadership Education Research Agenda and was awarded the 2014 College of Agricultural and Life Sciences Teacher of the Year at the University of Florida.

Skye Burn is Founder and Former Director of The Flow Project offering research and education in art-infused leadership. A visual artist, she has published and presented widely on the relevance of art to leadership, understanding the world as a work of art, and the psychology of the creative process. Community Board member, UNESCO Crossings Institute for Conflict-Sensitive Reporting and Intercultural Dialogue, University of Oregon; International Associate, UNESCO Chair, St. Petersburg Branch of the Russian Institute for Cultural Research.

Susan Cannon, Ph.D., Interdisciplinary Scholar-Practitioner and Futurist brings 25 + years to innovation, learning, and change in human systems. Currently a certified integral master coach/consultant, Vollett Executive Coaching and Evolucent Consulting; adjunct professor Organizational Development and Leadership, Fielding Graduate University; and pioneer in women's integral leadership development, Kore Evolution. Work history includes engineering/senior executive positions, and patents. B.S. Engineering Physics, Texas Tech

University; M.S. Chemical Engineering, Purdue University; Ph.D. Integral Studies, California Institute of Integral Studies.

Cathleen Clerkin, Ph.D., is a member of the Research Faculty at the Center for Creative Leadership. Her research topics include creativity and innovation, applied social cognitive neuroscience, holistic leadership, and social identity. Cathleen's work has received numerous accolades, including recognition from the National Science Foundation and the American Association of University Women. Cathleen holds a B.A. in psychology from the University of California, Berkeley, and M.S. and Ph.D. degrees in psychology from the University of Michigan, Ann Arbor.

Barry A. Doublestein, DSL, has spent the entirety of his vocational career serving various positions in undergraduate and postgraduate medical education. Presently, he is Clinical Associate Professor at Nova Southeastern University College of Osteopathic Medicine, Adjunct Instructor of Healthcare Administration at Belhaven University, and President of the Osteopathic Institute of the South. He earned his doctorate in strategic leadership from the School of Business & Leadership at Regent University with emphasis on strategic leadership in medicine. His research interests focus on physician professionalism development.

Lisa Endersby, M.Ed., combines professional passions in assessment, technology, and leadership to help institutions and individuals ask better questions. She holds a Master's in Education from the University of Victoria and a Bachelor's degree in Psychology from the University of Toronto. Lisa has written for several journals and professional publications, and speaks internationally about (re)defining success. Her current research interests include intersections of technology, identity, and leadership, the assessment cycle, and online communities.

Philip A. Foster is a Futurist, Leadership/Business Consultant and an Adjunct Professor at Middle Tennessee State University. He holds an M.A. in Organizational Leadership and a Doctorate of Strategic Foresight (Regent University). He is a thought leader and best-selling author of The Open Organization. A New Era of Leadership and Organizational Development. Gower Publishing and Organization 3.0 − The Evolution of Leadership and Organizational Theories Toward an Open System for the 21st Century. Maximum Change Press. He resides in Middle Tennessee and can be contacted at philip@maximumchange.com or on twitter @maximumchange and @openorgs.

Kathy L. Guthrie, Ph.D., is an Associate Professor at Florida State University, where she coordinates the Undergraduate Certificate in

Leadership Studies. Guthrie currently serves as Associate Editor of the *New Directions in Student Leadership* series. She coauthored *Cultivating Leader Identity and Capacity in Students from Diverse Backgrounds* and currently serves as Chair-Elect for the ILA Leadership Scholarship Member Interest Group. Guthrie focuses her research on undergraduate leadership education and use of technology in teaching and learning.

Jean Houston, Ph.D., Scholar, Philosopher, and Researcher in Human Capacities; one of the principal founders of the Human Potential Movement; a past President of the Association of Humanistic Psychology; instrumental in developing the field of Social Artistry; Senior Consultant to the United Nations; and author of 19 books, including *A Passion for the Possible, Search for the Beloved, Life Force, The Possible Human, A Mythic Life: Learning to Live Our Greater Story,* and *Jump Time.*

Bruce H. Jackson is the Principal of the Institute of Applied Human Excellence, a training firm dedicated to individual, team, and organizational performance using "Flow" and "Attentional Leadership" to increase focus. With master's degrees in psychology, business, and public administration, and a doctorate in Human and Organizational Systems, Dr. Jackson works with professionals and students alike – using corporate, education, and high adventure arenas – to facilitate their "zone of excellence" and highest functioning.

Daniel M. Jenkins, Ph.D., is an Assistant Professor of Leadership and Organizational Studies at the University of Southern Maine. He earned a doctorate in Curriculum and Instruction with an emphasis in Higher Education Administration from the University of South Florida. Dan's chief research focus is leadership pedagogy and he has presented internationally on leadership education and curriculum. Dan presently serves as the Past-Chair of the ILA Leadership Education Member Interest Group and Secretary of the Association of Leadership Educators.

Karen K. Johnson, Ed.D., is a state, regional, and internationally recognized leader, innovator, coach, and mentor. After four decades of coaching leaders on how to sustain and grow organizations, her work in professional organizations, businesses, manufacturing firms, universities, and charter schools has earned her regional, state, and international awards. Dr. Johnson mentors doctoral students at the University of Phoenix through their dissertation research. She has mentored over 30 students to successful completion since 2007.

Walter T. Lee, MD is Associate Professor of Otolaryngology-Head and Neck Surgery at Duke University Medical Center, Co-Director of the Head and Neck Program, Duke Cancer Institute and Staff Surgeon at the Durham VA Medical Center. He holds a BA in Philosophy (ethics) and MD from George Washington Medical School. Dr. Lee completed his residency and subsequent fellowship at the Cleveland Clinic. His areas of research include professional formation and integrating a virtue based approach to healthcare delivery. He also is involved with medical student and resident education as well as global health education and development.

Timothy C. Mack is the Former President of the World Future Society (2004–2014) and Executive Editor of *World Future Review*. His previous experience includes research and analytical work with: the John F. Kennedy School of Government at Harvard; the National Academy of Science; the US General Accounting Office; and WPP Ltd. (the largest business strategy firm globally). While working in the private sector, Mr. Mack has assisted organizations in the manufacturing, healthcare, insurance, and energy fields, as well as foreign nations. Mr. Mack has written extensively in the public policy, marketing, and technology areas, and has been published by such presses as MIT press, National Academy Press, the U.S. General Accounting Office, and the Greenwood Publishing Group. Mr. Mack is now Managing Principal at AAI Foresight (www.aaiforesight.com).

Whitney McIntyre Miller is an Assistant Professor of Graduate Leadership Programs at Chapman University. She received her Ph. D. in Leadership Studies from the University of San Diego, and holds masters degrees in International Development and Social Work. Dr. McIntyre Miller centers her research on peace leadership and issues of community development and leadership. She is a member of the International Leadership Association and co-convener of its Peace Leadership Affinity Group, while also active in the Community Development Society as co-chair of its International Committee, and the Peace and Justice Studies Association.

Mindy McNutt is an Associate Professor of Leadership in the Department of Leadership Studies at Wright State University, where she teaches in the bachelors, masters, and doctoral leadership programs. Throughout her career she has held a variety of leadership positions, which have included, among others, academic vice president, college dean, and dean of student services. Her research interests include leadership education, transformational leadership, women in leadership, leader values, and the future of leadership.

Maureen Metcalf, MBA, Founder and CEO of Metcalf & Associates, Inc., brings 30 years' experience to support her clients' leadership and organizational transformations. She is recognized as an innovative, principled thought leader who demonstrates operational skills coupled with the ability to analyze, develop, and implement successful strategies creating thriving organizations. She combines intellectual rigor and discipline with an ability to translate theory into practice. She is co-author of the award-winning *Innovative Leadership* books series.

Michael Morrow-Fox, MBA, has over 20 years of experience in leading technology and human resources operations for health care, education, banking, and nonprofit organizations, as well as several years of university teaching. His bachelor's degree focused on Industrial Psychology and Employee Counseling and his MBA focus was on Organizational Leadership. He is currently completing his Doctorate in Educational Leadership. He is a contributor to several books in the award-winning *Innovative Leadership* books series.

Susan Elaine Murphy is currently the Chair in Leadership Development at the University of Edinburgh Business School. Previously she was Director of the School of Strategic Leadership Studies at James Madison University. Her current research examines leadership requirements, effectiveness, and development across different contexts and organizational levels and identifies ways in which organizations encourage "the leadership development mindset." She has consulted with numerous organizations as well as national and local government and other public sector organizations.

Donnette J. Noble, Ph.D. earned her doctorate at the University of Nebraska-Lincoln before joining the faculty at Roosevelt University in Chicago. She is an Assistant Professor of Organizational Leadership in the Evelyn T. Stone College of Professional Studies. Before entering into the ranks of academia, Dr. Noble (www. noblenuggets.com) accrued considerable management and executive leadership experience in healthcare, marketing, and public broad-casting. She is a strong advocate for social justice and passionate about access to education.

Richard M. Pfohl, DSL, is an anticipatory thought leader recognized for transforming organizations through his strategy, innovation, and leadership solutions. Presently he is President of Navigos, an Adjunct Professor of Leadership and Course Writer with LeTourneau University, an Adjunct Professor of Leadership with Eastern University, and an entrepreneur, aligned with SCORE, helping small businesses start, grow, and succeed. He earned his doctorate in strategic leadership from the School of Business & Leadership at Regent University with an emphasis on anticipatory leadership in healthcare. His research and practice currently focuses on anticipatory leadership, entrepreneurship, healthcare transformation, and healthcare professionalism development.

Michael A. Piel, D.M. is a Senior Partner and Consultant at the *IceBridge Research Institute* and a Visiting Professor at the *Universidad Autónoma de Manizales*. Driven by passion and compassion to continuously listen, learn, create, and share knowledge, Dr. Piel is helping others around the world achieve professional and personal success by realizing their own distinctive levels of leadership excellence and encouraging individuals to see their unique and positive potential to improve our shared planet.

Sebastian Salicru is a Business Psychologist based in Sydney, Australia. His work is about taking leaders and their teams to new levels. He works with C-level and other senior executives on building the leadership capability required to succeed in the increasingly competitive global economy, where hyper-complexity is the new normal. Sebastian also assists emerging and high-potential leaders in Australia, Europe, UAE, China, Singapore, and the United States to fast-track their careers, unleash their potential, and achieve their career aspirations.

Rian Satterwhite serves as Director of the Holden Center for Leadership & Community Engagement at the University of Oregon. Long-time member of the ILA, Rian has served as Chair of the Leadership Education MIG and co-founded the Sustainability Leadership Learning Community. Author of the Deep Systems Leadership Model (in Redekop (Ed), *Leadership for Environmental Sustainability*, 2010), Rian is actively engaged with others exploring how leadership theory and practice is evolving in response to our increasing awareness of our participation within a multitude of complex and natural systems.

Kate Sheridan is the Associate Director of the President's Leadership Program and has served as an Adjunct Faculty Member in the Department of Leadership and American Studies at Christopher Newport University. She received her Masters degree in Leadership Studies from the University of San Diego and is a member of the International Leadership Association. Kate has a growing research interest in innovative practices of leadership development and education that equip individuals to confront the future with greater self-awareness and systems capacity.

Matthew Sowcik is an Associate Professor in Leadership Studies and the Director of Leadership Education at Wilkes University, where he has worked professionally for the past 11 years. His research specialization is in humility, leadership and the emergence and sustainability of Leadership Studies programs. Aside from his research and administrative duties, Dr. Sowcik also currently serves as a consultant to *The New York Times*, focusing on the newspaper's educational programming for leadership studies faculty and students.

Nicole L. P. Stedman is an Associate Professor of leadership in the Department of Agricultural Education and Communication at the University of Florida. Her Ph.D. is in agricultural education and communication from UF with a specialization in leadership development teaching courses at the undergraduate and graduate levels. Dr. Stedman is an active scholar publishing and presenting her work and has partnered for $1.6 million in funded grants. She has teaching awards from the University of Florida (2010, 2013), the American Association for Agricultural Education Southern Region (2013), and as a NACTA Teaching Fellow. Her current research interests include evaluating teaching and learning practices for their ability to build capacity for critical thinking.

Jeffrey L. Suderman is a Futurist, Adjunct Professor, and Consultant who works in the field of organizational development. He partners with clients to improve leadership, teamwork, organizational alignment, strategy, and their FutureReadiness. He completed his M.A. Leadership degree at Trinity Western University (Langley, Canada) and his Doctorate in Strategic Leadership at Regent University (Virginia Beach, VA). He resides in Palm Desert, California and can be contacted at jeff@jeffsuderman.com or on twitter @jlsuderman.

Icarbord Tshabangu is an Education Lecturer at Leeds Trinity University, UK and a former Senior Lecturer and Coordinator of Educational Foundations and Management at the University of Namibia. Previously he has also lectured in M.Ed. and MBA programmes at the University of Arusha, Tanzania and was also associated with the University of Liverpool Online doctoral development programme in education as an Honorary Senior Lecturer.

Index